HISTORY OF THE LEMEN FAMILY,

OF ILLINOIS, VIRGINIA,

AND ELSEWHERE

(1656-1898)

Collinsville? Ill.

[1898]

FRANK B. LEMEN.

Table of Contents of the Illinois Branch.

Portraits and Illustrations.

BIOGRAPHIES.

PREFACE.

In placing this work before the family we are conscious of the fact that it is not allotted any man to attain perfection. It is not our purpose to set forth all the works of all the family, but only those that will be most instructive and elevating to the present and coming generations. In condensing the history of a large family, covering a period of two and a half centuries, it becomes necessary to select only the chief incidents, leaving out much that would be of interest, hence criticisms will arise; let us ask that they may be made in the spirit of charity. The facts herein given are the result of much research and are as extensive as the scope and purpose of a single volume will permit.

The Lemen family is large and influential, and when we consider that, as a family, we form a part of a great nation, the history becomes in part the history of that nation; thus our family history necessarily becomes a matter of importance to both Church and State, and can profitably be reviewed by those who would correctly understand the complete history of this great nation. This book, therefore, will not be strictly confined to private distribution.

The historical and other facts presented herein are sustained by authentic records, and if due allowance be made for the varied conception of the human mind, they may be accurately harmonized with other authentic works.

In gathering the biographical sketches and genealogical lists of the different branches, we have found some persons who would not, even after many solicitations, respond. Such persons surely cannot censure us if when reading the history they find that they and theirs have been left out.

In many families there will appear those who have a pride in the achievements of their ancestors, and who set out to investigate the history of those who have preceded them. Such investigators of our family have appeared from time to time, and it is to those that we are indebted for much of the data used in this work. As a family we must acknowledge our obligations to Rev. James Lemen, Jr., and to Mr. Joseph B. Lemen, his son, who have successively gathered data for three generations, and who have had access to old and valuable manuscripts which have been prepared by a competent antiquarian at large cost.

Among those who have contributed to the completeness of this work are intelligent men and women, members of the different branches of the family, all of whom are to be commended for the careful and concise way in which they have preserved their family records. As a family we are especially indebted to Mr. Joseph B. Lemen for the vast amount of labor expended on the historical division

of this book.   In this connection I wish to mention
Mr. J. Baker Kearfott, who prepared, by great
labor, a genealogical list of about 600 names of the
Virginia branch of the family, and who by referring
to and examining old legal records helped to establish
the connection of the Illinois and Virginia branches.

I wish to urge all to whom a volume of this book
may come to keep a record of all births, marriages
and deaths; also that all events worthy of note be
made a matter of record.   With many the history of
their grand and great-grandparents is almost a
blank; and it is often the regret of one's life that he
does not better understand the history of his family.
It often happens that important litigations hinge
upon the authentic knowledge gained through family
records, and in such an event one may lose a
fortune because there are no records to meet the
conditions of the bequest.

In the compilation of this work it has been our
purpose to bring together such facts as will per-
petuate in the minds of succeeding generations those
sterling and unswerving principles that have actuated
our ancestors in Scotland, Ireland and America.   If
a single mind is quickened, by a moral lineal parentage, to emulate the principles that elevate humanity
to a higher plane of civil and religious life, our work
will not have been in vain.

FRANK B. LEMEN.

CHAPTER I.

ORIGIN OF THE LEMEN FAMILY.

There is an early tradition which assigns the origin of the Lemen family to the continent of Europe; but the family in Illinois and the larger branch of the family in Virginia cannot with absolute certainty, through an unbroken line of ancestry, trace their origin beyond Robert Lemen of Scotland. He and the other members of his father's family in that country were ardent followers and adherents of Oliver Cromwell, Lord Protector of the Commonwealth of England, and Robert Lemen and his brother, William Lemen, were soldiers under him, and assisted to banish for a time royalty and its attendant tyrannies in England and to place the affairs of that country under the control of their great chieftain; and at the time of Robert Lemen's marriage in Scotland, Cromwell, who was then in that country and community, attended his wedding and presented Robert's bride with a beautiful little box richly inlaid with pearls and silver.

In 1656, Robert Lemen and his wife, with his brother William Lemen and the other members of the family, moved from Scotland and settled in the North of Ireland. Among Robert Lemen's children, born in the North of Ireland, was Nicholas Lemen, who married in Scotland, but settled and reared his family in North Ireland; and in 1708 three of his (Nicholas') sons, James, Robert and Nicholas Lemen, came to America and settled in Virginia. All were married there and had families. There was a Stephen Lemen who settled in Virginia at an early day, but he belonged to another branch of the family. Prior to their sailing for this country the three brothers, James, Robert and Nicholas Lemen—though the permanent home of the family was in North Ireland— spent much of their time in Scotland, and they came here directly from that country. They brought with them many souvenirs of the early family, among which Nicholas brought the little box presented to his grandmother by Cromwell, James brought a little silver dish of his grandmother Lemen's, and Robert brought a cane which had belonged to his grandfather, Robert Lemen. The box is now in the possession of some of Nicholas Lemen's descendants in Kentucky, the little silver dish is held by some of the Lemens in Ohio, and until recently the cane was in the keeping of Robert Lemen of Williamsport, Md., who has now given it to his grandson, Robert Lemen.

Of the three young men, James, Robert and Nicholas Lemen, who came from Scotland and settled in Virginia in 1708, and who were married and reared their families there, the daughters only of Robert's family survived, his sons having died in infancy; Nicholas' family consisted of both sons and daughters, and of James Lemen's family two daughters and four sons survived, the latter being John, Robert, Nicholas and Thomas Lemen. Three of them finally lived near Harper's Ferry, Va. Nicholas, who was born in Virginia in 1725, was married there in 1747. In 1746 he had made a survey of a tract of land in Frederick County (now Jefferson County), West Virginia, where he and his wife settled and had their family. This tract of land was confirmed to him by a grant from Thomas Lord Fairfax, Baron of Cameron and Lord Proprietor of the Northern Part of Virginia, under the seal of the crown, and bearing date September 5, 1756. The tract comprised 570 acres.

The children of Nicholas Lemen and Christian Lemen, his wife, were John, born December 14, 1749; Robert, born November 6, 1750; Nancy, born March 4, 1754; Mary, born January 7, 1756; Thomas, born February 4, 1758, and James, born November 20, 1760. The latter was the Rev. James Lemen, Sr., who became the founder of the Lemen family in Illinois. He was a son of Nicholas Lemen and Christian Lemen, his wife, and not a son of Robert Lemen, as some of the earlier and more meager sketches of the Lemen family in Illinois have, through a mistake, stated. He had an uncle Robert and a brother Robert, but his father was Nicholas Lemen, as is conclusively shown by Mr. Joseph Baker Kearfott, a member of the family who resides in Martinsburg, W. Va., by deeds, wills and other legal papers on record in the archives of the

counties where the early family lived. Mr. Kearfott
is an excellent antiquarian and a trained investigator,
and his great services have been of incalculable
importance and assistance in the preparation of this
family history; as have also the many important
facts obtained through the correspondence of the
venerable Robert Lemen of Williamsport, Md. The
large collection of facts, records and family notes
which that learned divine, historian and great investigator, the late Rev. John M. Peck, D. D., gave to
the late Rev. James Lemen, Jr., were also of great
assistance in preparing the histories of both the
Lemen and Ogle families; as they referred to the
early history of both, and particularly to the latter
family, giving their early connection in England with
the reigning family, their castles, estates and titles,
such as dukes, lords and other dignitaries, early and
modern, with many other important facts, which
later investigators in the West, East and South have
confirmed, and who have also been of much help in
making a correct family history.

Nicholas Lemen died at his home in West Virginia
on July 20, 1761, and in due time his widow, Christian
Lemen, married Rev. Henry Eaty of Virginia. From
this union there were two children born, namely,
Sebastian Eaty and a little daughter who died in
infancy. As Rev. James Lemen, Sr., married a
member of the Ogle family, namely, Miss Catharine
Ogle, a daughter of Captain Joseph Ogle, who was a
soldier and officer under Washington in our war for

independence, it will be necessary to give a brief sketch of her family.

The Ogle family have a well preserved history both in this country and in England. In England they were of early Saxon origin, having descended from an early line of the Saxon Kings. They finally held a vast landed estate on the river Blythe in England, which, by the royal decree of King William the Conqueror, was confirmed to them, the title vesting in Humphery Ogle; and continuing to hold the estate by feudal tenure, the family occupied it for a long period of time. The estate was called "Ogle," and there were two castles on it, Castle Bothal and Castle Ogle. The latter was built by Robert Ogle, a leading member of the early family, and it became the scene of many stirring events. It was at that castle that David Bruce, King of Scotland, was imprisoned after his defeat, before his removal to London. It stood for over four hundred years, and but recently its materials were put into other buildings near by; but the site where it stood is yet well marked.

Among the noted members of the family were seven Lords Ogle, barons and peers of the realm, and many others prominent in British history; and among their descendants are Sir William Cavendish, Marquis and First Duke of Newcastle; Sir William Bentick, Duke of Portland, and several other prominent English leaders. The succession of the Lords Ogle occupied Bothal Castle, and, with their brothers and sisters, were descended through a female branch from Edward the First, King of England, by his second marriage, and not Edward the Second, as the types make it in some former sketches.

In 1666 John Ogle, a descendant of the younger brother of the first Lord Ogle, with his wife, Elizabeth, came from England to America and settled in what is now Newcastle County, Delaware, where they reared their family. They were the great-grandparents of Captain Joseph Ogle, whose daughter, Catherine, married Rev. James Lemen, Sr.

Captain Joseph Ogle was born in Delaware in 1741. He removed to Virginia in early manhood and married Miss Drusilla Biggs. From this union there were five children born, namely, Catherine, Nancy, Prudence, Benjamin and Joseph. After her death he married Miss Jemima Meiggs, and they had several children. Captain Joseph Ogle, under a commission from Governor Patrick Henry (bearing date June 2, 1776, and which is now in the hands of Dr. Edward C. Lemen, of Upper Alton, Ill.), was an officer in the war for independence, and commanded the American forces in the battle at Fort Henry, Wheeling, Va., in 1777 against the British and Indians, and he was also in several other engagements, some of which were under the direct command of Washington. In 1785, with his family, except Catherine, he removed to the Illinois Territory, and settled near New Design, now in Monroe County, In 1802 he removed to and settled on his farm in

Ridge Prairie, St. Clair County, Illinois.   He died at his home in Ridge Prairie in February, 1821, aged four score years. Captain Ogle was a devout member of the M. E. Church, and was greatly esteemed for his many noble traits. Among these were some of the ancestors of Catherine Ogle Lemen.

The descendants of Rev. James Lemen, Sr., and his wife, now number several hundred, with about the usual per cent. living, and they represent every calling, trade and profession in which people seek an honest living; while it is creditable to say of the patriotism of the family that there has not been a war since our Declaration of Independence in which some of its members have not enlisted in defense of the country and the old flag.

CHAPTER II.

35—REV. JAMES LEMEN, SR.

REV. JAMES LEMEN, SR., fourth son and sixth and youngest child of Nicholas Lemen and Christian Lemen, his wife, was born at the homestead of his parents in Frederick County, now Jefferson County, West Virginia, on November 20, 1760. Before James was a year old his father died, and in due course of time his mother married Rev. Henry Eaty, a member and minister of the Presbyterian Church in Virginia, and he was brought up in strict accordance with the tenets of that faith. He acquired a common s.·hool education and also a practical knowledge of farming. His family were friends and associates of some of the Lee family of Virginia, of revolutionary note, and he, with some of his brothers, particularly his brother Robert Lemen, often reaped wheat with some of them. Before his majority he enlisted for a period of two years in the Army of the Revolution, and was a soldier under Washington, receiving at one time his special commendation for a noted act of bravery. He was in the battle of White Plains and several other engagements. His enlistment had expired previous to the siege at Yorktown, but with the view of re-enlisting, he joined his old comrades and was in the ranks at Yorktown when Lord Cornwallis surrendered; after which, our officers thinking the

RESIDENCE OF REV. JAMES LEMEN, SR.,

where the first Baptist Church of Illinois was organized on May 28, 1796. The porch and
some rooms to the right have been added; but the room shown in the left is the
part of the original building where the organization was effected.
This was the first brick building west of the Ohio River.

fighting was well over, James, with his brother
Robert Lemen, who was also a soldier under Washington and who was in the American army at Yorktown, returned home without being again mustered in.
In Virginia, in 1782, he married Miss Catharine Ogle,
a daughter of Captain Joseph Ogle and Drusilla Ogle,
nee Biggs; and with his wife and first two children,
Robert and Joseph, he came to the Illinois Territory
in 1786, and finally settled at New Design, now in
Monroe County, having previously lived for short
intervals in Fort Piggott some miles from New
Design, and in some other neighboring and temporary
forts, to protect the family against the hostile Indians.

On his farm at New Design, where they settled,
and where he built a small temporary house, was a
beautiful swell of prairie with a heavy forest on each
side, and near by was a beautiful, clear and deep lake
of some forty acres in extent, abounding in fine fish,
and at times almost literally covered with water fowls.

Later the family erected there a substantial brick
house with two large lower rooms and two small upper
rooms; the house is still standing, with some additions, and is yet in good repair. It is situated near
Waterloo and is regarded as an object of considerable
historical interest. There was a fine grove of sugar
maple near by, from which the family made their
sugar, and the farm and family residence were thus
favorably situated for many material comforts; and
in all respects the family was a singularly happy one
for the pioneer days. Mr. Lemen was a good provider

and his wife was an excellent manager, and though
they were not wealthy, they secured everything
which their pioneer wants required, and they gave
their children good religious, and even very fair educational, training for those early times.   There was a
pleasant family tradition that Mr. Lemen and his
wife at their first meeting and acquaintance, had the
impression that Providence had ordained them for
partners in life, and the happiness and harmony of
their married lives afterward seemed to confirm that
conviction.   On their voyage from Virginia to Illinois,
which was made on the Ohio River in a flat-boat, the
boat was partially submerged at a point down the
Ohio, and the family lost nearly all their goods, and
Robert, their eldest son, was only saved from drown-
ing by the heroic efforts of his father.   But the great
loss only urged Mr. Lemen to greater efforts, and
they finally reached their destination safely and in a
short time had built their little cabin home.   Of their
children, Robert and Joseph were born in Virginia,
and James, Nancy, William, Josiah, Catharine and
Moses were born at New Design, Monroe County,
Illinois.

Mr. Lemen was a Justice of the Peace, and also a
Judge of the Court of Common Pleas for some time,
and an intelligent and faithful discharge of his official
duties always marked his efforts.   He was waited
upon by a confidential agent of Aaron Burr and asked
to join the scheme of the latter for the organization
of a Southwestern Empire, but he publicly exposed

the scheme and denounced it as treasonable. He was
in one battle against the Indians, in Monroe County,
where the whites killed several of the braves without
loss to their own side. He was intensely anti-slavery,
as were all of his sons, and when William Henry
Harrison was Governor of the Northwestern Territory
he resisted his personal and persistent overtures to
introduce slavery, and he assured him that "while his
blood was warm" he would oppose that purpose; and
the future labors of himself and sons proved how
faithfully he kept his vow. He was one of the leaders
who directed the petitions from the people to Congress, bitterly opposing even the temporary introduction of slavery in the Territory; and acting largely
upon those petitions Congress finally refused to sanc-
tion the introduction of slavery here. Judge Lemen
was also an earnest advocate of temperance, which he
inculcated by both precept and example.

The next contest for the introduction of slavery
in Illinois was but a few years before Illinois became
a State, and in this Judge Lemen was a leader of the
anti-slavery sentiment and forces. In 1809 he became
a Baptist minister, and he opened this last anti-slavery
contest in a sermon which he preached in the Richland
Baptist Church, of which he was a member, and which
church had been, until 1807, an "arm" of the New
Design Baptist Church. In that sermon he denounced
the practice of slavery as a crime which the church
should not tolerate, and the church divided on that
issue, and the anti-slavery element finally withdrew

from the Richland Church and organized Bethel Church, and from that event the anti-slavery senti-ment spread so rapidly that a few years later Illinois entered the Union as a free State.

For some years previous to 1787 Judge Lemen had been a Baptist in principle, but in that year he made a public profession of religion, and in February, 1794, he, with his wife, Catharine, John Gibbons and Isaac Enochs, in the order named, were baptized in Fountain Creek, Monroe County, by the Rev. Josiah Dodge, an eminent Baptist divine of Nelson County, Kentucky, who had for some weeks been holding a successful revival meeting at New Design. They were the first persons baptized by immersion in Illi-nois, and the ice had to be cut and removed before the solemn rites were performed. They united with the New Design Baptist Church in 1796, composing a part of its constituent members. It was the first protestant church organized in Illinois. Judge Lemen was licensed to preach on July 9, 1808, and his ordi-nation took place at Bethel Church shortly after its organization; his son, Rev. James Lemen, Jr., being one of the council officiating. Judge Lemen was an earnest, forceful and interesting speaker; was a man of liberal reading, and as a minister of the gospel he accomplished a good work in assisting to build up the churches of his faith.

For quite a number of years Mr. Lemen's house was a hospitable stopping place for strangers, and the late Colonel Dent, Mrs. General Grant's father, used

to tell a good story about his experience in stopping
there over night. He was carrying on horse-back
quite a large amount of silver with him to invest in a
home and business in St. Louis, and somehow or
other Mr. Lemen and his several stalwart sons, who
arrived in the evening from a hunt with a liberal
supply of venison blood on their deer-skin hunting
suits and their guns and great hunting knives in their
belts, impressed Colonel Dent that he would probably soon become the victim of assassination and
robbery. And in the evening when the family all
gathered in and closed the door and Mr. Lemen
walked toward the mantel-board, which was well
loaded with hunting knives and other deadly weapons,
Colonel Dent thought the awful crisis had arrived,
and he said he was just debating in his mind whether
he had better spring to the door and try and knock
down one of the stalwart sons who was standing
against it and try to make his escape, or whether he
had better quietly surrender and plead for his life.
But just at that moment he said Mr. Lemen took
down the old family Bible, and having read a chapter
he made an earnest and excellent prayer, invoking
the divine blessing and guidance for "the stranger
who was with them;" and, of course, this dissipated
the Colonel's fears, and he said he enjoyed a fine
supper, a good night's sleep and an excellent breakfast, for which Mr. Lemen would not charge him a
cent, as he was an old soldier. When Colonel Dent
started on his journey in the morning he had become

a great friend and admirer of Judge Lemen, and
when his business called him to St. Louis, Colonel
Dent met him and he spent the night at the Colonel's
house and was treated in a princely manner; and,
when the latter told Mr. Lemen of his awful fears of
the night at his house, they both had a hearty laugh
over it. Colonel Dent used to relate this story to the
newspapers in such a way as to make an interesting
and laughable article of two or three columns, but our
limited space forbids details.

The pioneer times were not without their jokes
and humors. Upon one occasion Judge Lemen was
officiating at the marriage of a young couple, a Mr.
Clover and his bride, and Clover, not being familiar
with the ways of polite society, had appointed one
Biggs, as master of ceremonies, one of whose duties
was to stand near Clover and touch his shoulder at
the time that he should kiss his bride. Judge Lemen
had proceeded but a little ways with the marriage
ceremony when the mischievous Biggs gave Clover
the signal and he sprang at the bride to kiss her, but
she resisted and the Judge kindly reprimanded him
and was proceeding again with the ceremony, when
Biggs again gave Clover the signal, and the same confusion followed his second effort to kiss his bride,
while the guests were convulsed with laughter. At
this crisis Judge Lemen said: "Ladies and gentle-
men, I had intended to marry this interesting couple,
but the uncontrollable affection and enthusiasm of the
bridegroom renders it impossible unless the master of

ceremonies, Mr. Biggs, will hold him until the marriage rites are completed.'' At this point quiet was
restored and the ceremonies were finished in due
order. The bridegroom gave Judge Lemen a dressed
deer skin for his fee, but the Judge gave it to the
bride as a token of his kind wishes and as a bridal
present.

In the innocent and athletic sports of the early
days Judge Lemen's sons made good records with the
gun, rod and oar. The six brothers were all successful, Moses Lemen, perhaps, being rather the better
hunter; but each of them killed many deer, turkeys
and water-fowls. With the ball and bat and in running, wrestling and jumping, William, James and
Joseph rather excelled. It is said that William and
James could very easily jump over a cord or line held
exactly at their own height, which was six feet and
six feet two inches.

The two daughters, Nancy and Catharine, were
attractive, happy and vivacious young ladies, and fine
singers for their day; and altogether they were as
happy a family, perhaps, as lived in the Territory of
Illinois. Judge Lemen's family discipline was almost
as exacting and precise as military rule, so far as the
obedience of his children to his commands was con-
cerned; but he was remarkably conscientious and
careful in first knowing himself that his commands
were expedient and right; but he never denied them
any reasonable pleasure. There was a mutual love
and respect between parents and children which made

their humble home exceedingly pleasant and their
lives happy and contented.

In politics Judge Lemen was a Federalist. In
Virginia he was well acquainted with the Lees and
Thomas Jefferson, and he was a great admirer of the
old author of the Declaration of Independence. But
when he (Jefferson) disagreed with Washington and
Hamilton on the tariff, national sovereignty and
one or two other important national issues, Judge
Lemen followed the lead of the latter, believing
with them in that constitutional construction which
recognizes National sovereignty as distinguished
from State sovereignty, and a tariff for both revenue and protection as opposed to a free trade
tariff or a tariff for revenue only; and when the
second law which Congress passed under our present
constitution, which expressly declared for protection,
was signed by President Washington, Judge Lemen
expressed himself as greatly gratified that both Congress and the President had thus formerly declared
for protection. Judge Lemen was a man of fine
physical proportions, standing a little over six feet.
He had a head a little above the medium size for a
man of his proportions; had dark blue eyes, slightly
auburn curly hair and slightly Roman nose with a
broad, full forehead; in his mental composition he
was quick of perception, kindly disposed, but rather
sedate, firm and brave but not revengeful; while in
his moral attributes he was honest, fearless in the
right and thoroughly devoted to his religious duty

and faith as he understood them. As husband,
father, friend and citizen Rev. James Lemen, Sr.,
performed his duties well; as a leader and officer
among the early pioneers he was brave, capable and
true, and as a Christian teacher and clergyman his
labors were intelligent, devoted and largely successful
in the great field of his Divine Master. After a life
of great usefulness, in his 63rd year he died at his
home in Monroe County, Illinois, on January 8, 1823,
and his ashes repose in a cemetery at New Design.
His son, Rev. James Lemen, Jr., preached his funeral
discourse.

CATHARINE LEMEN, the wife of Rev. James
Lemen, Sr., and a daughter of Capt. Joseph Ogle
and Drusilla Biggs Ogle, his wife, was born in Virginia in 1764. She married Mr. Lemen in 1782, and
they settled for a time in Berkley County, Virginia,
but they removed to New Design, Ill., in 1786, where
they finally made a permanent home and reared
their family. In complexion she was a brunette with
slightly curly hair as black as a raven, finely-formed
features, blazing black eyes, of straight and perfect
form, a little above the medium in height, and to
these good physical traits she added a strong, practical mind and a happy, even temperament. As a
wife, she was thoroughly devoted to her husband's
happiness and interests, and to his every enterprise
in society and church she gave his efforts an intelligent
and successful second; as a mother, she was devoted
to her children's best interests, and as a Christian

she was faithful to her vows and an active worker in her church. Like her husband, she was a member of the Baptist Church. At a ripe old age and in full possession of all her faculties, she died at her home in New Design, Ill., on July 14, 1840, and was buried by the side of her husband. Her son, Rev. Joseph Lemen, preached her funeral discourse.

CHAPTER III.

37—ROBERT LEMEN, SR.

ROBERT LEMEN, SR., first child and son of Rev. James Lemen, Sr. and Catharine Lemen, his wife, was born in Berkley County, Virginia, on September 25, 1783, and came with his parents to New Design, Ill., in 1786. He received a common school education for that early period, and on July 2, 1805, he married Miss Hester Tolin, and the same year they settled on their farm in Ridge Prairie, St. Clair County, Ill., where they built themselves a permanent home and reared a large family. Robert Lemen was Justice of the Peace for many years, and under John Quincy Adams' administration he was appointed United States Marshal for Illinois, and served very acceptably until he resigned the place from his own preference. He was a member and clerk of the Richland Baptist Church, and when Bethel Church (then Canteen Creek Baptist Church) was organized on December 10, 1809, he and his wife were two of the constituent members, and for thirty-six years he was the clerk of that church. In every position in life, official and otherwise, he discharged every duty faithfully, was a liberal and active supporter of religious and educational interests, and was greatly esteemed throughout the community and State. In politics he was a Federalist until that party merged into the Whig party, and as its principles were about identical he became a member of the latter party, and when that gave place to the Republican party in 1856 he became a prominent and earnest member of that party, as its principles of anti-slavery, protection and national sovereignty were the very principles which Robert Lemen had always embraced. This may also be said of his five brothers. They all became Republicans in 1856. They were not only radically anti-slavery men, but for the most part, they were thoroughly devoted to the cause and progress of temperance, and Robert, Joseph and James were leaders in that cause, and in a future chapter will be found a discourse in full on that most important question by Robert Lemen.

Robert Lemen was an expert and excellent weaver, but his chief occupation was farming. He was a good farmer, and he and his wife secured a good, large farm and made themselves a very comfortable residence. He was a bountiful provider and a man of warm and large affection for his children, but like his father was strict in his family discipline, inculcating and insisting on strict obedience to all his family rules, and his children yielded a ready, loving and willing obedience. He had a large and wisely selected library for the times, and was a man of large religious and general reading. He was a sound, interesting and practical speaker, and good writer in the secular and religious press, and was justly esteemed a safe and worthy leader in the community and church circles; and we here reprint one of his

37—ROBERT LEMEN, SR.

articles on Pioneer Times in Illinois, from the *The Pioneer*, published by Mr. Green at Rock Spring, Ill., January 8, 1830. The article was one of a series written by Mr. Lemen at that early date, and it contains many incidents of interest. The article is as follows:

"RIDGE PRAIRIE, ST. CLAIR COUNTY,
"January 1, 1830.

"MR. GREEN:

"Being confined to the house for several days in consequence of a wound I received by the fall of a tree, and finding it disagreeable to my feelings to be entirely unemployed, it may be of interest to your readers to be made acquainted with some incidents which occurred after I came to this country, it being forty-three years and six months since. My father, with a few others, perhaps not exceeding twelve families, were under the necessity of collecting in a small fort called Piggott's Fort, about nine miles below Cahokia, at the foot of the bluff adjoining the Mississippi Bottom, as a safeguard against the hostility of the Indian tribes, whose murderous arms were uplifted against us. The heads of families were chiefly farmers, who were delighted with the beauties which the prairies seemed to present in their black rich soil, the tall grass, the yellow flowers and the song of the lark. 'I wept,' said one, 'when I beheld the sight, to think there were so few in this country to praise God.' The prairie sod has since closed over his remains. But to proceed: notwithstanding all the caution and pains that were taken, we were from time to time visited in a most solemn and distressing manner.

"As a young man about nineteen years of age was driving his team with a load of hay, a ball from the gun of an Indian broke his right arm and entered his body, and seeing another gun presented at him, being active on foot, he made an attempt to spring from his horse; but his arm hanging down in consequence of being broken, prevented, and instantly a second ball was commissioned to perform the deed of death, but failing, the horses were alarmed, and running with speed an escape was made. The solemn tidings immediately reached his father, who, when beholding his son, embraced him in his arms and cried, 'O Benjamin, my son, my son, would to God I had died in thy stead.' But to the inexpressible joy of his father, after suffering a long time he recovered from his wound.

"Another remarkable circumstance: 'A certain woman, after having four husbands killed by the Indians, lastly was killed herself.' The towahawk and scalping knife were our common dread. To use the words of the prophet Jeremiah: 'We got our bread by the peril of our lives, because of the sword of the wilderness.' Thus it was with the greatest difficulty we procured the necessaries of life, laboring with one hand while in the other we held a weapon of defense; our food and raiment being of the coarsest kind and scanty withal. No coffee nor whiskey, without which numbers think they cannot live in these days of plenty. In a manner we had all things in common; in one field we raised our grain, and a kind of kindred feeling possessed each breast, uniting us as brethren of one family. Among those who were then heads of families there are but four remaining, one male and three females.

"Our currency consisted of deer skins, three pounds being equal to one dollar in silver, and it was a lawful tender. Our amusements were the contemplation of better days. We had no minister of the gospel; our manner of worship was to assemble together on the Sabbath, read the Scriptures and sing a few Psalms or spiritual songs. In these times of distress we were visited by a Baptist minister from Kentucky by the name of James Smith. Being a man of talent and warm in the cause of religion, great power attended his preaching. Under his ministry several professed a hope; but as it is often the case with preachers of the gospel it was his lot to forego difficulties; being in company one day with three others, intending to go to Prairie du Rocher, at the road near Bellefontaine, now Waterloo, at an unexpected moment two were killed, one escaped and Smith was taken prisoner by the Indians. This was solemn news, and particularly so, the two that were killed being the wife and daughter of one of our neighbors, who in company with others hastened to the spot, beheld, wept over and committed to the earth all that was near and dear unto him. Pursuit was made

after the murderers, but slowly and with caution, not
wishing, however, to overtake, but to ascertain
whether they had killed or saved the prisoner alive.
At length discovering the track of his shoes to continue for some considerable distance they returned.
Some months after news came that for a certain sum
Smith would be brought back. No questions were
asked if less would suffice, the ransom was paid down
and language fails to describe the joy that was felt at
Smith's return.

"We afterwards moved back to New Design, to a
place selected by Captain Joseph Ogle and others,
suitable for that purpose, being surrounded by excellent timber and good water. After our removal to
that place the most distressing circumstance which
occurred was the murder of the wife and four
children of the family of Robert W. Mahon, himself
and oldest daughter being taken prisoners by the
Indians; and such was the unfeeling conduct of these
barbarous sons of the forest that when camping at
night they placed before the fire, for the purpose of
drying, the scalps taken from the heads of his wife
and children. Mahon made his escape, but the
weather being cold and somewhat mistaking his
course, he had liked to have perished in the snow.
After returning he immediately visited the solemn
place where his wife and children were all interred in
one grave, and falling prostrate on the yellow pile, he
uttered these words; 'They were lovely in their
lives and in their deaths they were not divided.'

"Although since the occurrence of those scenes years have passed away, yet while I am pursuing the subject I now and then feel a tear kindling in the eyes that once beheld them. Sometime after moving to New Design we experienced a great revival of religion, both Baptists and Methodists aiding in the work. It was then that I for the first time beheld the ordinance of baptism by immersion administered. It was in Fountain Creek, by Rev. Josiah Dodge, a Baptist preacher from the State of Kentucky. Although young I shall never forget the solemn impression of mind. Four persons were baptized, James Lemen and Catharine, his wife (my parents), being the first two, and they were the first persons baptized by immersion in Illinois. He who administered the ordinance and those who were baptized are all sleeping in the dust with the exception of one. Thus I have seen Illinois in a state of infancy, have beheld her growth, have been jealous for her character, which she has preserved unsullied; have seen her form a healthy constitution, and strangers beholding her have been made to say, 'half was never told us;' and I have no doubt but that in a few years she will be able to vie with the tallest of her sisters, and it will no doubt be said of her: 'Many daughters have done virtuously, but thou excellest them all.' I can now sing these beautiful lines from Dr. Watts:

" 'Happy the country where the sheep,
 Cattle and corn have large increase;
Where men securely work or sleep,
 Nor sons of plunder break their peace.'

"An old Settler in Illinois. R. L."

The young man whose arm was broken by the Indian's bullet was Benjamin Ogle, a son of Captain Joseph Ogle, and an uncle of Robert Lemen. He was a pioneer leader of note, was one of the constituent members of (Canteen) now Bethel church, and was ordained as a Baptist minister by a council of ministers of that church, and became a preacher of large influence and fine ability.

Robert Lemen was not only a good general writer, but he could write very creditable poetry. He had a good voice for music, and for more than forty years, by general consent, he led in the congregational singing at Bethel church; and succeeding him the congregational and choir music at different times were led by William P. Bowler, James Hogan, Cyrus Begole and others. At this time the church has an organ, and the choir singing is generally conducted by the younger members, several of them being the descendants of Robert Lemen and his wife.

The children of this worthy pioneer couple were Milton, James H., Catharine, Emma, John T., Miriam, Robert, Isaac, Joseph L., Hester, Josiah, Moses, William E., Gideon S. and Rachel. Milton Lemen died shortly after marriage. Robert died in infancy, Rachel in childhood and William and Moses in early manhood. Each of the others were married and reared families. They were all members of the Baptist faith, or believers; were successful in the accumulation of a fair living, and all have passed to their final rest. Professor Clarence J. Lemen, Cap-

tain James Garretson, Lieutenant Cyrus A. Lemen
and Robert Price, grandsons of Robert Lemen and
wife, were soldiers in the Union army in the late war.

In stature Robert Lemen was about of medium
height, compactly built and muscular for a man of
his weight. In temperament he had a fine equipoise,
but quick and resolute to resent an injury, but also
quick to forgive on reasonable apology. As citizen,
officer, husband and father he discharged all his
duties faithfully, and as a Christian and active laborer
in the cause of the Divine Master he has left a
monument and record of faithful and intelligent
services which all respect and honor. For some
years before his death he suffered much inconvenience and finally great pain from the growth of a
tumor on his neck or throat, and later he submitted
to a surgical operation by Dr. McDowell, Sr., an
eminent surgeon and physician of St. Louis, but
without permanent benefit. He met his sufferings
heroically, but continued to fail, and he died at his
home in Ridge Prairie, Ill., on August 24, 1860, aged
nearly 77 years. His funeral services were attended
by a large concourse of sorrowing friends and relatives, and he was laid to rest in Bethel Cemetery by
the side of his beloved wife, who had preceded him
by several years to the Better Land.

HESTER TOLIN LEMEN the wife of Robert
Lemen, and a member of the noted pioneer Tolin
family, possessed every attribute of noble womanhood
which goes to make up the faithful wife, the devoted

mother and the true Christian. In early life she united with the Baptist Church, and she adorned her profession by a blameless and noble life. In the arduous duties of providing for a large family of children amid the privations and hardships of the early pioneer days she did her part well, and in every enterprise of her husband she always gave him a hearty and intelligent second. It was said that the young and old and rich and poor all loved "Aunt Hester Lemen," and that she never lost a friend except by death. She did not live to a remarkable old age, but when the summons came she was not unprepared. She died at the family residence on November 21, 1849, aged nearly 63 years.

CHAPTER IV.

38—REV. JOSEPH LEMEN.

REV. JOSEPH LEMEN, second child and son of Rev. James Lemen, Sr. and Catharine Lemen, his wife, was born in Berkley County, Virginia, on September 8, 1785, and with his parents moved to New Design, Ill., in 1786. He received a common school education, and on January 19, 1809, he married Miss Mary Kinney, and they settled on their farm in Ridge Prairie, St. Clair County, Ill., in the early years of the century, where they made a permanent home and reared a large family. In their early lives both he and his wife united with the Baptist Church, and obeying the call of his Divine Master to enter the ministry he was duly licensed to preach the gospel, and at a little later period his ordination followed by a council of duly authorized ministers at the Bethel Baptist Church (then called Canteen Creek Church), of which he and his wife were two of the constituent members. His brother, Rev. James Lemen, Jr., assisted at his ordination; the same council ordaining his father, Rev. James Lemen, Sr., and Rev. Benjamin Ogle at the same occasion at Bethel, or then Canteen Church. Like his father and brothers, Rev. Joseph Lemen was intensely anti-slavery in his views, and like them he did his share in setting in motion the causes which finally secured Illinois in the sister-

hood of the Union as a free State. Formerly a
Whig in politics, he became a Republican when that
party was merged into the Republican party; and,
like all his brothers, he had a profound respect for
Abraham Lincoln. In common with them he also
had a high regard for Stephen A. Douglas, regarding
him justly as a great national leader and as a true
patriot in the then coming peril of the Union, and as
a man of profound ability. The patriotism and profound love for the Union and the old flag by Rev.
Joseph Lemen were as true as the needle to the poles;
and when the news was flashed across the country
that Fort Sumter had fallen under the hostile guns
of South Carolina the old patriot declared "that he
would rather give the last drop of his blood than to
see the Union perish or one star stricken from the old
flag." He called on his brother James, at the home
of the latter, on the same evening, and before departing
—the members of the family being present—the Rev.
Joseph Lemen made a most touching and eloquent
prayer that the Union, in the awful conflict impending, might be saved from final dissolution. The venerable patriot passed to his final rest and reward long
before the conclusion of the war; but his prayer has
been answered in the restoration of the Union and
flag to a place of loyal love and devotion in the hearts
of the people of all sections of our common country.
His brothers and sisters were also equally and
intensely loyal in their love for the Union and the old
flag, but Nancy, William, Moses and Robert did not
live to see the Union assailed by civil war.

38—REV. JOSEPH LEMEN.

Rev. Joseph Lemen was a man of considerable general information and a close and devoted student of the Bible, and with a musical voice he delighted in singing the sacred songs of the grand old poets, Dr. Watts being his favorite poet, and for whom he named one of his sons. He was a feeling, devoted minister in his discourses, and an active and successful laborer in the cause of his Master—his ministerial field extending to Iowa and Missouri; but St. Clair County and Southern Illinois were his chief fields of labor, where, for a period of more than a half century, he successfully called men to seek repentance and salvation. In the course of his labors he assisted to organize many churches and he accomplished a great general work. For many years, and down to 1851, he, with his brother James, supplied Bethel Church with pastoral and ministerial services (except for a period when Rev. Moses Lemen was pastor), and their labors were blessed, as the church increased greatly in numbers and strength. He was a lover of good poetry, and it is said he composed one or two poems in sacred verse. In common with some of his brothers, particularly Robert and James, he was an active worker for the temperance cause in St. Clair County, and he delivered an excellent and able temperance address in connection with that cause in Bethel Church, which was said to have been published in the cotemporaneous press, and which we should be pleased to publish here, but we cannot find the papers containing it. Rev. Joseph Lemen and his father and brothers gave previously careful study to their sermons, but always delivered them without writing, unless they were designed for publication.

In their dress in later life, when in society, the pioneer Lemen family, Joseph and his brothers and sisters, were always well and tastefully (but not vainly) clad, and with stately and fine manners, and a graceful, easy carriage, they were well at home in polite and cultured society. In his family government Rev. Joseph Lemen was very strict, but always reasonable, and his children yielded a ready obedience; and like all the other pioneer Lemens, he always maintained family worship. He and his wife were good providers, and they gave their children good religious training and opportunities for common school education. They built a very comfortable residence and secured a good farm, where they lived, and they also had a farm a few miles south of Bethel Church on the Belleville road, but disposed of that eventually.

In stature Mr. Lemen was above the medium in height; not of a heavy, but a compact frame, straight and muscular; in disposition generous, but brave, and always a defender of the right as he understood it. He was a careful, good farmer, and as a father, husband, citizen and Christian he discharged his duties faithfully and successfully. On a quiet summer day, June 29, 1861, at his home in Ridge Prairie, Ill., he reclined upon his bed to rest for an hour, though in his usual health, when the summons came, and peace-

No. 55. { 220—Marta E. Burnette. 223—Nellie E. Guion. 222—Ida R. Beatty
224—Joseph E. Lemen. 221—Catharine Dripe.

fully the old pioneer passed to his final rest in the
76th year of his age. The funeral services were held
at his residence, attended by a vast concourse of his
friends and relatives, after which the remains were
interred in the family cemetery at the old homestead.

The children of the Rev. Joseph Lemen and Mary
K. Lemen, his wife, were Sallie, James, Benjamin,
Joseph, Isaac W., Polly, Robert C., Eliza, William
K., Catharine, Elizabeth, and three which died in infancy unnamed. Catharine died in childhood. Each
of the others united with the Baptist Church in early
life and all were married and reared families. The
only survivors are William K. Lemen, who, with his
wife, lives at the residence on his farm near Collinsville, Ill., and Elizabeth, who, with her husband,
Charles Leslie, lives in Missouri. Rev. Joseph
Lemen and wife had a son, Joseph K. Lemen, who
was a captain in the Mexican war and a major in the
Union Army in the late war, and also two grandsons,
Capt. William K. Murphy and Joseph, his brother,
who served in the late war for the Union.

MARY K. LEMEN, the wife of Rev. Joseph
Lemen, was a member of the distinguished pioneer
Kinney family, a sister of the Hon. William Kinney,
who was Lieutenant Governor of Illinois from 1826 to
1830. She possessed a fine figure and marked personal attractions, and, like the Lieutenant Governor,
she was quick at humor and repartee; but after her
marriage she was not satisfied with her limited learning, and under the kind advice and instructions of

her husband she improved her education. She gave
her husband a ready and intelligent support in all his
labors and enterprises, and in religion she was a Baptist from early life. She was a faithful wife, a loving
mother and a devoted Christian, and with her husband
was an active supporter of religious interests. She
died at Mount Vernon, Ill., on June 1, 1863, while
visiting relatives and friends there, aged about 71
years. The remains were brought to her home in
Ridge Prairie, St Clair County, Ill., by members of
the family, and after appropriate funeral services,
which were attended by the family, relatives and
other friends, she was interred by loving hands by
the side of her husband in the family cemetery.

CHAPTER V.

39—REV. JAMES LEMEN, JR.

REV. JAMES LEMEN, JR., a son of Rev. James Lemen, Sr. and Catharine Lemen, his wife, was born at the home of his parents in New Design, Monroe County, Ill., on October 8, 1787. He was the pupil of Rev. John Clark, a Scotchman by birth, and a man of a good, classical education; and under his instructions James Lemen completed a liberal course of study, comprehending the French, mathematics and many of the other higher branches. In early life he was baptized by Rev. David Badgeley and became a member of the Baptist Church, and in early manhood he was regularly licensed and shortly afterwards ordained as a minister of the gospel of that faith. Soon after entering the ministry he was called to Vincennes, Ind., on business with General William Henry Harrison, and at that time he was present at the war council held by General Harrison and the old Indian Chief Tecumseh and his warriors. In council he saw the old chief, Tecumseh, pass the lie to Harrison and raise his tomahawk, but without flinching Harrison flashed out his sword, and the great chief stepped back and apologized. On the following night he told his warriors that he had heard that Harrison was a "squaw" and would not fight, and that he gave him the lie to test him; and he added, "Harrison no squaw, he fight to kill;" and after that Tecumseh was very polite to General Harri-

son. From Vincennes Mr. Lemen, in company of Rev.
John Baugh, proceeded to Kentucky, the two ministers having been delegated by the early Baptist
churches in Illinois to represent them in a Baptist
association in that State; and having executed their
mission, and preached several sermons at a revival meeting and elsewhere, they returned home.
While in Kentucky Mr. Lemen visited a relative, a
daughter of Nicholas Lemen, one of the three emi-
grant brothers who settled in Virginia in 1708. She
had married and settled in Kentucky in early times.
She held the little box which Cromwell had pre-ented
to her great-grandmother at her marriage in Scotland, her father Nicholas having brought it to
America with him in 1708, and Mr. Lemen saw it.

At a later period he was an admirer of Kentucky's
greatest citizen, Henry Clay, and although differing
with him on the great doctrine of protection—Mr.
Clay being an ardent protectionist and Mr. Lemen
then being a free trader—they were warm personal
and political friends, and when Mr. Clay visited St.
Louis upon one occasion he wrote Mr. Lemen to meet
him, which he did, and they then consulted as to the
programme of conducting a general election canvass,
then pending, in the best interests of their party.
Mr. Lemen also received a letter from his great and
warm personal friend, Abraham Lincoln, in 1862,
urging the cause of protection, in which he said that
" protection was not only necessary for the benefit
of the whole country, but that it was absolutely

39—REV. JAMES LEMEN, JR.

demanded in behalf of our great laboring, industrial
and farming interests.'' But Mr. Lemen could never
see his way clear to indorse it until his warm personal
friend, the Senior Congressman McKinley, of Ohio,
President McKinley's father, satisfied him of its
necessity and soundness by his ar uments in a
masterly letter which he wrote him, after which Mr.
Lemen was always a firm and unyielding advocate for
the great doctrine of a protective tariff.

Like his father and brothers, particularly Robert
and Joseph, Rev. James Lemen, Jr., labored for
temperance and the anti-slavery cause, as well as for
the higher mission of the gospel; and he had the
courage of his convictions wherever his duty called
him. In traveling and preaching in Kentucky he
chanced to pass the great plantation residence of a
planter who owned a great many slaves, and he was
whipping one most unmercifully for some trivial
offense, when Mr. Lemen rode up and quietly inter-
posed for mercy, at which the enraged planter became
frantic and threatened vengeance against him; but
he sat on his horse and kindly reasoned with the
planter, who was a professed Christian, which finally
so moved the man that he repented of his cruel act
and his rash temper, and calling all his slaves from
their quarters he asked Mr. Lemen to preach to them
and his family, who had meantime all come out to
the road; and sitting on his horse he preached to all,
slaves and masters, and some of the poor negroes
began to shout and a most interesting meeting was

held there on the road, the planter promising his
slaves to be tender and merciful to them in the
future. But this was not enough; he insisted that
Mr. Lemen should dismount and become his guest
for the night, and complying, the planter gave him
princely treatment and invited the neighbors in, and
at night Mr. Lemen preached to a large congregation
at the planter's house.

In 1810 Rev. James Lemen, Jr., with the Rev.
John Baugh, constituted the Canteen—now the Bethel
Baptist Church—from members who had withdrawn
from the Richland Baptist Church on anti-slavery
grounds; and with the organization of Bethel Church
began the anti-slavery contest which finally secured
Illinois as a free state. Mr. Lemen served for sixteen
years in the Territorial and State Legislatures and
was a member of the constitutional convention which
framed the first constitution for Illinois and which
made her forever a free State. He sat as a legislator
at the three capitals, first at Kaskaskia, then at
Vandalia and finally at Springfield, serving as State
Senator for the last two terms and previously as a
Representative. He also served several times as a
Federal grand juror at Springfield, and was one of
the Commissioners who located the St. Clair County
Seat at Belleville. At one time when serving as a
member of the General Assembly, he was waited on
at night by a committee of the joint caucuses of the
two parties and tendered an election as United States
Senator, with full assurance that at the joint meeting

of the two houses the next day his election would be
unanimous; but he declined the place, having formed
a resolution and recorded a vow to henceforth devote
his time and service more wholly to the duties of the
ministry.

On December 8, 1813, Rev. James Lemen, Jr.,
was married to Miss Mary Pulliam at the residence of
William Lot Whitesides near Belleville, Ill. They
settled on their farm in Ridge Prairie, Ill., the same
year, where they built a home and reared their
family. With their industry, frugality and good
management they finally secured a good large farm
and built a comfortable house of seven rooms. Like
his father and brothers, Mr. Lemen had a strict
family government, and their children always yielded
a ready obedience and mutual affection always ruled
their home. The parents provided well for their
children's wants and gave them careful religious
training and good educational advantages. They
always maintained family worship. Mr. Lemen had
a large general reading; his library contained several
hundred wisely selected volumes, among them a full
line of Commentaries on Holy Writ, a full list of
ancient histories and many of the works of the
modern authors and poets of England and America.

The field of the gospel labors of Rev. James
Lemen, Jr., extended into Indiana, Kentucky and
Missouri, but St. Clair County and Southern Illinois
comprised the chief field of his gospel labors; but
much of his time was given to his beloved old Church

of Bethel, and with his brother Joseph, for a long
term of years, he furnished that church with pastoral
services; but at the same time he made many preaching tours elsewhere in Illinois and assisted to organize
many other Baptist Churches.   Like his other brothers who were preachers, Rev. James Lemen, Jr.,
never received nor demanded any considerable
remuneration.   Souls were their recompense, and
the favor of their Divine Master was the great incen-
tive to their arduous toils and long years of service.
They considered these rewards better than gold.
Mr. Lemen enjoyed the acquaintance of a large circle
of the leading men in both church and State. Of the
ministerial co-laborers of the State who served with
the pioneer Lemens there were many prominent
divines whose memories will long be cherished; but
the only living and active minister in that list in
Illinois is the Rev. Justus Bulkley, D. D., of Shurtleff
College, Upper Alton, a preacher who for talent,
piety and devotion to the cause of religion has no
superior in Illinois.   He held a warm place in the
hearts of the pioneer Lemen preachers.   Mr. Lemen
enjoyed the acquaintance of every Governor and
United States Senator who ever served the State of
Illinois down to 1870; and though differing in politics from Senator Stephen A. Douglas, the latter
being a Democrat, and he first a Whig and then a
Republican, he regarded Douglas as a man of profound ability and personally esteemed him very
highly.   But Abraham Lincoln, with whom he was

more intimately acquainted, and who was often present in the courts in and around Springfield, where he met him, had a warm place in his personal esteem. Upon one occasion when Mr. Lemen was at Springfield, Lincoln, who was troubled with some doubts, came to his room and spent the night with him to converse on religious views. Lincoln was not a member of any church, but he there expressed a profound reverence for the divine economy and the word of God. The greater part of the night was spent by Mr. Lincoln and Mr. Lemen alternately stating their reasons in support of the truth of God's word. They retired at a late hour and in the morning Mr. Lincoln, with all doubts removed, expressed himself as very much gratified with their interview.

Upon another occasion when Mr. Lemen was called to preach the funeral discourse of a friend who lived and died a few miles from Springfield, both Douglas and Lincoln were present. After services they accompanied Mr. Lemen to a friend's house and dined together and spent a very pleasant afternoon in talking over old pioneer times in Illinois. In speaking about the organization of Bethel Church on an anti-slavery basis by the pioneer Lemens and their friends, and also of their anti-slavery labors in general, Mr. Lincoln said that it was these circumstances and facts which finally secured Illinois as a free State when she entered the Union; and he appealed to Mr. Douglas to know if he was familiar with the facts, and Douglas replied that he was, and that Lincoln's

judgment was correct. Senator Lyman Trumbull,
another acquaintance and friend of the pioneer Lemen
brothers, also expressed the same views to a friend
in Belleville, the late Sylvester Lemen, quite a number of years ago. But of all our public men, the
mighty achievements and tragic death of Abraham
Lincoln endeared his memory to the old pioneer,
Rev. James Lemen, Jr., beyond the power of words
to express; and when the news of Lincoln's assassination reached him at his home he called the members of his family and others present into his room
and made the following

PRAYER :

"Our Father in Heaven, we approach the Throne
of Mercy and Grace with hearts bowed down with
grief, because our nation's ruler and Thy chosen
servant, Abraham Lincoln, has fallen, and a great
life has gone out, not in the behests of honorable war-
fare, but to gratify the idle vagaries and the heartless vengeance of a pitiless monster and a brutal assassin. But in the depths of our grief we yet thank
Thee for the gift of Abraham Lincoln, under whose
leadership, by Thy guidance and blessing, the nation
has again reached the port of peace and a haven of
rest; and we praise Thee again for one country and
one flag. Bless our erring brethren of the South who
have grounded their arms and submitted to the national
laws, and in obedience to Lincoln's decree have
abandoned slavery. Build up the waste and ruin and

desolation of war. Grant that the rivers of blood
which have flown from the brave hearts of both the
North and South, and that perished in the conflict,
may be sanctified as a warning to our countrymen for
wisdom, patience and forbearance, and that precious
blood seal a peace that shall endure forever. We
thank Thee for the freedom of the slave. Plant anew
in the hearts of our Southern brethren a loyal love
for the Union and flag. Bless all efforts making to
build up Thy cause and kingdom. Bring hope and
peace and prosperity to every heart and every home
in our broad land. Remember all here in divine presence. Guard, guide and keep us, and finally save us
in a world without end, for Christ's sake. Amen.''

The above prayer is a verbatim copy of the original,
as at request Rev. James Lemen, Jr., repeated it, and
it was written down.

In addition to his occupation of farming, Mr.
Lemen and Jacob Ogle, Sr., his uncle, had a mill on
Ogle's Creek, operated by water power, for grinding
wheat and corn; but it was successful only at
brief intervals, by reason of insufficient water, and he
built a more substantial mill on his farm in
Ridge Prairie, which was operated by the power of
several horses, and which made the flour and meal of
the adjacent community for some time. From childhood until old age disabled him Mr. Lemen had a
busy life. He was the second child born of American parents in Illinois and the first native preacher
ordained in the Territory, and for more than half a

century he was an active minister of the gospel. But while he had a busy life between his secular and ministerial labors, he found time to devote to study. He was a close Bible student and also an extensive reader in general literature and poetry, also a good singer. He was a great lover of the early American poets and the old British poets, and he read them largely with much interest. He wrote largely for the religious and secular press on current subjects; he also wrote quite a number of poems, and we here reproduce the following poetical words which he wrote under the caption of

MY FATHER.

My Father is rich; the wealth of His stores
Abounds everywhere to far distant shores;
And His unclouded title to treasures untold
Holds fabulous mountains of silver and gold;
With a Father so rich, need ever I fear
That hunger and want shall ever come near?
If I bow at His throne and tell my wants there,
Rich gifts will He bring to answer my prayer.

My Father has power; the world He commands,
He fashions the mountains and holds in His hands
The winds and the waves, and no tempest so wild
That it does not obey Him as a dutiful child:
With a Father Whose hand can thus still the storm,
Should I fear any foe or dread any harm?
I will bow at His throne, for His promise is sure,
And if only I ask He will keep me secure.

My Father is great; His crystalline throne
Is blazing with jewels of value unknown;
And as choirs celestial pour forth their lays,
Heaven's canopy rings with songs of His praise;

And though bright is the throng which near his throne
    stands,
And arch-angels are waiting to do His commands,
Yet amid all the homage that angels can pay,
My Father still hears me whenever I pray.

My Father is good; nor a sigh nor a groan
Has pain ever uttered unheard at His throne;
Not a woe can we suffer nor a tear-drop fall,
But He sees and pities and numbers them all:
With a Father so good, no harm can betide,
And when my frail craft on Jordan shall ride,
He will quiet the storm on the wild wave's crest
And bring me at last to a haven of rest.

In stature Mr. Lemen was above the medium in height, straight and compactly built and of fine physical proportions in every way. In temperament very resolute, but reasonable, generous and obliging; and in charitable and religious gifts (for fifty years) he always appropriated $50 a year in money, sometimes much more—in addition to giving large gratuitous services to the churches. For ten years before his death he was confined to his home on account of the physical infirmities of approaching age, but his mental faculties were unimpaired up to the fatal termination of his last illness. Morally and mentally, Rev. James Lemen, Jr., had a fine equipoise, and in his duties to his family, society, church and State, he was faithful, and in every sense his life may be said to have been a success. In his last illness his physician attended him, but without avail. At the death-bed scene his wife and some members of the family and other friends were present, and about one hour before his death his son, Sylvester Lemen, asked him to take some wine which the physician had prescribed, but he declined with this beautiful quotation: "Not till I take it anew in the kingdom of heaven," and these were his last words. The end was at hand, and just as the sun set and the shadows of twilight were gathering, on the evening of February 8, 1870, at his home in Ridge Prairie, Ill., the old pioneer, Rev. James Lemen, Jr., in his 83rd year, peacefully passed to his last rest and "his spirit returned to the bosom of that Divinity who gave it." On February 10th, brief services were held at his residence, his wife not being able to attend at the church, after which the cortege moved to Bethel Church, where, in the presence of a large concourse of friends and relatives, appropriate funeral services were held, Rev. W. S. Post and other ministers officiating, after which the remains were interred in Bethel cemetery. And thus he sleeps nearly under the shadows of the old church which he loved and for which he labored for so many years.

MARY PULLIAM LEMEN, wife of Rev. James Lemen, Jr., and a daughter of John Pulliam and Margaret Pulliam, his wife, was born near Richmond, Va., on April 27, 1794, and removed to New Design, Ill., with her parents in 1795, her mother dying in Mary's infancy. She was reared by her brother-in-law and sister, Mr. and Mrs. William Lot Whitesides, who lived near Belleville, Ill. Some years before moving to Illinois, her father and one or two of the

older children went to Kentucky to locate a home for
the family, but they returned to Virginia again and
then they all removed to Illinois. Her mother,
Margaret Stockton Pulliam, was a descendant of the
Stockton family, who came from England in the early
colonial days and settled in America, and several of
whose descendants were active in the war for independence against England, one of them, Richard
Stockton, signing the Declaration of Independence.
A few years after her marriage Mrs. Mary Lemen
united with the Bethel Baptist Church, and she had
been a member of that church for fifty-six years at
the time of her death. She was an affectionate
mother, a faithful wife and a devoted Christian and
friend to the poor, and beloved by everybody who
knew her. After a brief illness in which the best
medical services were of no avail, she died at her
home in Ridge Prairie, Ill., on February 23rd, 1876,
in the 82nd year of her age; and thus passed as loving a wife, as fond a mother, as faithful a Christian
and as noble a friend as ever honored the name of
true womanhood. Her funeral services occurred at
Bethel Church on February 25th, attended by a large
concourse of friends and relatives, Rev. W. S. Post
and others officiating, after which the remains were
interred in Bethel cemetery by the side of her husband.

The children of Rev. James Lemen, Jr., and wife,
were Lucinda, Sylvester, Catharine, Nancy, Jacob O.,
John C., James P., Robert S., Mary E., Joseph B., and

Moses P. John died in early manhood, unmarried, but he had become a member of Bethel Baptist Church before his death. Each of the others united with the Bethel Church, all were married and had families, and four of them yet survive: James, who with his wife and family live at Hastings, Minn.; Robert and his wife and son live at Cairo, Ill.; Mary Stebbins and her daughter live at Denver, Colo., her husband having died some years since, and Joseph B. Lemen and his wife live at their home near Collinsville, Ill. Rev. James Lemen, Jr., and wife had one son, Moses P. Lemen, who served for a short time as assistant surgeon in the Union Army; and two of their grandsons, Lieutenant Edward C. Lemen and Judge Cyrus L. Cook were also in the Union Army. In the Black Hawk war they had a son-in-law, Captain Samuel Bowman, killed by the Indians while leading his company in battle.

CHAPTER VI.

41—WILLIAM LEMEN.
40—MRS. NANCY TOLIN.
43—MRS. CATHARINE HARLOW.

WILLIAM LEMEN, a son of Rev. James Lemen, Sr., and Catharine Lemen, *nee* Ogle, was born at the home of his parents in New Design, Ill., on May 1, 1793. For strength and form he was a child of remarkable development, as he walked at seven months old. In early manhood his phenomenal strength was such that he could easily tilt a barrel of cider on his knee and take a drink from it; and upon one occasion, upon the wager of a miller, he carried a nine-bushel sack of wheat on his shoulder; and when wrestling in the army when a soldier, the managers of the sport nearly always pitted two men against him and usually he won the prize.

He acquired an ordinary education for the pioneer days. He was a good reader, wrote a fair hand and had some knowledge of mathematics; and in later life he was a close bible reader and could quote every word from memory in the Book of Psalms without one omission. His wife, Miss Mary Miller, a daughter of Mr. Henry Miller, who lived near where the city of Belleville now stands, was of German extraction, could read and speak both the German and English languages fluently and was a noble Christian woman whom everybody esteemed. They were married on

October 10, 1810, and from this union there were nine children, three sons and six daughters.

In the war of 1812 he enlisted as a soldier in the company of Captain James B. Moore and served until the close of the war, being in several engagements against the Indians who were the allies of England in that war. He was one of a small party who followed and killed several of the Indian band who had murdered the families of Moore and Reagan in the Wood River settlement. He was in the campaign of Governor Edwards, of Peoria, when they burned the village and killed and dispersed the last fragment of that once powerful tribe, the Kickapoos. He stood near Major Murdock, who shot an Indian who was trying to shoot one of them, and saw him walk up and put his foot on his neck and then calmly reload his rifle with the remark: "Bill, that is the way to serve the redskins."

Mr. Lemen was in General Zachary Taylor's command when they ascended the Mississippi River to Prairie du Chien. On that expedition General Taylor landed his troops on an island near the foot of the Lower Rapids. The island was covered with a dense growth of weeds and willows, and a vast body of Indians managed to reach and conceal themselves therein, and when General Taylor discovered their presence he ordered Captain Daniel Whitesides, with a detachment, to dislodge them. The order was a fearful mistake, and it is difficult to see why General Taylor made it. Captain Whitesides knew it, but he was a brave leader,

41—WILLIAM LEMEN.

and he selected tried soldiers, William Lemen among
them, and made the assault. But a few minutes
revealed the fearful odds. The unseen foe in tremendous forces was mowing our men down, and Captain
Whiteside, seeing the hopeless and useless sacrifice,
ordered a hasty retreat. Many of our men were
killed. A soldier fell by the side of Mr. Lemen and
pleaded not to be left, and nobody seemed to heed
his prayer; but Mr. Lemen called another comrade to
help him, and, though the bullets were raining like
hail around them, they carried the poor fellow back
to the boats, but he died in a few hours.

In the morning the enemy was greatly increased,
and to ascertain their purpose General Taylor ordered
his men to hoist the black flag. As soon as this was
done the roar of cannon was heard suddenly and
unexpectedly as a peal of thunder from the clear sky.
A hasty retreat was ordered, but the boats were
necessarily slow in getting out, and the long boat of
General Taylor had her steering oar and six of her
side oars cut away and her hull pierced by a cannon
ball just above the water-line. No one ever dreamed
of a cannon up in that section, but the British, antici-
pating Taylor's movements, had brought several
heavy guns across the lakes with which to oppose
him. The boats floated slowly down the river, sometimes turning around in the currents, all the time
under a heavy fire from the enemy until they passed
out of reach; but the shouts of our men and the roar
of their musketry showed that they were neither

alarmed nor idle. Having passed down the river
beyond the present reach of the enemy Taylor and
his command disembarked on the east bank, where
they constructed what was then called Fort Adams.

In his duties as a soldier, Mr. Lemen was fearless
and faithful, and for these noble qualities he enjoyed
the confidence and good will of his officers and comrades; but his inordinate disposition and love for
practical jokes and his consummate and phenomenal
talents for planning and executing them, gave the
officers some anxious concern; but at the same time
they were generally so amused with his usually harmless jokes that they could not reprimand him without
breaking down with laughter. An event in this line
occurred at the building of Fort Adams. Mr. Lemen,
with a number of Frenchmen, were hauling a wagon
load of timbers up an incline, when suddenly he pretended to become frightened, and breaking out of the
harness the wagon descended and a Frenchman was
injured, for which offense the Colonel, though an
ardent friend of Mr. Lemen, had to send him to the
guard-house. But pending his brief detention there
he, with his musical voice of tremendous volume,
sang the national airs, and among them, "Yankee
Doodle," with such wonderful accent and effect that
the whole army heard him, and General Taylor
almost took a fit of laughter at it. The Frenchman
soon discovered that Mr. Lemen was singing himself
into universal favor with both officers and men, and
he petitioned Taylor to turn him out and reprimand

1250—E. T. Edwards.   874—Dim Wid Lemen.   1218—Peck Cooksey.   1217—John T. Cooksey.

873—Laura L. Edwards.   871—Hattie B. Lemen.   860—John B. Lemen.   872—Minnie B. Cooksey.

1221—Waldrip Edwards.   1219—Fannie Cooksey.

him. So, accordingly, he called him before him and asked him if he could proceed with assisting to haul the timbers for the fort? To this Mr. Lemen replied that he would try; but he told General Taylor that as he, in doing so, was filling the place of a horse for the Government, and to make it true to nature and realistic it would be necessary for him to shy and scare at such objects as would naturally frighten a spirited horse; and that he would greatly oblige him if he would detail the Frenchman to remove the black stump which frightened him, and such other objects as might involve the safety of the team by preventing a second affright which might be more disastrous than the first. By this time General Taylor was so overcome with laughter that he could scarcely command his dignity, and he afterwards said that "Lemen was worth a regiment of men to keep his army in good cheer, besides his excellent fighting qualities as a soldier." But the recitation of all of Mr. Lemen's practical jokes would fill a volume. In humor he was Davy Crockett's equal, in will-force and courage, General Jackson's; in honesty, General Taylor's; in natural oratory, second only to the best, and in off-hand poetical instincts and capabilities, a match for Robert Burns.

While living a soldier's life Mr. Lemen unfortunately contracted the habit of intemperance—that demon which has wrecked so many brilliant lives—and which largely prevented him from attaining to what he might have been.

In disposition he was humane, generous and obliging, often feeding the poor and unfortunate from his own limited means, and of course anti-slavery in his views. He possessed a vigorous mind; his physical characteristics were a dark complexion, hair and eyes black, height six feet, and weight 185 pounds. He was quite a natural poet. While in the ranging service with him an Indiana soldier composed a poem in honor of his captain, and Captain Moore offered a prize to any of his men who would compose a poem for him that would excel the Indianian's verses. Many competed, and among them William Lemen, who, in the space of half an hour, presented his poem of some ten verses to his captain, and when all the poems were in the judges gave Mr. Lemen the prize. As indicating his great endurance Mr. Lemen once cradled, bound and shocked three acres of heavy wheat in one day. At another time he swam the Mississippi River near St. Louis, then over a mile wide.

About the year 1821 Mr. Lemen reformed, was converted and baptized into the Baptist Church, and after a trial of some years he was ordained as a Baptist minister of the gospel by Rev. John M. Peck, Rev. W. F. Boyakin, Rev. James Pulliam, and two other members of the council of ordination; and for some years he circulated in St. Clair, Randolph and Monroe counties; and in Missouri, preaching and doing good work. He organized a small church in Monroe County, near which he lived and died, at which he often preached and where many converts were baptized. He died November 2, 1858, and was buried in a place of his own selection in Renault Grant, ten miles south of Waterloo, Ill., where the remains of his worthy wife were also buried.

NANCY (LEMEN) TOLIN was born at the old homestead of her parents, Rev. James Lemen, Sr., and wife, in New Design, Ill. She received an ordinary education and in early life married John Tolin. They settled on a farm in Monroe County and built themselves a permanent home, where they reared a family. Parents and children were all members of the Baptist Church. They were good providers and kind Christian parents, and they gave their children good religious training and a common school education. Mrs. Tolin was a fine singer, was of fine personal appearance, a noble Christian woman, a faithful and loving wife and a devoted mother. She was active in church duties and was greatly esteemed by all her friends and acquaintances for her many neighborly and excellent characteristics. She survived her husband for some years, and at her death was buried by his side in a cemetery at New Design.

John Tolin, her husband, was a member of the early pioneer Tolin family, noted for their many manly and noble deeds and popular traits. He was a good farmer, a great and brave hunter; and as a man and Christian he was highly esteemed by all his acquaintances. Of their children who survived to their majority, one daughter married Joseph Hilton, and the other daughters were all married and had families, as were also their three sons, Luster, James and Brackett. All were members of the Baptist Church and all have passed to their rest. Their names will all appear in full in the genealogical tables in another part of this book.

CATHARINE (LEMEN) HARLOW was born at the home of her parents, Rev. James Lemen, Sr., and wife, in New Design, Ill., and in childhood received a common school education. She was married in early life to Joseph Kinney, and they lived on a farm in Monroe County and reared a family. After his death she married Sylvanus Harlow, but there was no issue. In her early years Mrs. Harlow was a lady of fine personal attractions, and down to her latest years she was a sweet and beautiful singer. In both her marriages she was very happy in every respect, as each of her husbands was a good Christian, a good provider and in every way worthy, excellent and noble men, honest, industrious and highly esteemed by all their acquaintances. As wife, mother, Christian and friend, Catharine Lemen Harlow discharged every duty faithfully and cheerfully; and when the last summons came she passed to her final rest leaving a memory and record worthy of her Christian life. She survived her last husband, Sylvanus Harlow, for some years and died in Missouri. Of the children, Samuel, Catharine, William, James, Polly and Maria Kinney were married and reared families. Of the three survivors, William and family live in Missouri,

Catharine lives in Monroe County, Ill., and Maria with her husband, Mr. Slattery, and her family live in East St. Louis, Ill. Mrs. Catharine Lemen Harlow and her two husbands, with all her children, were members of the Baptist Church. The names of all the children will be found in the genealogical tables in another part of this book.

CHAPTER VII.

42—REV. JOSIAH LEMEN.

44—REV. MOSES DODGE LEMEN.

REV. JOSIAH LEMEN, a son of Rev. James Lemen, Sr., and Catharine, his wife, was born at the home of his parents in New Design, Ill., on August 15, 1794. He acquired a practical education, and on August 3, 1815, he married Miss Rebekah Huff and settled at their home on a farm in New Design, Ill., where they reared a family and acquired a very comfortable competency. Both were members of the Baptist Church, and Mr. Lemen became a minister of the gospel of that faith. He was well read, a fine singer, made a warm, eloquent prayer and delivered a feeling and sympathetic sermon. In every way he was a useful and active worker in the great cause of the Divine Master.

His gospel labors covered a large field and he assisted in organizing and building up many churches. Like his father and brothers, he was an advocate of temperance and thoroughly anti-slavery in his views. He had a considerable library, was a writer of fair ability and was fond of good poetry, of which he read a great deal, and he wrote several poems of considerable merit. Like his brothers, he was a Republican in politics, and a great admirer of Abraham Lincoln and General Grant.

42—REV. JOSIAH LEMEN.

Some years after the death of his first wife he was married again, but from this union there was no issue.   In stature Mr. Lemen was above the medium in height, was well proportioned and very active.   In his mental and moral characteristics he was well equipped for the faithful discharge of the duties of his high calling; and as a minister, man, citizen and friend, he was greatly esteemed.   In rearing and providing for his family he and his first wife met their wants bountifully, and he gave his children good religious and educational advantages; and all, parents and children, were members of the Baptist faith, or believers.   Mr. Lemen was a kind neighbor, a good and successful farmer and a liberal supporter of all good causes; and after rounding out the period of a useful, honorable and religious life, he died on July 11, 1867, aged about 73 years.

Of the children, John, Catharine, Harvey and Josiah were married and had families.   Jemima died in early life, and Noah, in early manhood, was killed by a falling rock at a quarry.   Harvey, who is the only survivor, lives with his family at Lincoln, Neb. Among the grandchildren of Rev. Josiah Lemen and wife are numbered some of the leading members in the higher professions of medicine, teaching and other noble callings, and the names of all will be found in full in the genealogical tables.

REV. MOSES DODGE LEMEN, a son of Rev. James Lemen, Sr., and Catharine, his wife, was born at the home of his parents in New Design, Ill., on

September 3, 1797. In early life he united with the Baptist Church and was ordained as a Baptist minister of the gospel on March 24, 1822. He acquired a good education and was married to Miss Sarah Hull, of Monroe County, Illinois, on February 24, 1817, from which union there were three children. After her death he married Miss Sarah Varnum, and from the latter union there were nine children. He was a preacher of wonderful natural power and an eloquent speaker. He was also a good writer, and many of his articles were published in the secular and religious press. He was a great admirer of good poetry, having composed several poems himself. He was a kind, indulgent parent and faithful husband, and justly inspired and enjoyed the love and devotion of his wife and the dutiful affection of all his children. He was of excellent physical proportions, above the medium height, of heavy build, but active and strong, and of a kindly disposition and social temperament which made everybody his friend; but he was brave and quick to resent an injury, and equally prompt to forgive on reasonable apology. With every attribute which the term *manhood* implies, Rev. Moses Lemen was well equipped to secure and hold the confidence of all his acquaintances. By occupation he was a farmer. He died at his home on his farm in Montgomery County, Illinois, on March 5, 1859, aged about 62 years.

At the death of Rev. Moses Lemen, his brother, Robert Lemen, wrote and published the following sketch of his life and labors in the St. Louis *Western Watchman:*

A PIONEER DEPARTED.

Elder Moses Lemen died at his residence in Montgomery County, Illinois, on March 5, 1859, in the 62nd year of his age. Elder Lemen was born at New Design, Monroe County, Ill., on September 3, 1797. He was the youngest son of Rev. James Lemen, Sr. His father was one of the first pioneers in what was then our Northwestern Territory, and was also among the first four persons who were baptized by immersion in the country now forming the State of Illinois. This baptism occurred more than three score years ago. He was one of the few constituents of the first Baptist Church in Illinois, and was for several years immediately preceding his death one of the pioneer preachers of the country.

Moses Lemen indulged in a hope in Christ when but ten years of age. He joined the church when young and was ordained to preach the gospel on March 24, 1822. He continued his labors as a minister for the term of thirty-six years. At the age of 20, on February 24, 1817, he was united in marriage with Miss Sarah Hull, of Monroe County, Illinois. She was an agreeable companion, professed conversion, and united with the church. She died in a few years in the hope of a blessed immortality, leaving three children, of whom the youngest was about one year old. After a time Mr. Lemen deemed it advisable to make choice of a second partner and married

Miss Sarah Varnum, with whom he lived until his death. She was a kind and affectionate step-mother and she bore cheerfully the privations which her husband's ministerial labors imposed upon her. In this respect she is worthy of imitation. Shortly after her marriage she was converted and united with the church. May grace be given her to bear the heavy trial. Moses Lemen has left behind him four aged brothers and one sister, a wife and eight children, together with a numerous connection of relatives and friends. They mourn their loss, but they have the consolation that the Judge of all the earth will do right. He is too wise to err and too good to be unkind.

Elder Moses Lemen's natural temper and disposition caused it to be his study and delight to make all with whom he had intercourse happy and comfortable. He was always cheerful and pleasant, kind-hearted and willing to give a part of what he possessed to those who were in want. He was the poor man's friend.

Agreeably to pressing invitations of churches he was several times in pastorates, and was thus the means of erecting several houses of worship. Yet his desire for the most part seemed to be to travel from place to place and preach the gospel; he had a great anxiety to attend as many protracted meetings as possible, and he always took an active part in these meetings. His general rule was to attend the first day and continue until the meetings closed, laboring day and night.

44—REV. MOSES D. LEMEN.

Having an extensive acquaintance he was often called upon to preach funeral services. As illustrative of many of these labors of love we will mention the following circumstance: He was at one time requested by a certain brother to preach the funeral sermon of his daughter—a young woman. When he returned he had traveled over one hundred miles without receiving any remuneration for either lost time or labor. The parents of the daughter died soon afterwards leaving a fine estate without an heir to enjoy it.

Moses Lemen had a wife and children who looked to him for support and protection and his sympathies for his family were strong; yet the thought, "woe is me if I preach not the gospel," made such an impression on his mind that he was always in a strait betwixt the claims of his family and the claims of the gospel. His family felt the effects of his absence and loss of time. But such has been the lot of our pioneer ministers most of whom have gone to their reward above. Under the circumstances in which he lived and labored, moving from place to place, it was not his lot to possess a large share of the things which pertain to this life. But he was rich in faith.

He thought no calling greater or more honorable than that of preaching the Gospel of Jesus Christ. On one occasion, however, while residing in Monroe County, Illinois, at the solicitation of many friends, he allowed his name to be used as a candidate to represent said county in the State Legislature. He

was elected and served to the best of his ability, but
never afterwards would become a candidate for office.
He thought it his duty to give his time to the ministry. Towards the close of his life, as if impressed
with the near approach of death, he became more
and more spiritual, which was noticed by all who
were familiar with him. There seemed to be more
of the spirit in his preaching, praying, singing and
every-day conversation. In December last (1858)
he, with Elder Elijah Dodson, attended a meeting at
Bethel Church, St. Clair County, Illinois, which
continued three weeks, during which he enjoyed good
health. The meeting was interesting; several were
converted, baptized and added to the church. After
the close of the meeting at Bethel he returned home
and appointed a meeting in his own settlement which
lasted three weeks or longer. Several were converted, whom he baptized and received into the
church. He was often heard to say, " if it were the
will of the Lord he would prefer to die in the
meeting-house with the people of God around him."
He almost had his request granted. On the morning
of the day of his decease he informed his family that
he felt somewhat indisposed. He ate his breakfast
as usual and walked out of the house to attend to
some business. Upon his return he sat down, took
his Bible and read until meeting-time, it being the
day of their church meeting. He then took his
family with him to the meeting, took an active part
in the exercises, returned home and was a corpse in

two hours afterwards. He died, it is thought, of
apoplexy. He is now where the wicked cease from
troubling and the weary are at rest. Peace to his
memory.   ROBERT LEMEN.

Rev. Moses Lemen was traveling missionary in
Illinois for the Baptist churches in 1832; and at one
time he also served as the pastor of Bethel Church.
He was married to his second wife, Miss Sarah A.
Varnum, on February 14, 1825. She was born at
Belfast, Maine, August 16, 1804, and came with her
people to New Design, Ill., in early childhood. She
was a devoted wife, a loving mother and a devout
Christian. She survived her husband for some years
and died in Butler, Mo., on December 11, 1889.

Of the children of Rev. Moses Lemen, Hull,
Miriam and Louisa, by his first marriage, and Byron,
Moses, Judson, James, Sarah and Mary, by his
second marriage, all were married and had families,
and all were members of the Baptist Church. The
only survivors now are Mary, who, with her family,
lives in Kansas, and Sarah, who lives with her
husband, Mr. Kingston, at Black Rock, Ark. Rev.
Moses Lemen had one son, James, who was a soldier
in the Union army in the late war.

The following poem was composed in 1835 by
Rev. Moses Dodge Lemen, in memory of Miss
Emeline Reynolds, who was killed by lightning in
the 12th year of her age, in Monroe County, Illinois,
in the house of Mr. Justus Varnum:

How great, how solemn was the stroke
  In Providence Divine,
When God in dreadful thunder spoke
  To little Emeline.

How little did she think that day
  That God in storms would come,
And call her spirit far away
  To its eternal home.

What wond'rous mercy did abound,
  In judgment here we see;
For others, sitting all around,
  Sustained no injury.

The clouds appeared to thickly fly
  The angry winds did blow,
Which brought the dreadful moment nigh
  That laid the damsel low.

The lightnings flashed with dread alarm,
  The thunders loud did roar;
And down she sinks in death's cold arms,
  A corpse upon the floor.

Her friends still hoped she was not dead,
  And raised her in surprise;
Then laid her gently on the bed,
  For death had closed her eyes.

The golden bowl had scarcely broke,
  The springs of life undone,
Before her ransomed spirit took
  Its mansion near the Throne.

There with her Blessed Jesus reigns,
  Transported with his charms;
To pass no more such dreadful scenes,
  As death and thunder storms.

CHAPTER VIII.

THE LABORS OF THE PIONEER LEMENS IN THE CAUSE OF TEMPERANCE.

The old founders of the Lemen family in Illinois, Rev. James Lemen, Sr., and his wife, were ardent and active advocates for temperance, and, for the most part, their children finally were in hearty accord in the great reform. In their earlier years, however, in common with the pioneer custom of the times, they were not for the entire and total abstinence of wine and alcoholic spirits; but they always insisted on strictly temperate uses of the same, when it was necessary at all to keep them; and finally they excluded the use or the keeping of intoxicants from their families, except for medicinal purposes. For a number of years previously, throughout a wide section of our State, the pioneer Lemens, and a few of their friends, had been urging the cause and practice of temperance in their addresses and sermons; and on March 7, 1838, Robert Lemen, with two of his brothers, Joseph and James, and a few other friends, met at Bethel Church, in St. Clair County, and organized *The Bethel Temperance Society*, with David Lawrence as President and James H. Lemen as Secretary. The society was constituted by about forty members. Upon this occasion Robert Lemen and his brother, Rev. James Lemen, Jr., made formal and able temperance addresses, which the society, by

vote, ordered to be published; and we here reproduce
the address of Robert Lemen, which we copy from
The Western Pioneer, of Upper Alton, Ill., of April
6, 1838, published by Ashford Smith & Co., the
editors being Rev. J. M. Peck, Rev. E. Rodgers and
Rev. Washington Leverett. Robert Lemen's address
was as follows:

"FELLOW CITIZENS!—For the purpose of forming
a temperance society in this settlement, I have come
forward to address you. While performing this duty
I should do injustice to myself were I not to speak
plainly and boldly on this important subject, at the
same time not wishing to offend any, while it is my
desire to speak the truth, the whole truth and nothing but the truth.

"Being well convinced of the fact that the use of
ardent spirits is the source of more moral and physical evil to the human race than any other cause whatever, I may safely say that, all other causes combined,
it is this opinion which I shall first endeavor to im-
press upon your minds. I will confine myself to the
mentioning of facts which have either come within
your own knowledge, or are supported by evidence
sufficient to convince every unprejudiced mind. The
demon of intemperance draws forth his legions indis-
criminately from every rank, age, and condition in
life. To this tyrant the prince and the beggar bow
with equal submission. He is no respecter of persons; he brings under his control the lips of the
eloquent man, to whose accents assembled multitudes

have listened with admiration and delight. The tongue of the righteous, whose persuasive words have turned many from the errors of their ways and brings messages of peace to the miserable and wretched, has been palsied by his relentless power. By his corrupting influence the beauty and loveliness of woman has been converted into deformity and loathsomeness. The young, the ardent and the healthful by him are cut off in the midst of their promise. The aged and venerable by him are treated with contempt. Victim after victim he seizes and sacrifices, and yet he is not satisfied, but calls for more. He is encouraged by past success to increase his demands, and will enforce them, unless some revolutionary movement is executed in the dominions over which he shakes his horrid sceptre and triumphantly waves his fiery banner. Nothing will check his desolating career but an open revolt among those whom he is endeavoring to trample under his feet. With us there is no alternative than either submit to his exactions or hurl him from his throne.

"Intemperance is one of the most disgusting of vices. It converts him whom the Ruler of the universe has placed highest in the scale of beings that inhabit this vast earth into a thing more degraded than the brute; it undermines all those principles of men who hold society together; it saps the foundation on which the whole superstructure of human affairs rest. Who can safely rely upon the word of a drunkard? What business can safely be trusted to

his care?   We all know that losses, shiftlessness and
sacrifices attended all his operations.   He who is
gradually becoming a drunkard is gradually becoming
forgetful, negligent, careless, indolent and loose in
all those principles upon which you can rely with any
confidence in the intercourse of life.   These are some
of the consequences which are obvious to the public
eye.

"There are others which have their operations in
private and are fully known only to those who feel
them; and yet these are not the less pernicious and
lamentable in their effects upon the community, because they are working in secret, whilst they are
productive of the most severe misery and the keenest
anguish to those upon whom they directly operate.

"We meet a drunkard in a street of St. Louis or
Belleville, reeling from the dramshop at which he has
been drinking and carousing, as he perhaps would
say, 'taking a friendly glass with his companions,'
until he can hardly stagger along upon the unsteady
earth; he is one in whom we feel no particular
interest.   We have not known him long and therefore
cannot contrast his present condition with what he
once was.   We know nothing but as he now is.   His
grotesque appearance may cause a smile, or excite in
us a feeling of pity.   We pass along to attend to our
own business and trouble ourselves with no further
thought about him.

"Let us examine a little more particularly than
we are accustomed to do, into one of those cases;

let us go home with one of those characters and see what is there. We will find one who was formerly in the higher walks of life; one who, until he was called forth under the banners of intemperance, was an active and useful member of society. Every one who hears could point out a number in the circles of his acquaintances who would answer the description. Once this unhappy man could go home after having spent the day cheerfully and industriously performing all the duties which his various relations in society required of him, and find a happy and contented wife ready to welcome him to that retreat from which the cares, the suspicions, the jealousies and most of the temptations of life may be forever excluded. Now that being to whom he once swore eternal attachment, for whom he could once find words hardly strong enough to express his love; this being who once poured forth her soul in full confidence to him; who gave to him the warm affection of her heart and relied upon him as her best earthly support, now waits in her unhappy dwelling the late return of the unworthy object of her blighted hopes. Her mind wanders back in its lonely musings to the delightful scenes of years gone by and her recollection sends a keener anguish to her heart when she contrasts her present condition with what she looked forward to in brightness of her fond anticipations. She waits his return and as hour after hour passes away her imagination brings up before her a thousand frightful images. She trembles that she hears not his footsteps at the door, and yet, dreads his coming. At length, however, he staggers in, not the merry, jovial fellow that he was in the circles of his drunken companions, but a cross, disgusting brute in human form. She utters no complaint, but exercises all those kind and tender means of which woman is capable, to sooth and calm him into rest. For all her kindness she receives nothing but unfriendly treatment. He who once made every exertion to win her affection and fix it on himself, that very tongue which was once eloquent with words that delighted her ear and sent a thrill of happiness to her heart now insults and abuses her, until her cup is full; nothing can sustain her from sinking under the weight of such trials but a firm reliance upon those principles which religion holds out; but numbers finding themselves unequal to the trial, fall in the struggle and are brokenhearted.

"How many tears of anguish are wrung from the eyes of anxious parents, when they are convinced of the melancholy truth that their son is falling into the snares of intemperance. What greater misfortune can be inflicted on a family of children than for those who gave their existence to become drunkards. Better to have a sober parent dead than a drunken one living. Intemperance is the direct and natural result of what is called the moderate—the temperate use of ardent spirits. All the drunkards have come forth from amongst those who advocate and once made a moderate use. I never knew a man who has suddenly become a drunkard. It is always a gradual progress. No man intends to be intemperate when he commences his career of drinking; he always means to confine himself to the temperate use; and here lies the danger. Thus it is they deceive themselves.

"If every miserable drunkard now in the country could have foreseen in his youth what was to be the result; if he could have beheld himself in a glass as he now appears to the world, there would be very few who would not have entirely abandoned this prudent use. But so imperceptibly are we borne along on this deep and strong, but apparently smooth and peaceful tide, that we are not aware whither it is bearing us until we find ourselves amongst the rapids from which it is too late to escape, and like the Indian who went over the falls of Niagara in his canoe, we lie down in drunkenness and are pitched into the abyss below. But duty and interest both call upon us to awaken to this subject; we have slumbered over it too long already. Thousands and hundreds of thousands of our fellow-beings have already become the victims of intemperance. All this talk about moderate use, temperate use, innocent use, must be abandoned, and the only kind of use which we allow ourselves must be no use at all. It must be considered sinful to make, buy or sell it, or even to give it away.

"About fifty years ago good men, not to say the best of men, bought and sold human flesh and blood without thinking they were doing wrong. What would now be thought of a man who professed to know the will of the meek and lowly Savior, to buy and sell his fellow-man? And yet thousands of dollars have been made by the inhuman, heaven provoking traffic. Who now in our country talks of carrying on the slave trade prudently, or making a moderate use of slaves? The idea, fifty years ago, of keeping slavery out of the Territory of Illinois would have been considered unreasonable, as some pretend now to consider the abolition of ardent spirits. My prayer is, and I trust the time will soon come, when no respectable person will have anything to do with ardent spirits, either making, buying or selling them; when touch not, taste not, handle not, shall be the received maxim.

"The work of regeneration has already commenced and will go on. Some good has already been done in this settlement. We need not fear the result, as has wisely been observed. It will not do for us to talk soberly on the subject for one moment and make it a matter of merriment and jest the next. The evils of intemperance are no fit subjects for laughter; and some of us may yet be made to feel it. I have often wondered how a Christian, especially a preacher of the Gospel, who considers for a moment, can resist the idea that he ought to abstain from drinking ardent spirits.

"But perhaps I am trespassing on your patience. I shall come to a conclusion with the following remarks;

"First. I have been a resident of St. Clair County some little upwards of half a century, and at the early settling of Illinois, the inhabitants being few in number, were under the necessity of uniting and building a place of defense as a safeguard against the sword of the wilderness, from which they at sundry times suffered extremely; while some of the number (although few), in youth and health, found an early grave; yet some were permitted to see the enemy vanquished and peace and happiness restored.

"Second. In this peaceable and happy state we were permitted to live for many years, when all of a sudden our fears were excited and we became dreadfully alarmed at the appearance of an enemy; I mean slavery; but having increased in number and means, we again, as a band of brethren, came forward on the day and time appointed at an election held in 1818 and forever gained a complete victory over the enemy.

"Third and last. We have been and are now most alarmingly threatened by an enemy, ardent spirits, more formidable, more deceitful and more dangerous than the former. It therefore becomes our duty, and the only alternative left us, again as brethren to unite. Union is strength. We would, therefore, in behalf of our beloved country, call on all classes of men, no matter of what denomination, to come and join our standard. We call on the aged and the young, the father, the son, the mother and daughter. Although I am somewhat advanced in life, and have been in the first two mentioned struggles, yet I have again for the third time volunteered.

I have entered the field, and am resolved never to desert my post until the enemy is driven back to his own country whence he came and where he will forever remain harmless.

> " Who will come and join our standard,
>   Help to pull the stronghold down?
>   Temperance men unite; come forward—
>   Then the victory is our own;
>   Endless glory will our useful labors crown."

The Bethel Temperance Society became strong in numbers, and with several kindred societies in other communities and sections of Illinois, exerted a marked influence in arresting the tide of intemperance, and in every way was helpful to the cause of progress and morality.

CHAPTER IX.

THE ANTI-SLAVERY LABORS OF THE PIONEER LEMENS.

As deeply planted anti-slavery sentiments were one of the impelling motives which induced Rev. James Lemen, Sr., to leave his home in Virginia, with his family, where slavery prevailed, and to seek a new home in the then wilderness of Illinois, it was natural that he should here oppose the introduction of slavery. Before leaving Virginia he consulted with his great friend, Thomas Jefferson, who, at heart, was opposed to the institution of slavery, about his purpose to seek a home in Illinois, with the view of assisting to confirm the Northwestern Territory to freedom; and as Jefferson then thought that, sooner or later, there would be an effort and conflict made to introduce slavery here, he advised Mr. Lemen to seek a home here, in the then Western wilderness, and he acted accordingly. It was but a few years after he settled here when he began his great mission of opposition to slavery by assisting to originate, and by heading the lists of great petitions to Congress, asking that body to firmly deny all efforts then being made for the introduction of slavery in the North-western Territory; and thus he assisted to arrest for a time the spreading demands for slavery. But by degrees the persistent efforts of that evil institution strengthened its influence in the Illinois country or territory, and then Rev. James Lemen, Sr., and his

sons, several of whom had become ministers of the
Gospel, endeavored to call the influence and power
of the early churches here to aid in the contest for
freedom, and to assist in shaping the events with a
view of finally bringing Illinois into the Union as a
free State, with a constitution forever forbidding
slavery in her limits.

It will be necessary now to mention the first
churches, largely organized by the influence and labors
of the Lemen pioneers in Illinois, and how they were
finally turned to account in the arrest and exclusion
of slavery; and then the story of the contest and
their final victory for freedom can proceed more
understandingly for the benefit of the general reader.

The first Baptist Church, which was also the first
Protestant church in Illinois, was organized at New
Design, Ill., on May 28 and 29, in 1796, at the residence of Rev. James Lemen, Sr. It was called *The
New Design Baptist Church*, and was constituted by
Rev. Joseph Chance and Rev. Badgeley; the constituent members were Rev. James Lemen, Sr.,
Catharine Lemen, his wife, John Gibbons, Isaac
Enochs and twenty-four other persons. For some
years the church or congregation met in temporary
quarters for service, and in 1815 they occupied a
school-house, which served as a meeting-house until
1832, when they built a very comfortable house of
worship, which is yet standing. The one-hundredth
anniversary of that old church occurred on May 28
and 29, 1896, and the Baptists of Illinois appointed

a meeting, which was held there on the above dates,
to commemorate the organization of their first church
in Illinois. Many of the leading Baptist divines of
Illinois were prepared to attend and take part in the
exercises, and Prof. Lewis Lemen, of Columbia, Ill.,
a great-grandson of Rev. James Lemen, Sr., had written and compiled a vast number of extremely interesting historical facts from the lives of the old
pioneers, specially for the occasion; and there would
have been an immense concourse of people present,
but the great tornado in St. Louis and vicinity at the
time prevented a large attendance and the execution
of the full program. However, the meeting occurred,
and many of Prof. Lewis Lemen's historical contributions and pioneer facts were published in the newspapers, particularly in the Waterloo *Republican*.
Many of the descendants of Rev. James Lemen, Sr.,
and wife, at one time or another, were members in
the old New Design Baptist Church, and it accomplished a large and beneficent mission in its day;
but its organization lapsed some years ago and at
this time no congregation meets there.

The next Baptist Church, largely constituted and
organized by the pioneer Lemens, Rev. David Badgley,
Rev. Joseph Chance, and other friends, was the Richland Baptist Church, which was the first protestant
church in St. Clair County. It was organized in 1802,
but there were no formal records kept until June 14,
1806, at a regular church session or meeting at the
house of William Lot Whitesides, at which meeting

Rev. Joseph Chance was moderator, and Rev. Benjamin Ogle was clerk. At that time that church was an "arm" of the New Design Baptist Church, in Monroe County, and the style of their minutes ran: "Richland Arm of the Church of Christ, at New Design." On September 12, 1807, this church met at the house of Isaac Enochs and voted to form itself into a separate organization under the name of "The Baptist Church of Christ at Richland Creek." In church session at the house of Jacob Ogle, in Ridge Prairie, St. Clair County, on February 13, 1808, this church adopted resolutions declaring the faith of the church against the belief and practice of slavery. In 1809 these people built a meeting-house on Richland Creek, some three miles northeast of Belleville; and at that time their church had a membership of some forty persons. Among the members were Rev. James Lemen, Sr., Catharine Lemen, Rev. Benjamin Ogle, Wm. Lot Whitesides, William Kinney, Isaac Enochs, Larkin Rutherford, Rev. Joseph Lemen, Robert Lemen, Polly K. Lemen, Hester Lemen, Ann Lemen, Ann Simpson, Ann Whitesides, Elizabeth Bageley, Mary Kinney, and others, a band of noble men and women whose pious lives and labors accomplished great results. This church was in session on July 8, 1809, when Rev. James Lemen, Sr., arose and referring to an anti-slavery sermon he had previously preached to the congregation, he denounced the practice of slavery as a wrong which he could not fellowship. He called the churches to plant themselves on the firm foundations of the New Testament as opposed to every form of wrong, evil and oppression. He boldly proclaimed that the mission for freedom had begun and the contest had opened that would never be closed until Illinois was firmly planted in the Union, with a constitution that would forever exclude slavery from her limits. This sermon, declaration and challenge created a profound impression in the church and community and a division followed. The conflicting sentiments, neither in that church nor in the association of the several Baptist churches then in Illinois, could be harmonized. However, both schools of opinion in the church met afterward in formal conference, and in church session on December 9, 1809, it was voted that as many as wished to withdraw, by reason of this difference of views on slavery, should have the privilege to do so; and five members signified their purpose to withdraw and form a new organization; and this was the first act in the origin of Bethel Church.

The third Baptist Church organized in Illinois by the pioneer Lemens and their friends was called "The Baptized Church of Christ, Friends to Humanity," now "Bethel Baptist Church," in St. Clair County. The five members who had formerly withdrawn from Richland Church the day previously, with two others, composed this church, and it was constituted by Rev. James Lemen, Jr., and Rev. John Baugh on December 10, 1809, under the name of "The Baptized Church of Christ, Friends to Humanity," on a strictly

anti-slavery basis. The constituent members were.
Robert Lemen, Hester Lemen, Rev. Joseph Lemen,
Polly K. Lemen, Rev. James Lemen, Sr., Catharine
Lemen, and Rev. Benjamin Ogle; Rev. James
Lemen, Jr., uniting with the church at the evening
session on the same day.

The declared faith of this church was the Old
and New Testaments; and for its friendship toward
men its constitution declared it to be "The Friends
to Humanity." And that simple, but grand declaration, right then, sounded the death knell of slavery
in Illinois; and from that event and that very hour,
the forces in the Territory began to gather under the
banners of freedom, and they marched on to final victory. From the peculiar surroundings of its organization, it is doubtful if there has ever been another church
organized which exerted such an influence in shaping
the destinies of the State as that of constituting the
Bethel Church has done. The church now, though
not numerically strong, is peaceful, progressive and
fairly prosperous under the pastoral control of Rev.
J. B. Webb at this time (December, 1897), and it is
only proper to add that several of the descendants of
the old pioneer couple, Rev. James Lemen, Sr., and
wife, are yet members of old Bethel Church, and
some of them belong to its corps of officers, dis-
charging their trusts faithfully and acceptably.

In the constitution of Bethel Church the founders
declared that the institution of slavery was contrary
to the spirit of the New Testament, and that the

churches in tolerating, the State in upholding and the people in permitting it, were wrong and inexcusable before God. And with the Bible as the pillar of their faith, they proclaimed their good will for the brotherhood of humanity by declaring their church to be "The Friends to Humanity, denying union and communion with all persons holding the doctrine of perpetual, involuntary, hereditary slavery." What a grand contest this was thirty years before the Abolitionists of the East dreamed of organizing against the wrong of slavery! A little band in the wilderness, humble and poor, but fearless, pious and trusting, laying the foundations for the glorious work which, at no distant day, was destined to plant a mighty State on the side of freedom, and to eventually fix in her constitution an everlasting decree against slavery. Where might our Union now have been had the imperial State of Illinois been for slavery, and launched her mighty armies in the late war against the Union instead of for it? From little beginnings what mighty consequences flow.

From the organization of Bethel Church until 1818, when the friends of freedom turned back the tide in the election and carried their State constitutional convention, the pioneer Lemens and the church were ever active and vigilant in the great contest for freedom which they had begun. In the canvass preceding the election, through letters, agents and every honorable means possible, they reached every district in the Illinois Territory, and saw that every can-

didate for a free State constitution, who was standing
for election to the constitutional convention, was
properly supported, and at last the victory was won
when the returns from the polls made an anti-slavery
majority certain in the coming convention. One
of the members of the church was among the
successful anti-slavery candidates, and everywhere
his party had won the majority. There was mighty
rejoicing in Bethel Church when she realized that
her brave stand for human rights had carried the
State; and when the constitutional convention met
in 1818, it completed the great act that made
Illinois a free State. That Bethel Church and
its founders set in motion the forces which made us
a free State was affirmed by Senator Stephen A.
Douglas, Abraham Lincoln, Senator Lyman Trumbull, and other great statesmen, and the historians of
the Baptist denomination also confirm that fact;
among whom are Rev. Justus Bulkley, D. D., that
eminent divine, historian and educator, with some
others. Rev. Dr. Bulkley has written some excellent sketches of the pioneer Lemens, father and
sons, which will take their places in the permanent history of the Baptist ministers and churches of
Illinois.

Mrs. Ellen Denny, of Vincennes, Ind., a grand-
daughter of the late Rev. Joseph Lemen, and an eminent advocate in the field of temperance, has also contributed some well written articles and facts on the
anti-slavery labors of her great-grandfather, Rev.

James Lemen, Sr., among which is the following fact relative to the overtures of General William Henry Harrison, when Governor of the Northwestern Territory, in which she says he personally sought the aid of Rev. James Lemen, Sr., to open the Territory for the introduction of slavery—his influence then being such that General Harrison thought it best to consult him. She says that General Harrison represented to Mr. Lemen that his personal interests, as well as those of the people, would be conserved should he lend his services and influence to induce Congress to open the Territory to slavery, by setting aside, for a time at least, the ordinance of 1787, which prohibits slavery. To this Mr. Lemen replied in firm, but respectful terms, that conscience and everything which he valued as a faithful and upright man and citizen stood in the way of his compliance; and "not while his blood ran warm" would he approve of or even submit to the consummation of a scheme fraught with such consequences of oppression and evil. And Mrs. Denny adds that when Mr. Lemen suffered a curtailment of half his rights in the distribution of bounty lands, afterward made, that it was on account of his firm and unyielding opposition to the introduction of slavery.

The pioneer Lemens, in common with mankind, were not free from the imperfections incident to human nature; but in the interests of religion, temperance, freedom and progress, in their day, they performed the full measure of their duty. Some might have accomplished more, while others would have achieved far less.

The present and preceding chapters in this work, comprising a history of the origin of the family and of the lives and labors of the pioneer Lemens in Illinois, were written by Jos. B. Lemen, at the request of Mr. Frank B. Lemen. And while he feels a profound respect and veneration for the memory of his ancestors and their families, he preferred to take the judgment of the eminent divines and of the great political leaders of both national parties in the State rather than his own, respecting the value of the services of the pioneer Lemen family as being less liable to that bias and favoritism which might naturally spring from affinity or kinship.

To write a full history of the pioneer Lemens would require a volume of many hundreds of pages; but the foregoing sketches will afford a connected, and it is believed, a faithful reflex of the chief incidents in their lives and labors, and as extensive as the scope and purpose of this work will permit.

The gratitude of the family is due and is cheerfully accorded to Mr. Frank B. Lemen, the compiler and publisher of this volume for making the same, and also for the vast labor and patient care and pains expended in making every part, incident and date as accurate as it was possible to procure after exhaustive and long protracted efforts.

Since writing this chapter thus far, a further perusal of Mrs. Ellen Denny's contributions to this work relative to the anti-slavery labors of Rev. James Lemen, Sr., record some details well worthy of mention: In 1803 the Northwestern Territory, with General William Henry Harrison as Governor, by a convention, memorialized Congress for a repeal or suspension of the clause in the ordinance of 1787, which prohibited slavery; but on March 3, 1803, a special committee under John Randolph, of Virginia, as chairman, to whom the matter had been referred, reported to the House adversely on the petition. At the next Congress a report was made to the House by special committee under Cæsar Rodney, as chairman, favoring a qualified suspension of that clause, but Congress took no action. The matter came before the House again and a special committee under Mr. Garnett, of Georgia, as chairman, reported in favor of granting the petition and repealing the clause prohibiting slavery, as the people, seemingly, were unanimously for it, but the House did not act upon it. At the next session of Congress a letter from General Harrison, inclosing a resolution of the Territorial council in favor of temporarily suspending the said clause in the ordinance of 1787, was received by the House January 21, 1807, and referred to a special committee with Mr. Park, delegate from the Territory, as chairman, who, on February 12th, reported for the repeal and formally for the petition; but the House did not act. At the next session of Congress

the matter came before the Senate on the apparently
unanimous action of General Harrison and his Legislature, by petition, for the privilege to temporarily
employ slaves in the Territory; but for the first time
there also appeared before Congress a remonstrance,
largely signed by the people, Baptists generally,
against the measure; and by a select committee,
under Jesse Franklin, of North Carolina, report was
made to the Senate as follows: "That it was not
expedient at this time to suspend the Sixth Article of
Compact for the government of the Territory of the
United States northwest of the Ohio river." The
Sixth Article was the clause in the ordinance of
1787, which forbid slavery. And here the long and
fruitless struggle for the introduction of slavery in
the Northwestern Territory ended. And Mrs.
Denny adds: "It was Rev. James Lemen, Sr., in
his journeyings to organize Baptist churches, whose
charters declared them to be the 'Friends of Humanity,' and circulating and obtaining signatures to the
great remonstrance, or petition, that finally induced
Congress to act, and thus saved the ordinance of
1787 and consecrated the Northwestern Territory to
freedom."

It was thus that Mr. Lemen had an honorable and
leading part in that great event; and thus in part
fulfilled his mission, and honored his vow made
before he left Virginia, to always oppose slavery.
When, under the advice of Thomas Jefferson, and
prompted by his own humane instincts to always

oppose oppression, he left his home in Virginia to
rear his family on free soil, he and Jefferson both
agreed that, sooner or later, there would be a mighty
contest made to fasten slavery on the Northwestern
Territory; and the battle and victory were by no
means won until the fierce and later contest to make
Illinois a free State was consummated in 1818. When
he left Virginia, with his young family, he had the
keen forecast to see and to say that the contest in
both the great Territory and in the narrower limits of
what was to constitute the State of Illinois at some
future time, would be bitterly waged for the spread of
slavery; and it might be said that two motives,
among several others, induced him to come West:
one was, to leave slavery behind him, and the other
was, to heroically resist its spread into the new
Territory. He made a vow to this effect before he
left Virginia, and his life work proved how well he
kept it, aided at last by his sons and other fearless
friends who served the cause of freedom.

CHAPTER X.

THE HEREDITARY MENTAL AND MORAL CHARACTERISTICS OF THE LEMEN FAMILY.

The law of heredity, or the transmission of marked traits of mind and body, from parents to children, through a long line of generations, operates with the certainty of any other natural law. Nor is this doctrine amenable to the charge of fatalism, which necessarily destroys all moral accountability, since it is the province or purpose of Christianity or true religion to cultivate the good qualities which come down to us, and combat and conquer the evil ones; and herein consists that conflict between right and wrong and good and evil of which the New Testament Gospel constantly speaks, and in the successful practice of which the true Christian constantly grows stronger.

The Lemen and Ogle ancestors of the Lemen family possessed marked individualities, and strongly accentuated mental and moral traits. In a large degree they possessed the attributes of courage, with stalwart powers of intellect, sensibilities and will, and a distinctive veneration for the Divine Power, or a strongly marked faculty of religious sentiment or conscience. When Robert Lemen, of Scotland, one of the ancestors of the Lemen family, and his brother William, enlisted as soldiers under Oliver Cromwell, they were prompted by their sentiments of religion to join his standard; and their Ogle ancestors, prompted by a like sentiment, had been the defenders of civil and religious liberty here and in England for many generations. The product of the union of two such families, according to the laws of heredity, ought to be strongly imbued with the religious sentiment, and with all the other attributes mentioned; and as the Lemen family of Illinois is the product or result of their inter-marriage, we find that in a large measure they are the faithful reproduction of their ancestors in this respect; and, as a consequence, that the moral attribute of conscience is a general characteristic of the family. Not that they are without the evil propensities common to human nature, or that they are better or more honest than many other families, or that sometimes some of them may not be tempted to do evil; but that, as a family generally, they are imbued with that religious sentiment that prompts to duty and controls the conscience. Of course, among the several hundreds of descendants of Rev. James Lemen, Sr., and wife, who have lived, or now live, there have been exceptions to this law, particularly in youth, under the impulse of temptation and inexperience; but generally their love of right, prompted by this religious sentiment, which has been a marked attribute of the family for generations, gets control, and the indiscretions and mistakes of youth are overcome and abandoned. That is not to say that the family members are always com-

municants of some church; but we are speaking of
that general prevalence among the family of that
religious tendency or moral sentiment which has
generally been an inherited trait among them.

The experience of this family in regard to this
religious sentiment does not bear out the atheistic
claim that its possession and practice tend to mental
insanity; but it confirms the contrary truth, which is
well established, that true religion is a safeguard
against that malady. It is the province and purpose
of true religion to develop that moral attribute which
gives a safe balance to our mental constitution, and
without which human nature has no safe equipoise;
and hence it necessarily follows that religion is one
of the chief safeguards against mental unbalance or
insanity; and experience fully demonstrates this
truth. Among the hundreds of the descendants of
Rev. James Lemen, Sr., and wife, there have never,
in more than a hundred years, been but three cases
of real, fixed, mental insanity, and they were caused
wholly from malignant fevers which wrecked the
functions of the brain; besides two or three other
cases of temporary insanity, caused by unexpected
debt or impending trouble; but the latter permanently recovered, and none of these cases had the
remotest relation to nor connection with their religious sentiment.

There have been cases in other families where
intense religious sentiment has been associated with
mental insanity; but intelligent investigation has

always discovered that in these cases there was an inherited tendency to insanity, or that it was the result of disease or some other cause, and that the victim in his delirium merely made his religion a hobby; just as he would have made the stage a hobby if acting had been his calling, or any other leading or controlling purpose or sentiment. These are cases in which insanity prevailed in spite of the religious sentiment, and not on account of it. In common with the Lemen family nearly all old American families have this religious sentiment in a sufficient degree to develop that balance and equipoise in the moral and mental powers which act as a safeguard, generally, for mental soundness, and almost as a sure preventive against the mania of suicide, of which very few cases occur among these old families. But we have an element of foreign population of atheistic or materialistic sentiments who are wanting in that religious tendency which generally gives immunity and safety against the mental unbalance, and particularly against that fierce mental mania of suicide; and in any great stress or disaster these atheistic classes are unequal to the stress, and often lift their own hands against their own lives; and this class of our population furnishes nearly all the suicides, as the newspapers show—as nearly all have foreign names. But that is not to say that the great masses of our foreign-born citizens belong to such classes; but on the other hand they are not without this religious sentiment in some form, and generally they are worthy and good citizens. But we only mention this fact to illustrate the grand truth already so well established, that true religion is a necessary element to develop human nature to a safe balance and proper model of what people ought to be. The truth is, when the Great Master gave His Gospel of Christianity to men He established a system that not only prepares them for future happiness, but which is also a shield and refuge against many of the fiercer and fatal ills of this life, and which lifts human nature to a higher and safer plane of civilization and progress.

The Lemen family inherited a distinctive and strongly marked power of habit from their ancestors, which may be turned to excellent account, but which, like all other advantages, is attended with more or less danger. With the members of the family, generally, repetition very soon fixes a strong habit in that direction. And this should warn them to cultivate habits of right and eschew all evil temptations, since it is infinitely easier to keep right than it is to get right after a wrong habit is once established. But on the other hand, the family have inherited a strongly marked will power, and this is a safeguard and a help in the cause of well-doing. There is also an inherited peculiarity or subjective trait, or psychological habit, not general with the family, but here and there a case. It is merely a habit, not akin to insanity, but bordering on a state of slight despondency, and it is always subject to and curable by mere will-force.

Captain Joseph Ogle, one of the ancestors of the Lemen family, and one of his sons, and several of his daughters, were subject to it; but by the persistent action of their will-power they entirely banished it, and became permanently cheerful and happy, and remained so throughout the balance of their lives. Captain Ogle called it a "family habit," and there have been a few cases among the Lemen family, though we are not aware that any member is now subject to it; but under all conditions it can always be banished by the continued and persistent power of the will, when the subject will apply that simple remedy. At worst, it never was any serious infirmity, and Captain Ogle used to say it was one of the penalties that often indicated strong mental powers, and that it could always be banished by the will-power and much easier than the habits of tobacco or rum.

Truth, honesty, courage, the love of country, the love or affection of the sexes, and ordinary family pride, with all other virtues esteemed and cherished by mankind, were present in the parent stocks, and have descended to the Lemen family in as large a degree as are possessed by most families, with, of course, about the usual per cent. of exceptions. As to courage and patriotism, there is no account of any of the soldiers of the family in battle—and there have been many of them—who, in the presence of probable death, ever deserted his post, or turned his face from the foe until the order for retreat was given by the officers. As to natural affection, or love, the family generally are good lovers. There is a pleasant family tradition that Rev. James Lemen, Sr., and Catharine Ogle Lemen, his wife, loved at first sight, and believed that Providence had designed them for each other, and their married lives were very happy indeed; but generally prudence and reason approve of a longer acquaintance before the purpose of marriage should be seriously considered. As a general rule the family are good lovers, good husbands and wives, good parents and good providers, with strong affection for their offspring, and generally they give them fair religious and educational advantages. Some of the family are quite well off, and generally they all provide good livings; but for the most part the love of wealth in a grasping way is not a very marked characteristic of the family.

In the purely intellectual faculties the parent stocks of the Lemens were generally well endowed, and in a fair measure these endowments were transmitted to their posterity. Of the children of Rev. James Lemen, Sr., and wife, all the six sons, Robert, Joseph, James, William, Josiah and Moses, had good capacities for composition in prose, and several of them had the gift of poetry in a very marked degree, and wrote some very good poems. Of the later members of the family, the late Benjamin F. Lemen wrote considerable poetry, and Robert S. Lemen also produced some very good poetical compositions, and one of his poems entitled, "A Burial by Nightfall," would rank well with the products of the best Ameri-

can poets; and there are several other members of
the family who have the gift.   Among other members of the family who were or are very good writers,
were Judge Cyrus L. Cook and Hon. Edwin H.
Lemen, deceased, also Mrs. Lillie Leavitt, Mrs. Ellen
K. Denny, Hon. William K. Murphy, Prof. Clarence
J. Lemen, Mr. Frank B. Lemen, Miss Ellen Bowler
(now Mrs. Ellen Beedle), Rev. Theodore A. Lemen,
Rev. J. G. Lemen, Prof. Lewis Lemen, and others.
As indicating the capabilities of several members of
the family as writers or speakers, we will here insert
a circular letter each, from the pens of the late Rev.
James Lemen, Jr., and Rev. Moses Lemen, which, in
the early days were addressed to the churches; and
these letters will be followed by extracts from the
speeches, sermons or writings of several members of
the family of later generations.   The circular letters
are as follows:

A CIRCULAR ADDRESS.

[Written by Rev. James Lemen, Jr., September, 1821.]

Dear Brethren: When by a retrospective glance
we retrace the roll of but a few seasons and realize
the commencement of our labors on the waters of the
Canteen and Silver creeks, contrasting those times
with the present, ought not the response of our
hearts to be, the Lord has done great things for us,
whereof we are glad.   In 1810 a small handful, seven
in number, withdrew their membership from the gen-

eral Union on account of involuntary slavery, believ
ing it to be an iniquity which ought not to be tolerated by Christian churches. Formidable, indeed,
were the powers which we then had to combat, and
alarming were the oppositions which we had to en-
counter. But none of these things moved us, being
sensible that unmerited, involuntary, perpetual, absolute, hereditary slavery is contrary to and a viola-
tion of the principles of nature, reason, justice, policy
and Scripture. In 1811 the Lord was pleased graciously to move the minds of a few faithful members
on Silver Creek (also seven in number), who called
for a constitution, and in February of the following
year were constituted, three of whom have departed
this life in the triumphs of faith. Several years were
spent in faithful labor ere there was a discovery of
any fruits thereof. At length Almighty God smiled
propitiously on our efforts, and almost instantane-
ously swelled our number to its present, and still
making daily additions. Beloved brethren, while we
behold that arm which quietly props the universe,
thus gloriously displaying its power in our defense,
do we not feel conscious that our cause is just? It is
the cause of oppressed humanity. We have seen the
sable sons of Africa torn from their native land by the
hand of a ruthless enemy and condemned to perpetual
bondage; to be driven at pleasure, like hogs and sheep,
to market, there to be disposed of for silver or gold;
where husband and wife, parent and child, are torn
from fond embraces of each other; where the groans

of the distressed father, or of the more deeply affected mother, the tear of the weeping child, are seen and heard only to be disregarded; let humanity drop a tear and blot from the catalogue of human offences the enormity of such crimes that it may not be told in "Gath nor published in the streets of Ashkelon, lest the daughters of the Philistines rejoice, lest the daughters of the uncircumcised triumph." Alas! This evil has not only found its way into our nation, and spread its poison there, but restless to obtain still greater victories has approached the portals of the sanctuary of the Most High; and, lamentable to relate, has found admittance there, and defiled even the temples of the living God; causing the children of light (who have been redeemed from cruel bondage and restored to the enjoyment of perfect liberty), to grow forgetful of the change and to impose involuntary servitude on their brethren in the gospel, and thus becoming masters can say to one brother, come, and he cometh; to another go, and he goeth—new maxims which the gospel knows nothing of. And will a God of equal justice rest quietly in his pavilion when "justice has fallen asleep and judgment gone away backwards?" while the poor are bought for silver, and the needy for a pair of shoes (Amos 8, 6). Has he not already declared that his people of late have risen up against him as an enemy, plucking off the robe with the garment from them that would pass by scarcely as men averse from war (Micah 2, 8). He has also declared what the conse-

quences shall be: Woe unto him that buildeth his
house by unrighteousness, and his chambers by wrong;
that useth his neighbors' service without wages, and
giveth him not for his work (Jer. 22, 13).   Behold
the hire of the laborers who have reaped down your
fields, which is of you kept back by fraud, crieth;
and the cries of them which have reaped are entered
into the ears of the Lord of Sabaoth (James 5, 4).
Seeing God hath taken cognizance of these things in
the archives of heaven, and is now looking through
the windows of his habitation to see whether any
will appear on the side of the oppressed, shall we re-
fuse to come up to the help of the Lord against the
mighty; will we not, like the men of Gideon, come
forth in haste, unappalled, before a host of oppositions, and exclaim in the consciousness of our recti-
tude: We struggle for liberty!   Our cause is just!
It is the cause which induced our forefathers to quit
their peaceful homes and go forth in martial array to
meet the enemy in the tented field (with victory or
death written on their foreheads), regardless of either
their blood or treasure, and although some unfortunately found an untimely grave in the desolate
wilderness and went down to the chambers of silence
without either change of apparel, a sheet or a coffin,
while the bones of others were left to bleach upon the
mountains without a burial, yet their cause being
righteous it still prospered in the hands of the survivors, who, at length, obtained a glorious conquest
which the pages of future history will be found to

relate. Thus the enemy being driven like a flock of frightened goats before an impetuous storm, back to their native shore to own the eclipse of their glory, the war-worn veterans of America could return in peace to their former habitations, bearing laurels of victory in their hands; at whose return the daughters of America could join in song with the daughters of Israel, and sing, Britain hath slain her thousands, but America hath slain her tens of thousands. Thus having obtained their freedom, could form a government of their own, the principles of which all nations are, or will be, proud to imitate; and we trust that under the influence of a just Providence, we shall be able to boldly and nobly defend our cause, and to build up a society the government of which will be a pattern for society yet unborn to follow. The Holy Scriptures are on our side, which will be seen from the passages to which you have been cited. Moreover, the Constitution of the United States, and of this State, are both in our favor. The former declares that all men are born equally free and independent, while the latter states that there shall be neither slavery nor involuntary servitude introduced into this State otherwise than for punishment of crimes, whereof the party shall have been duly convicted. Thus the scene is changed, and now, instead of being charged with flying in the face of authority, we can exhort our congregations to be subject to the higher powers.

A CIRCULAR LETTER.

[Written by REV. MOSES LEMEN in 1831.]

DEAR BRETHREN: What an immense debt of gratitude do we owe the great King and Governor of the universe for permitting us to have our existence in an age of such vast improvement, not only in the various arts and sciences, but likewise in the means and exertions employed in the glorious cause of the Redeemer's kingdom; and to live not only in a land of peace and plenty, but of civil and religious liberty, where each one may sit (as it were) under his own vine and fig tree and worship Almighty God according to the dictates of conscience, regardless of the sword, the inquisition and the rack. The time has been when even kings and princes bowed the knee before a corrupt and vicious tyrant who could make war or peace, who pretended to have the key of heaven to absolve men from sin and debar them from heaven. Superstition and ignorance had plunged almost the whole world into an abyss of darkness and woe, wretchedness, and in the name of religious wars depopulated the earth. Millions of men (led by subtle priests, whose robes glittered but to deceive), gave up their property and went to perish in the field of battle, while their wives and children fell victims to want. Religion yielded only a faint and glimmering radiance, as a light that shined in a dark and gloomy place. But at length the great Jehovah saw the time had come to favor Zion. He commanded and it was done. The gloom of ignorance and barbarism was dispelled, and religion began to revive in its pristine purity and glory. A numerous train of pious men awoke from their long slumber and engaged in the arduous work of reformation. Ever since the days of Calvin and Luther the work has been progressing, until thousands of heathen, who never heard of Jesus, have been made to rejoice in the merits of a crucified Savior. Thus, in contrasting past ages with the present, may we not exclaim with wonder and astonishment: "What hath God wrought, for sure the lines have fallen to us in pleasant places, a goodly heritage is ours!" Beloved brethren, let us awake and behold the signs of the times. The Savior reproved the Scribes and Pharisees for their blindness and stupidity, who could discern in the face of the sky the tokens of fair or foul weather, or in the vine and the fig tree, the near approach of spring, but could not see the omens that preceded the rise of His glorious kingdom, the downfall of their own nations, and the destruction of their city and temple. When we behold the rapidity with which the gospel is spreading over sea and land, the numerous train of gospel ministers that is visiting the dark and benighted regions of the earth, the many benevolent institutions, the object of which is to enlighten the ignorant and reform the vicious, the great revivals of religion in different parts of the world, the many ignorant children that have been taught to read the word of God, together with the noble exertions

of the various religious denominations to send the
Bible, without note or comment, to all nations of the
earth, and the flattering prospect that soon, through
the magnificent project of Sabbath schools, every
family in the vast valley of the Mississippi (in a
goodly degree) will be taught its glorious contents.
May we not reasonably calculate that the time is not far
off when "the wilderness and the solitary place shall
be glad, and the desert shall blossom as the rose;"
when the "watchmen of Zion shall lift up their voices
together, and together sing;" and the glorious sun
of righteousness burst forth from behind the hills of
bigotry, superstition and infidelity, and shine with
unparalleled brightness on Zion and make her the glory
and wonder of the whole earth?—that there is a time
of peace and prosperity drawing near, such as the
church has never yet enjoyed.   We think the Scriptures furnish abundant ground to believe, and this
time, according to St. John (Rev. 20, 2), shall continue a thousand years, in which the devil shall be
confined to the bottomless pit, and the dominion of
Jesus become univeral.   David, in reference to this
time, says: "All kings shall fall down before Him;
all nations shall serve Him."   Daniel, speaking of
this kingdom, says: "It shall stand forever, and shall
consume all other kingdoms," while Isaiah declares
all nations shall flow to it like a cloud, or as doves to
their windows.   It is then and there that all the people of God will meet, forgetful of former prejudice,
persecution and strife, and join hearts and hands in

one eternal union of friendship and love. Sects, parties and names will no more divide the world. Bigotry, superstition and prejudice will sink in the sea of oblivion, and all opposition to pious effort and religious truth will cease. Christians of every name will possess a perfect agreement in doctrine and worship. Friendship and harmony will pervade the land; the wolf shall dwell with the lamb, and the leopard shall lie down with the kid; there shall be none to hurt or destroy; war and bloodshed shall be forgotten by the nations of the earth; capital crimes and punishment be heard of no more; governments will rest on fair, just and humane foundations, and thefts, robbery and murder will be unknown. Before this happy period arrives, be it long or short, we may expect times of great tribulation and woe. Kingdom will war against kingdom, and dreadful revolutions arise, both in church and State; tears may fall like rain, and seas of blood may run, but the great work must and will go on. All tyrany and oppression must cease, and the church be cleansed from all pollution. We therefore, dear brethren, exhort you to awake to righteousness; be vigilant, be prayerful, lest like the sluggard we be found with folded arms, till destruction comes. It is highly probable that more is required of us in the present day than will be in any generation to come; a greater call upon our exertions and our charities, because it is a day of battle, that presents a prospect replete with victories and conquest. Let us, therefore, cast our eyes over the field

and behold the greatness of the heavenly harvest,
and see how many souls are perishing for the want of
the bread of life.   Let us join with the prophet in the
humble prayer: "O Lord, revive Thy work in the
midst of the years, in the midst of the years make
known; in wrath remember mercy," and let us strictly
examine ourselves and try to lay aside every weight
that we may run so as to obtain, for there never
was a time when the kingdom of darkness was making greater exertions than at the present.   Infidelity
has assumed a thousand forms, such as Deism, Athe-
ism, Campbellism, Mormonism, Parkerism and Drunkenness, which calls aloud for the friends of Zion to
rally around one common standard, concentrate all
their forces, lay aside all prejudices, join heart and
hand, and "earnestly contend for the faith once
delivered to the saints," which faith admits of no
division or separation of the children of God.   But
before this happy union can be brought about, and
the church enjoy her promised rest, rottenness must
be rooted out of the church and pollution out of Zion.
That there does exist some great and prominent evils
among churches professing Christianity, and which
must be laid aside, we think no one with an enlightened conscience will pretend to deny.   These evils
have locked the wheels of Zion and caused her to
move heavily for ages.   One or two of these we will
mention, as the most intolerable that ever disgraced
the human character.   First: That of African
slavery, the enormity of which no tongue can de-

scribe.   Such slavery has in it a sound at which
every principle of humanity revolts.   It presents a
state of degradation and misery unknown even in the
rigid code of military discipline, or the most despotic
government of Europe.   Ours is the boasted land of
liberty, yet this monster stalks through it, making
the life, liberty and happiness of the unoffending
African his prey.   Beloved brethren, let one simple
view of this horrid practice suffice.   When the
poor African is brought to our peaceful shores, he
comes strongly pinioned and hand-cuffed, his heart
bleeding with the thought of his happy home and
friends that he has lost forever, his body sinking
under the toil and afflictions of the middle passage,
and his soul stricken with horror to find himself surrounded by a host of Christian friends, who approach
him, not to deliver, but to oppress.   He comes, indeed, to a land of freedom, but he comes to wear the
galling chains of bondage.   He comes to a land of
milk and honey, but he comes to drink the bitter cup
of oppression.   He comes to a land of Bibles, but the
laws of Christians doom him to ignorance, and make
it a crime to teach him to read the word of their God.
He comes to a land of gospel light, but what must
be his opinion of such Christian acts.   Thus brought
to the destined port, now set up as sheep to be sold,
where Christian, Pagan or Turk may have him for
silver or gold, while at the same time he beholds his
wife and children disposed of in like manner, while
their cries and lamentations denote the anguish of

their souls, and here they finally part to meet and know each other no more till they meet beyond the grave. And is it not most wondrous that many who profess to enjoy the mind of the meek and lowly Saviour, should suffer their hands to be polluted with this unhallowed practice, and still continue amidst the blaze of gospel light, to hold it in their churches as a matter of small consequence? Would not the heathen, whom we are attempting to convert to our religion, hear with astonishment that in our land two millions of souls are kept in slavery, debarred by our laws from learning to read the word of God? What will Christians in the millennium think, when they read the history of the nineteenth century, and learn that a highly Christianized people (so called) met once a year to celebrate their independence and freedom, for the purpose of inspiring their sons with the love of liberty, while at the same time they held in miserable bondage two millions of their fellow-creatures, with their hearts and backs all bleeding, whenever a despot wills it? Will heaven be always deaf to their cries? We think not. God will hear and deliver. The storm is fast gathering; its thunders are already heard in the distance, and soon, unless justice is done to that injured race, will it burst upon our devoted heads. We therefore earnestly exhort our brethren to keep in mind that it was this that produced a division at first amongst some of the Baptists in the West, and have nothing to do with churches that hold fellowship and countenance this nefarious practice.

Next to this appalling evil, is inebriety, or drunkenness, which, like a mighty conquerer, has pushed its victories to the ends of the earth, invading all ranks, high and low, rich and poor. This brutal practice has broken more hearts, beggared more families and cost more lives than the American revolution. Much has already been said on this subject from the bench, the pulpit and the press; but still this dreadful foe moves through the land with gigantic march.

"Like a staunch murderer, steady to his purpose,
Nor misses once the track; but presses on
Till forced at last, to the tremendous verge."

The friends of religion have long felt and deeply lamented their condition, and have inquired with tears what can be done. In answer to this we would remark that a victory over this formidable foe never can be obtained by single combat, by the powers of a few faithful individuals, nor yet by a few well fought battles. Our forces must be concentrated, and our plans and system must be universal. Let the President in his message, the judge from the bench, the politician from the stump, the minister from the pulpit and the editor from the press, all unite in raising the warning voice. Let leading men in every neighborhood raise their buildings and reap their fields without the morning bitters or the evening sling. Let the mother in her parental instruction admonish her sons to shun the deadly poison. Let young females, when offered a companion for life, turn aside from the young man who uses it. No matter how well spiced or minted it may be, or in how small quantities. Let the professors of religion quit the use of it in any shape whatever. Let churches exclude from their fellowship speedily all drunkards, and receive no more unless they give satisfactory evidence that they have finally quit the disgraceful practice, and we think before the present generation shall have passed away this mighty monster will fall by the sword of public opinion, and sobriety, temperance and peace will reign throughout the land.

We will now close this address with the beautiful prayer: "Our Father which art in heaven, hallowed be thy name; thy kingdom come, thy will be done in earth as it is in heaven. Give us day by day our daily bread; and forgive us our tresspasses as we forgive them that tresspass against us; and lead us not into temptation, but deliver us from evil; for thine is the kingdom, the power, and the glory, forever. Amen."

We copy the following beautiful extract from a memorial address of Professor Clarence J. Lemen, of Morganfield, Ky. The address was made May 25, 1890, in the Presbyterian Church at Shawneetown, Ill. It is as follows:

"The one great blessing handed down to us from the past is the inalienable boon of liberty. It is as right and as sacred to man as the tie that binds him to life itself. Yet how few have a true conception of its idea? It behooves the present age to study its meaning. The anarchist and the nihilist clamor for liberty, and the mob surging through the streets of

our cities howl for liberty while desecrating every
principle enunciated in that Magna Charta of American Liberty—the 'Declaration of Independence.'

"The true greatness of any nation consists in its
intellectual power, and the diffusion of knowledge
among its masses. The nation that advances in
intellectual development will be the one that has the
most freedom; and it is safe to say that the people who put forth the greatest efforts in this diffusion
of knowledge will be the one that rises to the highest plane of liberty.

"If the free institutions of America would live
and be perpetuated it must educate. Their very lives
depend upon the dissemination of knowledge among
the masses; for the government is just what the people are. If they are ignorant, degraded and unthink-
ing, then will the government be weak, debased and
inefficient. If they are intelligent, upright and honest, then will the government be strong, vigorous
and enduring. The history of all the past has
already proven that liberty does not put into the
lands of ignorance—freedom."

The following is an extract from an able and
philosophical paper prepared and read before the
Illinois Association of Expert Judges of Swine, by
Mr. Frank B. Lemen, of Collinsville, Ill. It is as
follows:

"Color is not a property of matter, properly
speaking; yet it does, as we have said, indicate the

processes taking place in the tissue elements of the protoplasmic cells. There are certain elements which enter into the structure of the physical organism, which, when acted upon by the peculiar chemical or molecular properties of that organism, will produce pigment, which is capable of reflecting various hues of light. 'Beauty is but skin deep' is a falsification, as scientific research has shown that the clearness, smoothness and tints, or flush of the skin depends upon the conditions of the various organs which enter into the animal structure.''

The following excellent paragraph is from the writings of the late Edwin H. Lemen, of Pinckneyville, Ill. It is as follows:

"Our free school system is the great source of our country's safety. The children who now fill the ranks in the school-house will soon be the men and women who are to shape the country's destiny. It is, therefore, of infinite importance that a sense of high morality, honesty, and the duties of good citizenship be impressed upon their minds. There is a wide room for improvement in the general course of instruction in this respect. If the course in our free schools were made what it ought to be, the children would be trained and confirmed to such safe and honest habits of thought and responsibility that in later years the libertine, with his tenets of immorality, the socialist with his sinister dogmas and the anarchist with his doctrines of murder and hate, would find no sympathy, support or adherents in this country."

The following beautiful truth is from a sermon of Rev. J. G. Lemen, of Council Bluffs, Ia.:

"The scheme of redemption of our Divine Master for the salvation of men is as far above all the inventions of human skill as divine wisdom is above mere human agency. For ages the sophists, sages and philosophers were vainly trying, by the process of unaided human reason, to pierce the gloom that shadowed our future life; but no sound, nor token, nor promise of immortality ever came across the dark gulf to dispel the dark doubt. In the presence of the awful problem, how helpless and hopeless were all human efforts until the Savior brought his message of mercy and mission of peace and good will to men and the sure proof and glorious promise of life and immortality beyond the grave."

The following paragraph, embracing a stalwart truth, is from a speech of the Hon. Wm. K. Murphy, of Pinckneyville, Ill.:

"The people are the source of all power. There is no mockery here, such as 'the divine right of Kings'; but the people both reign and rule. They are the masters and the officers are their servants. If the masses are honest, intelligent and patriotic, our government will be strong, secure and beneficent. If the masses become dishonest, ignorant and unmindful of the duties of citizenship, the government will be insecure, weak and corrupt. The Congress is what the people make it; the judiciary, indirectly, is what the people make it; and, in fact, government in all its manifold branches and phases is just what the people make it, and no peril can ever come to our institutions while the people are honest, vigilant and intelligent. To always be secure, the people must rule in fact as well as in theory. The combined armies and navies of the world may hurl themselves against us, but they cannot prevail. Our downfall will never come except by the fault, folly or corruption of our own people, and in that event all the armies and navies of the world would not avail to save us."

The following practical idea is an extract from the writing of the late Professor Lewis Lemen, of Columbia, Ill. :

"The school teachers are a class who, through the influence of their teaching upon the minds of their pupils, are largely shaping the future stability and safety of our country. It should, therefore, be their aim and purpose, as it is their duty, to inculcate in the children's minds and habits of thought a deep sense of the importance of morality, honesty, and a patriotic regard for all that is good in our popular institutions. With this end in view, the course of study in our free schools, and the character and scope of our school books, could be greatly improved. 'Knowledge is power.' But since power may be evil

685—Andrew B. Smiley.　　686—Frank B. Smiley.　　200—Susan C. Smiley.

and perilous, as well as good, safe and patriotic, it behooves all classes interested in our free schools to give a more careful and intelligent attention to the courses of instruction taught in our public schools.''

The following excellent thought is from the writing of Miss Mary Cook, deceased; who was a sister of the late Judge Cyrus L. Cook, of Edwardsville, Ill.:

"Were it not for the hope of immortality this life would be infinitely more sad and gloomy than what it is. But the belief and realization in the soul, that it is only the first stage of the morning of our existence, inspires a hope that doubly sweetens the joys of this life and cheers us with the promise of unending happiness beyond the grave.''

This excellent paragraph is an extract from an essay on "The Art Gallery and its Exhibits," of the World's Fair, at Chicago, read by Miss Mary L. Lemen, before the Uniontown Reading Club. Miss Lemen is a daughter of Professor Clarence J. Lemen, of Morganfield, Ky. The extract is as follows:

"We are a nation, not only free in literal fact, but have been gradually and surely freeing ourselves from the charms of superstition and ignorance. That polish and culture which, in Europe, is only attained by individuals and classes, we, as a nation, are acquiring through the fostering of music, literature and painting. And this will prove, in the course of years, to be a step, nay, a flight of stairs, by which we will have reached the highest civilization ever known in the history of the world.''

The following sentiment, as beautiful as it is true, is from the pen of Miss Ellen Bowler, now Mrs. Ellen Beedle, wife of Samuel Beedle, Esq., of Caseyville Township, Ill.   It is as follows:

"The golden memories of our childhood days come to us in later life, across the bosom of the intervening years, with a sacred light and a fragrance pure enough and sweet enough to be akin to the celestial joys.   The enjoyment of station, wealth and honor, which may come to us in later years, have no such unalloyed joys for the mind to record and the memory to retain as were the golden moments of childhood, the recollections of which come down to us through the by-gone years with a happy light, which neither the joys of our later lives can dim, nor the shadows of misfortune extinguish.   And when those happy days of childhood are blended with the recollections of devoted, loving, Christian parents, they are, indeed, joyous, golden, happy events that can never be forgotten.''

This beautiful and touching poem was written by Mrs. Lillie H. Leavitt, of Ewing, Ill., upon the occasion of a visit to the old Bethel Church cemetery, where the remains of her only child, a beautiful and bright little boy of some seven summers, were buried. The poem is as follows:

IN THE OLD CHURCH-YARD.

The sumach had shed its crimson crown,
  Faded the maple's golden glow,
The leaves were lying dead and brown,
  The autumn winds whispered of snow.

I stood within a church-yard old,
  Where laid to rest were the sainted dead,
Some of the marbles were covered with mosses and mold;
  On some his wintry rays the sun had yet not shed.

I lingered beside a new made grave,
  That hid from sight a face—young, tender and true,
Whose smile was my joy; whose eyes sweet and brave
  Looked lovingly into mine when South-winds blew.

The autumn winds breathed of death and decay,
  My heart was heavy with grief and care;
I sought for solace; the place where he lay—
  For strength and grace I breathed a prayer.

A tender voice seemed to fall on my ear,
  "Why seek the living among the dead?
Your boy is risen—he is not here,
  On the bosom of the Father he rests his head."

The message I heed; I look above,
  And strive to enter the "mansions of heaven,"
Where I shall find the son I love,
  Who left me here, as a boy of seven.

Not in the church-yard gray and old
  Are gathered the dear, loved friends of yore;
But in the "City Celestial," with streets of gold,
  Where pain and care, toil and tears, they know no more.

The following practical and forcible poem is from the pen of Robert S. Lemen, of Cairo, Ill.

SPEAK KINDLY.

Speak kindly to your fellow-man
Where ere you meet him, brothers,
And thus let each do what he can
In making happy others:
A kindly word and friendly smile
With helping hand attended,
Will always raise a sinking heart,
New joy and hope to it impart,
And glorifying love, new start
In it when thus befriended.

Where'er you find a woe-worn one,
No matter what his nation,
Pass him not by, but look upon
His need, and not his station;
Then place yourself within his stead,
'Tis but the rule that's olden;
Your heart with tenderness will flow,
Your tongue and eyes with kindness glow,
Your hands themselves find what to do—
Such sympathy is golden.

Pause not to parley with the thought,
" 'Tis sorrows self contracted,"
'Tis but the outgrowth of what ought
Have ever been enacted:
For shame! Such heartless thoughts subdue,
'Tis not to mortals given,
To pass in judgment on their kind,
To bruise their wounds instead of bind,
But rather heal them where they find,
And leave the rest to heaven.

When in life's weary race there come,
As come misfortunes will;

Who then shall cast the weary sum
Of all thy woes and ill?
Will some dead-hearted man presume
To stand and give their rise,
And pin each one of that dread roll
Upon this sin-distracted soul,
And say, "At last you've reached the goal"
For man beneath the skies?

Oh! vile, inhuman, undivine—
Such doctrine's not for man:
Speak kindly then, Oh! brothers mine,
And heal what woes you can;
Since every mortal man must stand
The brunt of woe and ill—
Since every mortal of the race
Must meet misfortune face to face;
Let every man stand in his place
And manhood's mission fill.

Speak kindly to your fellow-men
In every grade of life;
Speak always kindly, husband, when
You're speaking to your wife;
Speak kindly, woman, to the man
You have chosen for your lord;
Kindly, children, sister, brother,
Kindly speak you to each other,
Kindly speak to father, mother,
Kind be every spoken word.

The following beautiful, poetical words are from the pen of the late Judge Cyrus L. Cook, of Edwardsville, Ill.:

THE BREVITY OF LIFE.

How brief our lives—the years go by
Swiftly as weavers' shuttles fly;
The circling decades come and go
Like fleeting tides which ebb and flow,

And though in prospect long they seem,
In retrospect they are but a dream.

Three score and ten—the Psalmist's song
To youth would make our lives seem long;
But soon, too soon, we reach that span
Of years allotted unto man,
Because the fleeting years go by
Swift as the weavers' shuttles fly.

Oh, Immortality—how blest,
When we shall reach that heavenly rest,
And ending here life's weary round,
Lay down the cross to take the crown;
Then let the fleeting years go by
Swift as the weavers' shuttles fly. .

The following poetical words are from the pen of
Joseph B. Lemen, of Collinsville, Ill.:

THE BIBLE.

I like the literature of men
And oft peruse their books with pleasure;
For delving much, I now and then
Exhume a thought or gem of treasure;
If this rewards my weary hand,
It scarce requites my toil's renewal,
To delve in seas of sterile sand
And gather now and then a jewel.

Not so this book for age and youth
Which God sends down the line of ages;
For open where I may, the truth,
Like diamonds, shines through all its pages:
This book of books—this priceless gem
Reflects in radiant streams of glory
The golden light of Bethlehem
And Calvary's undying story.

CHAPTER XI.

BETHEL BAPTIST CHURCH.

"The groves were God's first temples," says Bryant in his Thanotopsis; and the groves were where the first act of worship was offered by the Baptists in St. Clair County. In 1787, Rev. James Lemen, Sr., and a few of his Baptist friends, who were seeking homes in the West, were prospecting for lands in this region. They camped for the Sabbath in a grove near the present city of Belleville; songs and prayers were offered and the Scriptures read. This was probably the first act of associated worship performed by the Baptists in what is now St. Clair County, Illinois.

This event preceded by some years the organization of the Baptist cause in St. Clair County. At that time a few early settlers had located in Monroe County, who shortly afterward organized a church called the New Design Baptist Church, and from which eventually sprang the Richland Creek and Canteen Creek Baptist churches located in St. Clair County; this latter church is now called Bethel Church.

Among the supporters of the New Design Church who interested themselves in organizing a Baptist Church in St. Clair County was Rev. James Lemen, Sr., five of whose sons became active laborers in the

Baptist cause, four of them becoming ministers. The labors of this pioneer, with a few other faithful members of the Baptist faith in Monroe County, gave much encouragement to the first Baptists who settled in St. Clair County when they were organizing their first church here.

Rev. John Clark, a native of Scotland, and a Baptist minister, gave the Baptists of St. Clair County much encouragement in organizing their first churches. He died in St. Louis County, Missouri, October 11, 1833, aged 75 years.

Rev. Joseph Chance, a pioneer Baptist minister of much zeal, also gave active aid in organizing the Baptist cause in this county; he died in 1840, aged 75 years. Rev. David Badgley and Rev. John Baugh, pioneer Baptist ministers here, were also faithful workers with those other devoted men at that early day. They were men of large influence and were successful laborers in their Master's cause.

The anti-slavery sentiment was prominent with these people, although they were mostly southern men or their immediate descendants. This sentiment was probably intensified by the logical results of that grand achievement of the Baptists in 1789, which preceded this period but a few years. The denomination had but recently pressed Washington to insist upon the adoption of an article in the amendments to the constitution which should declare for religious liberty, and he had complied; and it was probable that when the Baptists had succeeded in assisting to plant the sublime doctrine of religious liberty in the constitution by the declaration that "Congress shall make no law respecting an establishment of religion, or prohibiting a free exercise thereof," it gave the feelings of these pioneer Baptists an impetus in the direction of freedom for the limbs as well as liberty for the conscience of men.

The popular sentiment at that day favored a complete separation of Church and State, and it was an opportune period, while the great republic was yet in its infancy, to plant the grand truth of religious liberty behind the strong towers of its constitution, and that some of these pioneers, in common with their brethren elsewhere, demanded the recognition of this truth in the constitution will ever remain to their credit. It is not unlikely that such an event stirred the minds of some of those early Baptist leaders with a sentiment for universal freedom.

In church government the first Baptist Church here, as well as their later ones, were in harmony with the theory and practice of the denomination in general. It was founded on the plan of a pure democracy, representing in religion the exact application of that grand principle which, in true political science should, and, according to our theory of government, does, control the State. In their views on Baptism and communion, these Baptists were a unit with their faith elsewhere.

The Richland Creek Baptist Church was the first Baptist church constituted in St. Clair County. The record of its first proceedings is dated June 14, 1806. Its first meeting, according to this record, occurred at Wm. Lot Whitesides' residence a few miles northeast of the present city of Belleville. Rev. Joseph Chance was moderator and Benjamin Ogle was clerk. At that time the church was an arm of the Baptist Church at New Design, in Monroe County, and the style of their minutes ran: "Richland Arm of the Church of Christ at New Design." On September 12, 1807, this church met at the house of Isaac Enochs and voted to form itself into a separate organization under the name of "The Baptist Church of Christ at Richland Creek;" and this was the style of their minutes at their next church meeting. In church session at the house of Jacob Ogle, in Ridge Prairie, St. Clair County, February 13, 1808, the church adopted resolutions declaring the faith of the church against the belief and practice of slavery. In 1809 these people built a meeting-house on Richland Creek, some three miles northeast of Belleville, and at that time had a membership of about forty. Among the members were Benjamin Ogle, James Lemen, Sr., Wm. Lot Whitesides, Wm Kinney, Isaac Enochs, Larkin Rutherford, Rev. Joseph Lemen, Robert Lemen, Polly K. Lemen, Catharine Lemen, Ann Simpson, Hetty Lemen, Ann Whitesides, Sallie Whitesides, Ann Lemen, Elizabeth Badgley, Mary Kinney, and others—a band of noble men and women whose pious lives and labors did much in moulding the destinies of the young State.

This church was in session July 8, 1809, when Rev. James Lemen, Sr., who had been licensed to preach July 9, 1808, arose and denounced the practice of slavery as something which he could not fellowship. To this declaration a portion of the church objected, and several church conferences were subsequently called to compromise the difference in opinion, but without results. Within the church each wing of opinion sent delegates to the association of the several Baptist churches, which had then been organized in Southern Illinois, but the association refused admission to both sets of messengers, and finally itself divided on the issue here presented. However, both schools of opinion in this church met afterward in friendly conference and talked over their views, and agreed that an amicable separation would be the better course to adopt. In pursuance of this end, at regular session of this church, December 9, 1809, it was voted that as many as wished to withdraw by reason of this difference of views on slavery and organize another church, should have the privilege to do so; and five members signified their purpose to form a new organization. This was the first act in the origin of Bethel Church. After this division in Richland Baptist Church it continued for many years, and numbered among its members many men and women of much influence and greatly esteemed by all who knew them. Many of their descendants yet survive and are found in Illinois and elsewhere. At a later period this church became extinct, its members having died or joined other churches.

The Bethel Baptist Church is located two and a half miles southeast of Collinsville in St. Clair County, in a beautiful and fertile farming district. It was constituted December 10, 1809. The five members who had formally withdrawn from Richland Church on the day previous, with two others, composed this church, and were constituted by Elders James Lemen, Jr., and John Baugh, under the name of "The Baptized Church of Christ, Friends to Humanity." The names of the constituent members were James Lemen, Sr., Catharine Lemen, Robert Lemen, Hetty Lemen, Joseph Lemen, Polly K. Lemen and Benjamin Ogle, who was an uncle to Robert, Joseph and James Lemen.

The declared faith of this church was the Old and New Testaments; and for its good will toward men, its constitution declared it to be "The Friends to Humanity, denying union and communion with all persons holding the doctrine of perpetual, involuntary, hereditary slavery."

With the organization of this church began the contest of slavery and anti-slavery views in Illinois. The birth of Bethel Church was among the first notes in the contest which ended at Appomattox more than half a century later; and as some of the early members of this church were officers under the Territorial and State governments of Illinois, it was undoubtedly a potent factor in shaping the destinies of the young

State, and in bringing it into the brotherhood of the States as a free commonwealth.

This church, while it exercised at an early day a potent influence on the policies of the State, was not idle in propagating its faith. At Belleville, Troy, Collinsville, Pleasant Ridge, Oak Hill, O'Fallon and elsewhere were churches which acknowledged their maternity largely to Bethel Church. Of the constituent members of this church we have given sketches which may be found under their proper headings.

For many years, and from its organization down to 1851, Rev. Joseph Lemen, with his brother James, supplied Bethel Church with ministerial labor (except for a period when Rev. Moses Lemen was pastor of the church). The church was blessed and increased greatly in strength through their labors.

Rev. Benjamin Ogle was a native of Virginia. He came to the Illinois country in 1785, united with the Baptist Church and became a minister of the gospel and accomplished much good in those early days by his gospel labors. He died at a ripe old age, esteemed by all who knew him.

These were the men and women who founded Bethel Church and gave it their labors, prayers and tears. They have long since passed away, but the church which they founded has gathered many hundreds to its fold and has witnessed their grand declaration for the common brotherhood of humanity take its place in the grand edifice of our national constitution.

On March 3, 1810, this church, in session, passed a rule to be called Canteen Creek Church, and for some years after was known as "The Baptist Church of Christ, Friends to Humanity, at Canteen Creek." This style was generally used until July 2, 1825, when the members had completed a meeting-house, and at that time had met in the house in church session for the first time. The records of that meeting call this meeting-house "Bethel," and from that date they seemed to be gradually, by public usage, assuming the name of Bethel Church, or Bethel Baptist Church.

Their meeting-house had a capacity of about 250, and was located a few rods south and a little east of the present church building.

From 1809 to 1825 the church sessions and worship were held here and there at the members' houses; and it was no unusual affair for one of these old farmers to feed fifty horses and a hundred people on such occasions. Sometimes half a beef and other provisions in proportion would be consumed in one day.

In looking over the venerable records of this church, it seems there was much progress in numbers and strength during this period. Here and there was an old camp follower, who worried the good people with his native and uncultured rhymes and dreadful music, tried the patience of the real preachers by following their sermons with wild, windy and unprofitable harangues, and consumed their chicken and beef with the avidity of a Roman emperor or hyena; but these harmless old fellows were tolerated in Christian charity.

General progress continued to attend the church after they built their meeting-house in 1825; and preceding this and some years later, a large number of earnest and active workers had united with the church, and a larger house had become a necessity— and they proceeded to build their new house—the present church building—in 1838 and 1840 at a cost of $4,000. It is sixty by forty feet, and was built in accordance with the specifications of a committee on plan for a house, appointed in church session April 7, 1838. The committee were: Joshua Begole, Merlin Jones and Samuel Seybold. Making their new house was to call forth the best energies of their members; but a noble band of workers consisting of Joshua Begole, Merlin Jones, Robert Lemen, John Cook, Rev. James Lemen, Jr., Samuel Beedle, Rev. Joseph Lemen, James H. Lemen, Samuel Simpson, William Hart, Peter Bowler, Warren Beedle, Samuel Baird, Isaac W. Lemen, David Lawrence, James Hogan, Sylvester Lemen and others, carried the enterprise forward to success; and the new house was dedicated the first Saturday in September, 1840, the Rev. John M. Peck preaching the dedicatory sermon. On this occasion a vast concourse of people attended, and a series of meetings continued for ten days, resulting in the conversion of fifty persons, many of whom united with Bethel Church.

In 1851, February 1, Rev. John M. Peck was chosen pastor of Bethel Church. From its organization to this date Revs. Joseph and James Lemen, Jr. had furnished the pastoral services except for a period in 1846 and 1847, when Rev. Moses Lemen, their brother, was pastor. During this period of about forty years, while the Lemen brothers, Joseph and James, labored in the church, other ministers from every section of the country often preached and labored at Bethel, in revival meetings and at other times, and rendered great aid and encouragement to the church; but the labors of these two pioneer ministers were rewarded with a degree of success in advancing the interest and strength of the church, which brought with it a consciousness of duty well discharged.

John M. Peck, D. D., was pastor of Bethel Church in 1851, and the church prospered under his care. Dr. Peck moved from the East and located at Rock Spring, St. Clair County, Illinois, at an early day. He was a man of universal reading, and as a minister of the gospel of the Baptist faith was devoted, and commanded a wide influence. He was the founder of Shurtleff College, which sprang from Rock Spring Seminary, Dr. Peck's school. He died at his home at Rock Spring in 1858, before he had attained a very great age. The scene at his death-bed was very impressive. Several of his ministerial and other associates had visited him, and but a short time before his death he reached his hand to Rev. James Lemen, Jr., and shaking his hand, earnestly exclaimed ·

"The Saviour Reigns!" It was a beautiful and fit ending of a life whose labors had left their mark upon the literature and piety of his age, and which had made the name of John M. Peck a household word throughout the country. Rev. James Lemen, Jr., preached the funeral discourses commemorative of Dr. Peck's life and labors at Alton, Bethel, Belleville and one or two other points.

Since Dr. Peck's pastorate Revs. D. M. Howell, J. H. Heigh, E. J. Palmer, H. S. Deppe, J. M. Cochran, W. S. Post, L. C. Carr, W. Wright, W. R. Andereck, George Steele and J. B. Webb, have constituted the succession of pastors of Bethel Church; and during that period the church, at times, enjoyed great seasons of revivals and large additions to its membership, and at other times experienced depression and discouragement.

W. R. Andereck served the church successfully for almost nine years, and J. B. Webb, who has just received his eighth call from the church, has labored untiringly and with good effect for seven years.

Those early members who bore the heat and burden of the work in making Bethel what it once was and now is, to a certain extent, have passed away. They were noble men and women, whose memories it were well to embalm in gratitude. Among the last of these who died in Bethel community was Joshua Begole. He came to Illinois at an early day, and during a long life contributed largely of his time and means to build up Bethel Church and the cause of religion generally in this section of Illinois. Joshua Begole was a man of liberal reading, and served the people of St. Clair County as justice of the peace for many years; married Mary Terry, and settled in St. Clair County, where they accumulated a handsome competence—reared a large family of children, who were all believers, and seven of whom united with the Baptist Church and are earnest and liberal supporters of the cause. He was a liberal, earnest Christian, and was esteemed by all who knew him. He united with Bethel Church August 4, 1827, and for nearly half a century he stood by this old church with his means and his toils and his prayers. He died at his residence a quarter of a mile west of Bethel, March 2, 1874, aged 82 years. His widow, Mrs. Mary Begole united with Bethel Church October 6, 1827. More than half a century separated her from that day to the one when she crossed to the evergreen shores of eternity. Through these long years she contributed with a liberal hand and sincere purpose to the interests of Bethel Church, while she was a generous supporter of the cause of religion generally, and none, more justly than she, was esteemed for their piety and benevolence.

Bethel Church has sent out many ministers of the gospel of the Baptist faith. Revs. Joseph Lemen, James Lemen, Sr., Benjamin Ogle, Joel Terry and several other members of the gospel ministry have been ordained and have gone out from this church to preach the Word of God. The deacons of the church since its organization were: Stephen Terry, Gideon Scanland, Samuel McClain, John Hart, Elisha Freeman, William Hart, George C. Hart, Samuel Baird, Benjamin Scott, Warren Beedle, James B. Lyons, Augustus Beedle, Samuel Simpson, Levi Piggott, and the present deacons are Frank B. Lemen and John Bevirt. The clerks were: Robert Lemen, who served in that capacity for forty years, Sidney Hart, assistant clerk at one time, James H. Lemen, Geo. W. Bowler, S. Whitlock, W. L. Beedle, and the present clerk is Oscar Lemen. The treasurers were: John Cook, Joshua Begole, Warren Beedle, James H. Lemen, Gideon S. Lemen, and the present treasurer is F. M. Begole, with F. B. Lemen, assistant. From time to time the church has renewed its board of trustees by election.

Bethel Church is, and always has been, missionary in spirit. It has given thousands since its organization for religious and eleemosynary purposes and it has not been wanting in patriotism. By its records of July 3, 1847, we find an act relieving its members who were in the Mexican war from church expenses for some time, and when some of its members and friends were in the late war, the church or its members held festivals for the purpose of sending extra comforts to their friends at the front, and on one occasion, with Mr. William Begole as president of the evening, $400.00 were collected and donated for that purpose.

Ordinarly, when the pastoral supply is short the church holds meetings every Sabbath. Their church meetings occur monthly, the first Saturday, and their communion seasons are observed quarterly.

Bethel Church is now the oldest Baptist Church in Illinois. The church property consists of a church house and about ten acres of land, on which there are a comfortable house for the pastor, and a cemetery. The property is worth $4,000. The church house is in good repair, and has a capacity for six hundred comfortable sittings. The church is well supported and cared for by the descendants of its early members, who reside in the vicinity of the church, and who generally belong to it, together with other persons who have settled in that locality and united with the church. The financial strength of the membership generally is considerable, and in addition to meeting the obligations of maintaining the church, they con_tribute of their means to a liberal extent in other religious missions. The strength of the church at this time, January, 1897, consists of sixty members. Usually a Sunday-school is conducted at the church, at hours when worship is not in progress, and the interests of the children are thus looked after. At this time the Sunday-school is under the control of F. B. Lemen, who has superintended the Sabbath-school and devotional singing for about twenty years with an intermission of about two years when Oscar Lemen superintended the Sabbath-school work. In their music, congregational singing has always been the custom at Bethel Church, but for many years this has been reinforced by the organ.

We have given the scene where the early members of Bethel Church labored; it is proper to name the spot where they rest. The church has a cemetery near the northern limits of their land, neatly enclosed and taken care of; many of the early laborers of the church are interred elsewhere, but a large number of them rest here; and if the Christian's hope is not a myth, and his Bible an idle legend—and they certainly are not—they have joined that throng whose faith made the toils of this life, with death and the grave, but steps in their progress to a happier sphere and blessed immortality; they have gone to that reward which God has promised the faithful.

CHAPTER XII.

THE ORPHANAGE.

A brief history of the Orphanage clipped from the *Christian Home*, a weekly paper published by Rev. J. G. Lemen in the interest of the Orphanage, is as follows:

The history of a work is always of interest and importance to the friends of that work. The history of the Home is of special interest to all Christians, as it is a history of God's gracious dealings with His children, the reading of which cannot fail to cheer the heart and strengthen the faith. We have not time nor space now for a history in detail, but will give a brief outline, praying that it may be blessed to the good of the Orphanage.

While, from a human standpoint, we may justly be considered the founder of this work, we do desire here and now to declare that we deserve and claim no credit for the founding and maintaining of the Orphanage. We never planned for the work, never intended to personally engage in it, until the time the Lord compelled us to do so. It is all of the Lord. By marked, wonderful and special providences He led us into this blessed work.

In the spring of 1882, a mechanic, who some months before had taken the temperance pledge and violated it, in a fit of despondency committed suicide.

THE HOME COTTAGE.

We were called to preach at the funeral. The poor wife, with babe in arms, and five little children, standing around the coffin, was a sight never to be forgotten. O, cursed rum traffic! God have mercy on the man who votes to license it! The poor woman was left penniless and had to go out and wash for families in order to support her little ones, made fatherless by the licensed curse of rum. Her oldest child was only eleven. The babe had to be left in the care of this little one during the day. The little sister probably did the best she could, but was too young to properly care for the babe. The result was that the little one took cold, and, in just two weeks from the time of the funeral of the father, we were called to preach at the funeral of the babe. Two souls gone on before to witness in the day of judgment against every man who by voice or vote upholds the rum traffic.

In the fall of 1882 we announced a temperance lecture from our pulpit. During the lecture we naturally used the sad, thrilling incidents as illustratrations. We had no thought of making further use of them. But when the lecture was concluded we felt impressed that we ought to give it a practical turn for the widow, as winter was approaching and we knew her to be in great need. But we had lately taken up a number of collections for different objects, and pastors will know how to sympathize with us when we say that we feared that the taking of the collection would do more harm than good. So we were greatly

troubled in mind.   The congregation was singing the
last hymn and we were undecided.   The last stanza
is reached, and we are in a state of literal perspira-
tion, because of conflicting emotions.   The last verse
of the last stanza is reached!   The last word—the
congregation is waiting for the benediction!   Well,
we decided, we will dismiss them *now*, and collect
some privately for her.   And so we lifted our hands,
but the Lord would not have it so.   We could not
speak, but were choked with emotion.   Feeling the
overwhelming conviction that we must not dismiss
the.congregation, we used our uplifted hands to make
a downward gesture, and said: "Please be seated
for a moment."   We stated to them what we had in
mind, and received a liberal collection.

The next day we ordered supplies for the family
for the winter, and, moved by the Lord, visited a
large number of other poor families who were as des-
titute as the one in question.   Late in the evening,
returning home, happy in spirit, but very tired in
body, the reporter of the *Council Bluffs Daily Non-
pariel* met us and asked for a report.   After he had
received it he said:

"Why not let me announce in the morning that
you will be in your study from 10 a. m. to 12 m. to
receive any additional donations that citizens desire to
bring in?"

"Why, we can't do that," we replied.   "Those
are our hours for study, and we can't do it.   We
must look after the interest of the church."

" But look here." he said, "if you are the means of feeding and clothing these people, what better work can you do?"

The Lord blessed the words of that worldly man to our good. He meant them to be ironical, but we let that pass, and said, " Well, do as you like. I shrink from it, but if you see fit to announce it, I will do my part."

He did announce it. The citizens of this city responded most liberally. He came around daily, and each morning wrote up the work, because he took a special pride in it, having suggested it. The work rapidly grew into large proportions, until we had the chapel of the church open from 7 a. m. to 10 p. m.; had a man to attend to it; had committees; sometimes had a half dozen express wagons engaged in the service of the committees; fed and clothed scores of families; made extensive repairs on dilapidated houses, where the sick were; furnished stoves, beds and bedding; sent nurses to the sick; and, in short, by the co-operation of all the churches and charitable organizations of the city, did a work for the poor that winter that will ever be remembered to the credit of the good people of Council Bluffs.

While this work was at its height, about the middle of December, 1882, a drunken man staggered into the chapel one day. Approaching us, he said:

" I want you to take my three girls."

We explained to him that we had no way of caring for his girls, that we were simply dispensing food and clothing, and that, if he and his family were in need, and, in the opinion of the committee, worthy, we would assist.

"I don't want that!" he exclaimed. "My wife died a few days ago. I am a wreck! There is no hope for me! If you won't take my girls they will have to go to the poorhouse, and then God only knows what will become of them."

This language touched our heart, as God intended it should. We took the girls and hired their board, praise the Lord! As soon as it was noised abroad that we had so done, other homeless, forsaken little ones were brought to us. Having commenced, our heart was softened, and we simply followed on, as the Lord led. Soon we had more than we could afford to board out, and so we rented a little house and hired a matron. In the spring of 1883, March 16, we called some earnest brethren together and organized a legal association for the holding of the property. We may not here go on with the long struggle we then had before the Lord saw fit to lead us out into a comparatively large place. He knows all about that and why it was He tried us. We are well aware it was for our best good, and devoutly praise Him for the dark days of the work, as well as for the bright ones.

CONCLUSION.

He has most graciously led all the way. To Him we have looked day by day for the supplying of all our wants, and He has never left nor forsaken us.

At present we have 237 in the Home, and during the history of the Home He has enabled us in all to care for 1,500 of His homeless ones. The children range in age from infancy up to fourteen years.

The blessed results of this work eternity alone can reveal. For the manner in which the Lord hath led, and for all His gracious dealings with the Orphanage, our soul doth magnify His holy name. To Him be all the glory. Come, dear fellow-laborers, children of the King, and let us together praise the name of our God.

CHAPTER XIII.

BIOGRAPHICAL.

Rev. J. G. Lemen, B. D. (Goff, as he was known in boyhood days), was born in Salem, Marion County, Illinois, the 20th of February, 1848. He was the son of Benjamin F. and Mary P. Lemen, and a grandson of Rev. Joseph Lemen. His only brother, Putnam Lemen, died in infancy before Goff was born, and hence the love of his mother, a very spiritual woman, centered on him as a gift from God, in answer to fervent prayer for a son to train for God.

Night and morning she prayed that Goff would grow up to become a minister of the gospel. Early in life, at the age of eight years, he professed conversion and offered himself as a candidate for baptism to the Baptist Church. At that day the churches did not take kindly to receiving children so young, and hence the pastor and deacons advised him to wait. This he did without complaint, having, even at that age, high regard for the decisions of the church. He attended the church meetings, the prayer meetings, Sunday-school and all services. In the prayer meetings he often spoke and prayed. Thus he continued, everybody calling him the "little preacher." He would invite his playmates to his home and have prayer meetings and talk to them of Bible characters. And so pleasant did he make it for them that some of

230—REV. JOSEPH GOFF LEMEN.

the wildest boys, such as are generally called the
" hard cases," came to be his friends, and seldom refused his invitations.

At the age of thirteen he again presented himself
to the church and was baptized into the fellowship
of the Baptist Church of Salem, Illinois.

At the age of sixteen he entered Shurtleff College, Upper Alton, Illinois, and was a student there
for four years. While at college he became possessed
with a desire for worldly favor, and, after a great
struggle with his conscience, decided to study law.
So when he left school he studied law, attended one
session of law lectures at Harvard University and was
admitted to the bar by the Supreme Court of Illinois
when he was twenty-one years of age. He then
bought an interest in a newspaper, moved to Lebanon,
Mo., and conducted the paper and practiced law for
seven years. He was successful in business and accumulated there a valuable property, the whole of
which was given to the Christian Home Orphanage
some years later.

In the spring of 1871 he returned home for a visit,
and more than a visit, in accordance with a social engagement made before he left for Missouri. During
this visit, on the 2d of May, 1871, he married Miss
Florence Jane Hagee, of Carlyle, Ill. To them five
children were born. One died in infancy and
four are living—three sons and a daughter. His
wife is one of the noblest of women, and has been to
him, and is still, not only a loving companion but

also a real helpmate and partner in all his labors.
Their children are Christians and are actively and
earnestly engaged in the work of the Orphange.

During the years he was practicing law and conducting his paper his heart was not satisfied. From
his earliest remembrance he had prayed to God to
keep him from becoming too proud to be a minister,
and all of his success seemed to him but idle.   So
one week when his paper came out, without warning,
with the announcement that it was for sale, and that
the editor had decided to give his life to the ministry,
his new-made friends were surprised and shocked,
but his old friends of boyhood days simply smiled,
and said " We knew it would be so."

The church at Salem, Ill., where he was born and
raised, at once asked the privilege of ordaining him,
which was granted; and so he was ordained at the
age of twenty-eight by the church which baptized him
when he was thirteen.

He then spent a year or more in missionary labor
among the churches of Missouri, and in that time
founded a Baptist College at Lebanon, Mo., which
was later moved to Bolivar, and set influences in motion that resulted in the founding of the Baptist College at Pierce City, Mo.   He was prominent at all
associational meetings, and many flourishing churches
in that vicinity date their birth from the time of his
labors during the first years of his ministry.   After
a little more than a year of most earnest labor given
to the cause he loved, as he often did not receive

747—FLORENCE J. LEMEN.

enough remuneration to meet his expenses, he accepted the call of his old home church at Salem, Ill., to become its pastor.

After a pastorate at Salem of two years, he was called as pastor of the Baptist Church at Bunker Hill, Ill. He resigned at Salem and accepted the call to Bunker Hill, in order to be near to Shurtleff College, as he desired to enter that school again and take a thorough theological course. This he did and graduated from the Theological Department of Shurtleff College, receiving the degree of B. D.

The winter following his graduation in the Theological course, in January, 1881, he was called to the pastorate of the First Baptist Church of Council Bluffs, Iowa. He remained pastor of this church for four years. At the close of the second year of his pastorate, he founded the Christian Home Orphanage. Two years later he resigned the pastorate, and since that time has devoted himself to the care of homeless children, often preaching here and there, as time and strength permits. Of his life now, and since the founding of the Orphanage, it is quite unnecessary to write as it is an open page known and read of all men To-day he and his work are known and loved in every civilized nation of the globe.

125—MRS. AMIRA LEMEN KING.

Amira Lemen King was born in Monroe County, Illinois, January 17, 1823. She was the second

daughter of Rev. Moses Lemen and Sarah Hull
Lemen, grand-daughter of Rev. James Lemen, Sr.,
one of the first American settlers of Southern Illinois.

The subject of this sketch spent her childhood in
Monroe County, being born on the old Lemen homestead, and in 1834 moved with her parents to Greene
County, Illinois. Her father became pastor of the
old Kane Baptist Church where he preached for ten
years. It was during one of these meetings that she
accepted Christ as her Savior, and was baptized by
her father into the Baptist Church, and remained a
member of this same organization for over fifty
years, until her death.

On January 14, 1841, she was united in marriage
(her father performing the ceremony) with Lucian
King, a native of New York State, and who came to
Illinois in 1840. Seven children were born of this
union, three only of whom are now living: Mrs. C.
E. Neeley and Mrs. Frank McClure, of Arkadelphia,
Arkansas, and Mrs. Theodore Jones, of Kane, Illinois.
She was a faithful wife, a loving mother, and strongly
devoted to her religion and church, ever ready to
lend a helping hand to the cause of Christianity and
Temperance. Although her early education was quite
meager she was an exceptionably intelligent woman.
In her later days she was a great reader and was well
informed upon all the subjects of the day.

In the summer of 1894, disease laid its hand upon
her, and she was a great sufferer for three weeks,
when death came to her relief. On June 15, 1894,

125—AMIRA KING.

surrounded by loving children and grand-children, her happy spirit took its flight to join husband and children that had gone before. Her last words were, "Oh the happy faces."

> 'Twas in the bright month of the roses,
> That we laid our dear mother to rest,
> And we decked her dear form, ere we laid her,
> With the flowers she always loved best.

192—MR. AND MRS. GEORGE W. BOWLER.

George W. Bowler, the eldest son of Benjamin F. and Hester Bowler, *nee* Lemen, was born in Ridge Prairie, St. Clair County, Illinois, January 8, 1838. He attended several district schools and made the most of his opportunities. On February 10, 1859, he married Miss Harriet E. Simpson (671), daughter of Rev. Gideon Simpson, whose residence was near Bethel. They settled on their farm in Ridge Prairie, and have so vastly improved the place that it is now one of the best, if *not* the best, that Ridge Prairie affords. There were born of this union two children, N. Ella and Thomas Jefferson, of which the elder only survives. The younger was born September 25, 1863, and died August 25, 1864, age 11 months. Mrs. H. E. Bowler embraced the Baptist faith and joined Bethel Church, December, 1870, was baptized by Rev. W. S. Post, and has proved herself a willing worker in her Master's vineyard. After

twenty-five years of wedded life they celebrated their
silver wedding anniversary, receiving a number of
costly and elegant presents from their many relatives
and friends, proving thereby the high esteem with
which they were regarded. Among many other
notable events or pleasure trips, the two that leave
the brightest impression on their minds, and the one
that "Father Time can ne'er obliterate," is their visit
to the World's Fair and their trip South to Atlanta,
Ga.

* * *

1180—MR. AND MRS. J. HARVEY KING.

Mrs. Ella King, *nee* Bowler (672), only daughter
of Geo. W. and Harriet E. Bowler, was born in Ridge
Prairie, St. Clair County, Illinois, February 14, 1860.
She entered Almira College, Greenville, Ills., September, 1874; after completing her studies she returned
to her home in Ridge Prairie. She was united in
the holy bonds of matrimony by Rev. W. S. Post, of
Chicago, Ill., on February 7, 1878, to J. Harvey
King, of O'Fallon, Ill. After enjoying a very pleasant wedding trip they returned to her parents' home
where she proved herself to be an able assistant in
beautifying and decorating her already pleasant home.
One of the many pleasure trips that Mr. and Mrs.
King enjoyed was their visit to the World's Fair, but
the one that Mr. King holds the most sacred is their
trip South, October 23, 1897, where they visited

671—HARRIET E. BOWLER.

1181—JAMES H. KING.

67²—ELLA KING.

19²—GEORGE W. BOWLER.

Nashville, Murfreesboro, battle-fields of Missionary Ridge, Chickamauga and also Lookout Mountain. He being a soldier such scenes brought vividly back his soldier life. He entered the Union army May 10, 1861, at the early age of 16 years and two months. He enlisted in Company H, 21st Illinois Infantry, Grant's Regiment. He fought in many battles, among the most notable are Fredericktown, Mo., Corinth, Miss., Perryville, Ky., Dalton, Ga., Rocky-face Ridge, Kingston, Resaca, Allatoona Hills, Pine Mountain, Kennesaw, etc.

Very few veterans escape with their lives, much less without scars, to tell of the battles they fought. Mr. King was severly wounded at Stone River or Murfreesboro, Tenn., and being unable to escape he was captured, and recaptured there, and lives to tell the story.

Mr. and Mrs. King are regular attendants at Bethel Church, where Mrs. King, being possessed of a good voice and ear for music, aids greatly in all the musical programmes of that church.

Mr. and Mrs. King celebrated the tenth anniversary of their married life by giving a reception to their many relatives and friends, who pronounced it a grand success. Many milestones have been passed thus far in their journey of life, but not a shadow of regret clouds the sunshine of their wedded bliss, and we trust *many more* milestones may be passed ere their journey is finished.

276—J. B. LYON.

J. B. Lyon was born May 11, 1811, at or near Shelbyville, Ky. Having strong anti-slavery ideas he moved to Illinois when a young man. He married Catharine, daughter of Rev. James Lemen, Jr., March 25, 1841. They lived for a number of years in St. Clair County. His wife died March 3, 1860. His health being very poor he moved his family to Hastings, Minn. On October 3, 1861, he married Miss Almira Vantamee. He lived at Hastings the remainder of his life.

His death occurred June 19, 1872. He lived an upright and consistent Christian life, well beloved by all who knew him, and died in full hope of a "blessed immortality."

277—MARY M. LYON.

Mary M. Lyon, oldest daughter of James B. and Catharine Lyon, was born March 16, 1842. On November 24, 1863, she married Dr. H. O. Mowers. They had one son, W. H. Mowers, who now lives at Deland, Fla. They resided at Hastings until the fall of 1876, when the family removed to Macon County, Alabama. The wife dying there in 1880, the father and son removed to Deland, Fla., where they still reside. Mary Mowers was greatly beloved by the people of both her Northern and Southern homes. She was a faithful wife, mother and sister; a good neighbor and a consistent Christian.

282—LOUIS A. LYON.

810—JAMES BERNARD LYON.　808—CARRIE L. LYON.

805—LOUIS AMOS LYON, JR.　811—MARY MARGUERITE LYON.

James, William and John Thomas Lyon were born in St. Clair County, Illinois, and partially educated there. The best part of their lives were spent in Minnesota. Both were splendid business young men, beloved by all, and popular in both business and social circles.

That fell destroyer, consumption, who has taken so many of our kindred, claimed them for his victims, and at a time when the world looked most fair to them they passed to that land to which our fathers have gone. Nancy Josephine and Lucy Irene Lyon both died in infancy.

282—LOUIS A. LYON.

Louis Albert Lyon, the youngest child of James B. and Catharine Lyon, was born in St. Clair County, Illinois, September 16, 1855. He is the only one of the family now living. He was educated in Minnesota, but as soon as he reached his majority sold out his possessions and went to Macon County, Alabama, where he has since lived.

Two years after his arrival in Alabama, he married Carrie Lanham Tuttle, daughter of A. G. Tuttle, of Montgomery, Ala. They have lived together in peace and happiness for almost twenty years.

Three children have blessed this union of North and South: Louis Amos, age 14 years; James Bernard, age 10 years, and Mary Marguerite, age 8 years. He is engaged in milling and farming, and has one of the vineyards in South Alabama.

74—CATHARINE LEMEN LYON.

Catharine Lemen Lyon, a daughter of Rev. James Lemen, Jr., and Mary Lemen, his wife, was born at the home of her parents in Ridge Prairie, Ill., on November 26, 1818. She acquired a common school education, and in early life united with the Bethel Baptist church. She married James B. Lyon, and they settled on their farm in Ridge Prairie, where they reared their famil . Their children were Mary M., James W., John, Josephine, Nancy and Lewis. Mary M. became the wife of Dr. H. O. Mowers, of Hastings, Minn. She is now dead, and their only child, William Mowers, now lives with his father in Florida. Lewis Lyon, the only living member of the family, married a very excellent lady, and he and his wife live in Alabama, where they have reared their family. The mother, Catharine Lemen Lyon, died at her home in Ridge Prairie on March 3, 1860. Her husband, James B. Lyon, removed to Hastings, Minn., where he was married again, but there was no issue, and where he died some years since.

240—DR. JOSEPH ROBERT LEMEN.

Joseph Robert Lemen, M. D., St. Louis, Mo., was born in Madison County, Illinois, near Collinsville. His father was Robert C. Lemen, a good and pious man who spent most of his life on a beautiful farm not far from the old Lemen settlement. Dr.

240—DR. JOSEPH ROBERT LEMEN.

Lemen, the subject of this sketch, attended school in Collinsville until about fifteen years of age, when he went to St. Louis, attending Washington University, afterwards going to the Missouri Medical College until he graduated in 1874. Being one of the successful candidates for the City Hospital, he was almost immediately assigned to that place. For two years, after being greatly benefitted by his experience at the hospital, he attended lectures in New York and Philadelphia, and then settled in St. Louis, where, up to date, 1897, he is one of the prominent practitioners, enjoying the esteem of the best physicians. Dr. Lemen was on the Board of Health from 1887 to 1891; has been for a number of years consulting physician to the City and Female Hospitals; is on the staff of the Rebekah Hospital and Deaconess Home —two flourishing institutions; is professor of diseases of the chest and physical diagnosis at "Marion Sims College." He has a clinic of his own at the college, and another on Grand and Easton avenues. With a large practice, and so many other calls on his time, Dr. Lemen is always a very busy man; he has also been physician to the Methodist Orphan's Home for the past twelve years; has written quite extensively on his specialty—diseases of the chest— and his writings have been published in the Eastern and Western journals. At present he is treating many consumptives with "Serum," and has effected quite a number of permanent cures, and has a wide reputation for helping and curing those afflicted with that dreaded disease.

Dr. Lemen was married to Miss Ida May Chick in 1885, a beautiful young woman, who has aided her husband greatly in gaining the high and enviable position which he occupies, not only in the medical but social world. They have two lovely children, Eugenia and Robert, aged respectively eleven and six.

157—ROBERT L. McKINLEY.

Robert Lemen McKinley was born in Clinton County, Missouri, May 22, 1844; he was taken when a small child by his parents to Texas, and thence to California, to Sacramento City, where he commenced his education which was finished in Solano County, where he went with his parents. He was a noble-minded, moral young man of more than ordinary intelligence, he had many friends and was highly esteemed by all who knew him for his good qualities. About the year 1867, in the month of September, he married Miss Jennie Hall, of Silveyville, by whom he had two children, a daughter and son—Catharine (deceased), and William B., who is now living in Waco, Texas. Robert McKinley while traveling in Colorado received injuries on his head, a fracture of the skull, caused by the overturning of the stage he was traveling in, which finally resulted in his death. He died in Waco, Texas, leaving a wife and two children. His wife after remaining a widow for several years married again. His son owns quite a nice piece of land near Waco.

135—MARY CATHARINE DAUGHERTY.

Mary Catharine (Lemen) Daugherty, the subject of this sketch, was born in Kane, Greene County, Illinois, October 17, 1843. She is the youngest child of Rev. Moses Lemen, and at the early age of eight years professed a hope in Christ, and two years later united with the Walshville Baptist Church, in which she was a faithful and consistent member.

In 1866 she with her husband, Wm. T. Daugherty, and her mother, Sarah A. Lemen, moved to Kansas. She has ever been faithful to the cause of temperance; has been a member of the I. O. G. T. over twenty-two years. In politics she is a thorough Republican, and through all the trying scenes of life has ever held the glorious cause of Christ high above everything else; choosing to suffer affliction with the people of God rather than enjoy the pleasure of sin for a season, striving ever to live up to the blessed teachings of our Savior; strong in the Baptist faith and ever true to its principles and teachings, she is ever kind and loving to those around her, speaking, when she can, a word for *Jesus*. She is fully satisfied that when this life's work is done that she will have a crown of glory and a place among the blessed, for she is resting on this promise.

753—JOHN SOBIESKI, Sr.

Hon. John Sobieski, the genial and popular Good Templar worker, lecturer and organizer, has become well known to temperance workers all over America. He has an interesting history. He is a lineal descendant of the great warrior King, John Sobieski, of Poland, and son of Count John Sobieski, who commanded the notable Polish uprising in 1846.

When the Polish army was defeated General Sobieski was taken prisoner by the Russians and confined in a dungeon, by order of the Czar of Russia, for thirteen months, and was then executed, as was also his father-in-law, the noted soldier Gen., Joseph Bemme, and the latter's two heroic sons; the youngest daughter starting the same morning on the dreary march to Siberia. The wife of Gen. Sobieski, the Countess Sobieski, indignantly refusing to take the oath of allegiance to Russia, and allow her boy to be educated in the Greek Church, was, with her little son, banished from Russia forever and their vast estates were confiscated.

By the help of the Polish Exile Committee they were taken across the line to Prussia-Poland, that portion of Poland which was awarded Prussia as her part of the "swag," but were not allowed to stop. They were then taken to Galacia, in Austria-Poland. Here they were permitted to remain two weeks, and at the end of that time were again banished. They then went to Belgium, and in Brussels they found their first shelter. From Belgium they went to Switzerland, and from there to Genoa, Italy. The mother supporting herself and child by teaching music and painting. Genoa was at that time under

753—JOHN SOBIESKI, SR.

the administration of Austria, and that power, fearing a weak, though patriotic woman and her child, again placed banishment upon them for participating in the ovation to that gallant American, Captain Ingram. Shelter was then sought in England, but sorrow broke the young mother's heart, and she died in the fall of 1854, two years after arriving in England. In 1855, the son, then thirteen years of age came to America. He immediately entered the regular army as a bu ler.

He was with the Army of the Potomac during the great Civil War, serving in the capacity of Colonel, and participated in all its battles. When the war closed he went to Mexico, and, true to his love of freedom, enlisted in the Mexican army and was made General Escopodo's chief-of-staff. He served there until after the overthrow of Maximilian, and then returned to the United States and settled in Minnesota. In 1867 he was elected to the Legislature, and is the author of the bills to abolish capital punishment, to enfranchise women and to prohibit the liquor traffic.

Since 1870 he has occupied the lecture platform, speaking on temperance and literary subjects. Aside from his temperance lectures, his most popular one is on Poland—that land of misfortune and sterling patriotism. The American people, fired with the spirit of freedom, will always look upon the spoliation of Poland as one of the greatest stains upon the banner of modern civilization.

Colonel Sobieski has lectured in every State in the Union, in the British Provinces, throughout England, Ireland and Wales. He is now pledged to battle against the liquor traffic until that traffic is overthrown or death releases him from the obligation.

231—LYDIA GERTRUDE SOBIESKI.

Lydia Gertrude Sobieski, born in Salem, Ill., January 3, 1851, is the youngest of the family of Benjamin F. Lemen and Mary Putnam Rand Lemen. She was educated in Almira College, Greenville, Ill., graduating in 1876.

At the age of sixteen she united with the Baptist Church in Salem, Ill. In her youth she joined all movements for the advancement of the temperance cause.

June 3, 1879, she was married to Hon. John Sobieski, the well-known temperance orator.

In June, 1884, she was appointed National Superintendent of the Woman's Christian Temperance Union work among the Polish people, and later, National Superintendent of the Slavic Department of the Foreign Work for the Woman's Christian Temperance Union.

Since June, 1895, she has devoted her entire time to lecturing in the interest of the Prohibition movement, and doing everything possible for the circulation of Prohibition literature.

231—LYDIA GERTRUDE SOBIESKI.

In July, 1896, she was appointed National Lecturer and Organizer for the Armenian Relief Association, and devoted her time during 1896 and the first six months of 1897 to lecturing in behalf of the Armenians and in raising money to assist in relieving their distress.

With that exception, her entire time is devoted to the movement for the overthrow of the liquor traffic.

755—JOHN SOBIESKI, JR.

John Sobieski, Jr., born in Neosho, Mo., November 4, 1882, was the youngest child of Hon. John Sobieski and Lydia Gertrude Sobieski. He was converted at the age of twelve and united with the Baptist Church in Neosho, Mo. He was at that early age president of a temperance society for little boys, which he planned and organized. He was highly intellectual and intensely religious, a worthy descendant of his noble ancestors with whom he was united in that Eternal City, April 5, 1895.

754—MARY P. R. SOBIESKI.

Mary Putnam Rand Sobieski, born in Salem, Ill., September 2, 1880, is the oldest of the two children of Hon. John Sobieski and Lydia Gertrude Sobieski.

She was converted at an early age and united with the Baptist Church. She is receiving her education at Forest Park University, St. Louis, Mo.

739—COL. W. N. DENNY.

Col. W. N. Denny was born May 12, 1836, at Bruceville, Knox County, Indiana. He was educated at Vincennes University, and studied law with his brother, Judge Denny; enlisted in the 14th Indiana, May, 1861; was transferred to the 51st Indiana, February, 1862; was captured by the Confederates May, 1863, and was twenty-two months a prisoner of war. He finally succeeded in making his escape, and was mustered out of the army in Texas, January, 1866. As Colonel of the 51st Indiana he was one of the first to enlist and the last to be mustered out. Long and valued service he gave his country in her time of need.

228—MRS. ELLEN K. DENNY.

Mrs. Ellen K. Denny, nee Lemen, was born in St. Clair County, Illinois, April 8, 1843. She was converted at the early age of eleven years and baptized at Alton, Ill., in January, 1854, while attending school at that place, by Rev. Breckenridge. She graduated at the Southern Illinois Female College in June, 1860, at the early age of seventeen. She was married to

755—JOHN SOBIESKI, JR.

Col. W. N. Denny, late of the 51st Indiana, of Vincennes, Ind., May 24, 1866. There were born to them eight children: Willie L., Putnam C., Catherine Ogle, Florence Goff, Gertrude L., Nellie K., Mary Putnam and Carrie Conant.

Mrs. Ellen Denny has been prominent in social and literary circles, and a National leader in the temperance reform. Her husband is one of the political leaders in the State of Indiana, and a staunch Republican.

500—ANNA J. WIBEL.

Anna J. Lemen Wibel was born in Columbus, Kansas, March 3, 1865, while her parents were on a pioneer expedition through Kansas, Missouri and Iowa. The rigor of the unsettled country and the anxiety of the father for the condition of his family, were no doubt factors which led to the untimely death of the head of the family, and Judson Lemen succumbed to the inevitable and death claimed him while the subject of this sketch was only two years of age. By this sad event four children were left orphans: Chesterfield Lemen, Seigel Lemen, Anna Lemen-Wibel and Katie Lemen-Shaffer. Seigel Lemen was accidently killed in early age by the fall from a horse.

The residence of Chesterfield Lemen is unknown. Anna Wibel lives in Salem, Ill., and Katie Schaffer resides at Nokomis.   Anna and Seigel were adopted into the family of Rev. Benjamin and Mary Lemen of Salem, Ill., and the noble precepts of her foster parents have been precious examples to her life. She was married to John C. Wibel in June, 1882.   Soon afterward he became editor of the Monroe County Republican, and for several years was identified with that paper. Mrs. Wibel is the mother of five children : Mary, Blanche, Luella, Hattie and Charlie Wibel. She is the grand-daughter of Rev. Moses Lemen, of whom the *Globe-Democrat* said in a write-up of the pioneer ministers, that Moses Lemen was one of the most influential preachers in the early history of Illinois.   Her father was Judson Lemen, and her mother was Mary Eberline Lemen, now the wife of John Green, Walshville, Ill.   By reason of her orphanage many facts concerning her life and of her ancestors are obscure in her mind.   There are many beautiful traits of character and some acts of heroism in the life of Mrs. Wibel that should be mentioned, but which, in a short biography, must necessarily be omitted; but for the present we will add, that she is trying to inculcate right principles into the lives of her children and retain the good qualities of the Lemen family.

276—DR. HARRISON AUGUSTUS LEMEN.

Harrison Augustus Lemen was born in Ridge Prairie, ten miles northwest of Belleville, St. Clair

754—MARY P. R. SOBIESKI.

County, Illinois, at the farm residence of his parents, Sylvester and Susan K. Lemen, on the morning of September 26, 1840. He grew to advanced boyhood on the farm, and regularly attended the schools in the neighborhood, especially the one known as the Ogle's Creek School. Later in life he had the inestimable advantages of tutorage under that admirable teacher, scholar and upright Christian gentleman, James P. Lemen, fourth son of Rev. James Lemen, Jr. (102).

The young student, even in early life was fond of stalwart reading, and took much interest in chemistry, astronomy, zoology and ornithology. His scientific studies extended beyond the time of his graduation in medicine, and composed the higher mathematics, mental philosophy, logic, principles of the English language, comparative anatomy and physiology. He began the study of medicine in 1869 at Hastings, Minn., under Dr. J. E. Finch of that city, and continued to study until he matriculated at the St. Louis Medical College, St. Louis, under the preceptorship of Prof. John T. Hodgen, the eminent surgeon of St. Louis. He graduated in medicine at the above medical college in March, 1864. Later in life he pursued special studies in medicine and surgery in New York and Boston. In April, 1864, he located at Olney, Richland County, Illinois, and actively began the practice of medicine and surgery. During his career as a medical student he served his country gratuitously for three months as a medical cadet in the City General Hospital, St. Louis—a large Union Military Hospital, with Prof. John T. Hodgen as ranking surgeon.

Very soon after locating at Olney, he formed a partnership with Dr. Edward J. French, a celebrated local practitioner and half-brother of the late ex-Governor Augustus French of Illinois. In a short time, also, he received the appointment of Assistant Examining Surgeon for the Sixteenth Military District, Illinois, composed of some fifteen or sixteen of the counties adjoining Richland County, and served in this capacity until the close of the war. He was, also, at this time called on to organize, equip and take charge of a *Military Post Hospital*, at Olney, for the district, in which to receive and treat the military and recruits massed at the time at the headquarters of the district.

On May 16, 1866, he was married at Belleville, Ill., to Miss Virginia M. Thomas, youngest twin daughter of Col. John and Mrs. Isabella Thomas, of Ridge Prairie, six miles northeast of Belleville.

To the doctor and his wife was born one child, a son, Thomas Watson Lemen, on August 26, 1868. The son died at his father's residence in Denver, Colo., October 4, 1876.

After ten years of unusually successful and lucrative work at Olney he sought a larger field of work, and on May 22, 1874, located in Denver, Colo., and at once engaged in the practice of his profession.

Early in the summer of 1876, at the urgent solicitation of the Board of County Commissioners of Ara-

267—DR. HARRISON A. LEMEN.

pahoe County, of which Denver is the county seat, he took charge of the County Hospital, which was also the City Hospital of Denver, but not until the authorities had agreed to place at his command a resident assistant physician to be constantly in the institution, a skilled druggist and a *corps* of day and night nurses.

This institution, keeping pace with the then rapid growth of Denver, soon had accommodations for from 120 to 140 patients, and had a *clientele* for hundreds of miles in every direction from Denver, there being very few hospitals in the State at that time.

At the end of five years, owing to the demands of private practice on his time, at his own request, the Board appointed his successor.

Meantime he was appointed a charter member for eight years to the State Board of Health of Colorado, and engaged actively in this humane work as Secretary of the Board, until deficient funds in the State Treasury necessitated a discontinuance of the Board's efforts.

He was elected president of Denver Medical Association, and served the State Medical Society in the same capacity for the year 1882-3. His annual address before the latter society attracted wide-spread and favorable comment, and for the first time in the history of the society, it was ordered that a large number of copies of the address be published in pamphlet form for distribution to the public.

In 1880, "The Medical Department of the University of Denver," known as the "Denver Medical College," the first Medical College organized in Colorado, was founded. The doctor was a charter member of the faculty of this medical college. He was given the chair of "The Principles and Practice of Medicine and Clinical Medicine," and he fulfilled the arduous and responsible duties of the position to the entire satisfaction of the faculty and classes for a period of five years, when failing health admonished him of the necessity of resigning, which he did. Thereafter he was clothed by the trustees of the university with the mantle of "Emeritus Professor of the Principles and Practice of Medicine," which honor he holds to this date. He has also served as consulting physician to St. Luke's Hospital and St. Joseph's Hospital, Denver.

For quite a time he was surgeon for the "Denver Tramway Company," and has been one of the consulting surgeons of the Union Pacific Railway for a number of years.

He was medical examiner for the Ætna Life Insurance Company, of Hartford, Conn., for over twenty years.

He took an active interest in the medical societies of his city and State, engaging in the discussion of current medical topics, and often presenting elaborately prepared papers in line with the current medical and surgical themes of the day. He kept fully abreast of the times in his profession—never lagged.

782—VIRGINIA M. LEMEN.

He took special interest in medical microscopy, and for years stood at the head of the profession in this line, in his adopted State. He boasted somewhat, at the time of the purchase, of having one of the most perfect instruments West of the Missouri River. It was a Hartnack & Prazmowski Grand Stand, with Hartnack's most improved lenses up to a $^1/_{16}$ oil immersion, a camera lucida, micrometer eye piece, polarizing apparatus, selenite plates, etc.

He entertained exalted views of the dignity and usefulness of the guild, and had marked respect, amounting almost to reverence, for the great lights of the profession.

He was compelled to retire from active practice in August, 1893, on account of the development of a most serious and painful affection which has left him in a condition of hopeless invalidism.

Dr. Lemen ranks among the most capable, influential and successful physicians of his State. He enjoyed a large and successful practic·, and in both medicine and surgery he stood at the head of his profession. He was one of the pioneers among the few scientists in America and Europe who first urged the trained application of the microscope and other kindred agencies to discover and reveal the ultimate causes of disease; and the marvelous revelations attending that wonderful method, in the hands of trained experts, fully vindicate the doctor's judgment, that there was a wide field of truth in that direction which was of infinite importance to suffering humanity.

Dr. Lemen's place will be difficult to fill if ill health compels him to retire from the practice of medicine.

64—BENJAMIN F. LEMEN.

Benjamin F. Lemen, son of Rev. Joseph Lemen, was born September 28, 1813. In his thirteenth year he united with the Bethel Baptist Church, near his father's residence, and was baptized by Rev. Benjamin Ogle, his grandmother's brother. He was married in St. Clair County to Miss Mary P. Rand, April 28, 1842, by Rev. Mr. Davis. To them were born four children, two sons and two daughters. He spent much of his time in literary pursuits; he achieved quite an extensive reputation as a writer, especially of biography and history, was a natural poet, and a born statesman. He traveled quite extensively in this country, having twice visited California, pursuing different routes each time. He also visited Pike's Peak and many other sections of the United States, and noted and published his experiences and observations. In California he visited the savages and made the acquaintance of some of the chiefs, and such was his influence that on one occasion when the Indians had a "pale-face" stripped and tied down, the fires built ready to torture him to death, he stepped in and secured his release, and thus saved his life; he was fearless of danger. He went to Pike's Peak in 1859, and while there he not only held prayer and social

783—THOMAS W. LEMEN.

meetings, but organized a Baptist Church and kept services to God. There he built a stone house, especially for a place of worship; for the little church; always fearlessly braving danger whenever duty required, as numberless instances will attest. Returning from California, to his home in Salem, Illinois, immediately after the repeal of the "Missouri Compromise," when the entire country was shaken from center to circumference, and few dared to stand upon the broad principles of the "Declaration of Independence," all men are created free and equal, etc., faithful in this time that tried men's souls, with his pen, and with all his energy he worked for the overthrow of slavery. He labored for the principles embodied in the Declaration of Independence, when it was a stigma to be called an Abolitionist; when our Senators were felled to the floor in the Senate Chamber, and when the assassin's knife was hid in the hand of unseen foes. He stood almost alone for the cause of freedom in the town and county in which he lived, where a colored man dared not to come, but to be smuggled into an adjoining State and sold into bondage. He was a leader for years for the cause of freedom, speaking, writing and using his influence in every way that was legitimate. He was an active worker in the Fremont campaign, and years after, when Fremont's troops were entering St. Louis, he stood upon his mail car and waved his hand. The murmur of indignation was heard from hundreds of foes, and curses were heaped upon the man that

dared cheer that brave man who offered his life and
fortune to his country in her direst need. At one
time, during the war, a poor panting negro, chased
from St. Louis by scores of would-be brave men,
took refuge in his mail car, and with only an iron
rod he protected the life of that trembling creature.
One night in the cold winter weather he stepped from
his mail car into a passenger coach to warm, when he
witnessed a most outrageous scene—men that came
into the car from the South were abusing and talking
insultingly to two colored women, it was the chivalry
of slavery; no one daring to interfere to protect
these helpless women, even the conductor absenting
himself from the car, he immediately stepped up to
them and demanded of them to desist their unseemly
conduct; without a word, except a muttered "Abolitionist", they struck him with slung-shots and stabbed
him in the back. He was carried from the car in-
sensible, covered with blood. His faith was so strong
in God that he stood in the midst of the lions of
oppression that were thirsting for his blood without
a fear. Of such a man, though he said not a word
about dying, we should have no doubt in reference to
his future state; though he had scarcely a moment's
warning at the time of his death—he was with his
daughter in Vincennes, Ind.—he died with less than
an hour's sickness, May 10, 18   was taken from
Vincennes to his old home,   ll.,   there
was a large funer   Ba   urch,
the memorial ser   g   by   . M.

64—BENJAMIN F. LEMEN.

Billingsly. From Salem he was taken to St. Clair County, to the home of his brother, William, and thence to Bethel Church where his relatives and friends congregated, and Elders Carr and Dawson, and numerous friends participated in a memorial service. He was then laid to rest in the family burying-ground of his father, Rev. Joseph Lemen.

592—PLATT A. LITTLE.

Platt A. Little, the oldest child of W. D. and Virginia Lemen Little, was born on a farm in St. Clair County, Illinois, February 5, 1862. At a very early age he gave evidence of decided artistic talent, but in the busy work of farm life there was little time for its development. In 1878, he entered a commercial college in St. Louis. After completing the course he engaged in business at the National Stock Yards, in East St. Louis, and has ever since been identified with the affairs of that corporation. All his leisure hours were devoted to art, exemplifying the fact that true genius will find a way to manifest itself. Of late Mr. Little has become a pupil of one of the most prominent artists in the West, and his work has received praise from the best art critics in St. Louis.

He was married September 30, 1885, to Miss Marian M. Dill, the daughter of a prominent physician of Southern Indiana. Of this union but one child was born, a daughter, Oral Dill Little, born August 15, 1886.

Mr. Little is at present Inspector of Dockage at the National Stock Yards, and enjoys the friendship and esteem of all who know him.

389—DR. ARMENIUS F. BOCK.

Dr. A. F. Bock was born October 19, 1846. His father, Dr. F. B. Bock, of Waterloo, Ill., was a physician well known in the Southern part of this State. His mother was Catharine Lemen, second daughter of Rev. Josiah Lemen, of New Design, Ill. His early education was received in the common schools of Waterloo and from a well-known instructor, Rev. Dr. Steinert of that place, and later at the City University of St. Louis, Mo.

He then prepared for the Military Academy at West Point, but failing to receive an appointment as cadet he applied himself to the study of medicine and received his medical education in the University of Wuerzburg, Bavaria, graduating from the latter place in 1868.

He then spent a year in the hospitals of Vienna, and some months in visiting the hospitals of Paris, London and various European cities, after which he returned to the United States and located in St. Louis, Mo., where he has been practicing his profession ever since, and has met with remarkable success,

389—DR. ARMENIUS F. BOCK.

having won the respect and esteem of the profession and achieved popularity among the laity, two results by no means always attained by one man.

He is a member of the St. Louis Medical Society, American Medical Association, etc., and is surgeon to and chief of the staff of the Deaconess' Home Hospital, of St. Louis, Mo.

268—DR. EDWARD CLARK LEMEN.

Dr. Edward Clark Lemen, second child of Silvester and Susan (Shook) Lemen, was born in St. Clair County, Illinois, July 20, 1842. In boyhood he worked on the farm and attended district school, being himself a teacher at the age of eighteen.

In August, 1862, he enlisted in the 117th Illinois Infantry, was elected Fourth Sergeant Company I; served as Color-Sergeant of regiment for a year and a half; was promoted to First Sergeant of Company, and May 10, 1864, was commissioned First Lieutenant, which position he continued to hold until the end of the war, having engaged in many hard-fought battles, some of which were those of Pleasant Hill, Yellow Bayou, Nashville and Mobile. Returning home he spent three years in literary pursuits—one each at Shurtleff College, Rush Medical, Chicago, and St. Louis Medical, where he graduated March, 1868. After practicing at O'Fallon for two years, he removed to Upper Alton, where he is still located.

He has served for twenty-five years as a member of the Board of Trustees of Shurtleff College, two of which as president; was president of the Village School Board for six years, and twice elected Mayor; is surgeon of the Western Military Academy; a member of the Illinois State Medical Society, and of the American Medical Association, and Pension Examining Surgeon. He is a prominent and active communicant of the Baptist Church, and a member of the Odd-Fellows and Masonic orders.

On June 9, 1868, he married Miss Susan P., daughter of the late Rev. Ebenezer Rogers and Permelia (Jackson) Rogers, of Upper Alton, Ill. Their children were Cora Mae, who died in infancy; Henry Rogers, now associated in the practice of medicine with his father, and Mamie Permelia, now attending school at Monticello Seminary, Ill.

Dr. Edward C. Lemen ranks among the ablest and most successful physicians of this State in both medicine and surgery, has a large and successful practice, is a friend to the poor in gratuitous professional services, and in church and community has a large and helpful influence.

68—ROBERT C. LEMEN.

Robert C. Lemen was born near Bethel Church, in St. Clair County, Illinois, January 20, 1823. At the early age of seventeen he was converted and

268—DR. EDWARD C. LEMEN.

joined the Bethel Baptist Church where he remained a consistent member and lived, as he died, an humble Christian.

He was married near Waterloo, Monroe County, Illinois, to Miss Eliza J. Johnson, March 12, 1849. After marriage he removed from St. Clair County to Madison County, where he bought a farm and lived on it sixteen years. His health became so poor that he gave up farming and removed to Collinsville, Ill., where he died. Four children were born of this union, two sons and two daughters. A son and a daughter survive him. He died February 21, 1892.

770—REV. FRANK W. DOWNS.

Rev. Frank W. Downs, husband of Olivia E. Lemen, was born in Ohio, February 7, 1853; he was raised in Southern Illinois; in 1871 he entered McKendree College and graduated in a classical course, in 1878—two years later, he received the title of A. M.; in 1875 he took the citizens' prize in oratory, having been marked 100 above eight competitors; in 1878 he was elected to represent the college in the state oratorical contest, held at Monmouth, Ill., there being one speaker from nine colleges in the State.

In 1882 Mr. Downs entered Drew Theological Seminary, and while there filled a pulpit twelve miles from New York City; he preached several years in Southern Illinois, his last station in the State being

St. John's Church, East St. Louis. From that church, he, with his wife, went to Tucson, Arizona, to work in that mission field, and have remained there ever since. Mr. Downs has filled several of the leading pulpits in Arizona for more than twelve years.

241—MRS. OLIVIA DOWNS.

Mrs. Olivia E. Downs, nee Lemen, was born near Collinsville, Madison County, Illinois, January 6, 1856. She was converted in December, 1872, and united with the Delmar Avenue Baptist Church, St. Louis, May 6, 1876. In her eighteenth year, she entered Monticello Seminary as a pupil. In November, 1877, she met Rev. F. W. Downs, of McKendree College, Lebanon, Ill., and after a personal friendship of eight years, they were united in marriage September 17, 1885, at the Laclede Hotel, St. Louis, Mo. The same evening they took their departure for the far West, where they have been working ever since in the mission field of Arizona.

They have one child, a son, Robert Frances Downs, who was born in Safford, Graham County, Arizona, November 1, 1896.

154—HESTER McKINLEY DASHIELL.

Hester McKinley Dashiell was born near Alton, Madison County, Illinois, April 19, 1834. When about four years of age she moved with her parents

239—ELIZA J. LEMEN

69—ROBBRT C. LEMEN.

to St. Joseph, Mo.; leaving St. Joseph they went to Texas; while in Texas she attended the Gonzoles Seminary; after her graduation, at the age of eighteen, she went with her parents to Sacramento, Cal. In the year 1854, she married W. A. Dashiell, by whom she had twelve children, of whom, ten are living and two are dead. Becoming dissatisfied with Sacramento City, she with her family moved to Soland County, where they settled on a piece of land near Dixon. In 1873, when the railroad was built through Dixon they moved to that place, and her husband was employed as station agent by the railroad. After remaining in Dixon for nearly fifteen years, where they sent their children to school, they removed to Auburn, where they remained for nearly three years; leaving Auburn they returned to Sacramento City, where she still resides, with all her children living within a day's travel of her. She has five daughters and two sons married, and one daughter and two sons single; she has fifteen grand-children living and seven deceased. She is the sole remaining member of her father's family, and professes a hope in Christ, and feels that she is ready for the embrace of the Angel of Death, when it pleases the good Father to call for her.

144—LIEUTENANT CYRUS A. LEMEN.

Cyrus A. Lemen, a son of James H. Lemen and Catharine Lemen, nee Chilton, was born at the home

of his parents, four miles north of O'Fallon, St.
Clair County, Illinois, in 1841. He acquired a fair
education and in later years he was an extensive
reader, and became a man of large general information. Shortly after the beginning of the war, he
enlisted as a soldier for the Union, in Company F,
14th Regiment, Infantry, Missouri Volunteers. He
was a brave soldier, and was in several engagements,
in one of which he was severely wounded. He was
promoted to the office of First Lieutenant in his company by Governor Gamble, of Missouri, his rank to
date from March 5, 1862. Afterwards he and his
company, in part, were transferred to Company F,
66th Illinois Volunteers, and he still held the position of First Lieutenant, under commission from the
Governor of Illinois.

After his return from the army, Mr. Lemen was
united in marriage in 1864, with Miss Caroline E.
Meyers, of Collinsville, Ill. From this union there
were nine children, namely, Clarence E., Jenny E.,
Josephine K., Charles O., Cora B., Emma, Don M.,
Raymond and Grace M., of whom, all are living except Charles, Jenny and Cora. Lieutenant Lemen
was a farmer and owned the home farm on which he
was born. He enjoyed the sport of the gun and rod,
and when on a fishing excursion with his friends he
was always unusually lucky; and in hunting he could
wing a quail, duck or prairie chicken about as readily
and as certainly as could our great shooting sports of
national renown. He also had a surprisingly well-

241—OLIVIA E. DOWNS.   770—REV. FRANK W. DOWNS.
771—ROBERT F. DOWNS.

trained hand in mechanical skill, though he never
served an apprenticeship as a carpenter; the art
seemed to be natural with him. He was an exceedingly kind and accommodating neighbor, and in the
cases of sickness and death in his settlement no man
had a warmer or more sympathetic heart than he;
and in the sick-room he was not only very faithful
but he was also remarkably skillful in suggesting
and doing everything possible that might relieve the
sufferer.

The wound which Lieutenant Lemen received in
battle gave him more or less inconvenience and pain
in after years, and there is no doubt but that finally
it aggravated the causes which resulted in his death.
The chief cause in the train of ills which resulted fatally
was the breaking down of the functions of the liver,
which of course, eventually involved the other vital
organs; and though he was a man of a wonderful
constitution, the complications attending his last illness, which was protracted, were too much for nature
to withstand, and at his home, on February 5, 1894,
he passed from the scenes of life. The funeral services which were largely attended, occurred at Bethel
Church on February 7th, the Rev. J. B. Webb, officiating, after which the remains were buried in Bethel
Cemetery.

The widow, and her family, except Josephine,
who is married, reside at the old home, where
they are conducting the farm under the management of her eldest son, Clarence Lemen; and as

a loving mother and faithful Christian woman, Mrs. Lemen is doing all in her power to train her family to upright and pious lives.

262—MRS. LAURA LUCINDA PRIMM.

Mrs. Laura Lucinda Primm, a daughter of John A. Cook and Lucinda Lemen Cook, was born at the homestead of her parents, near Troy, Ill., on August 29, 1853. She united with the Baptist Church of Troy at an early age, and during her life was a devoted Christian, and an active member of religious circles. She received a liberal education, having attended school for some time at Almira College, at Greenville, Ill. On January 2, 1878, she was united in marriage to the Rev. J. W. Primm. From this union two children were born to them, namely, Ralph Cook, born September 21, 1879, and Clara Laura Primm, born April 17, 1883. The first child, Ralph, was killed in a runaway accident on November 23, 1880, and the second child, Clara, is now an excellent young lady, well advanced in her studies, and attending school at Shurtleff College, Upper Alton, Ill., and a worthy member of the Baptist Church, having been converted and baptized into that faith by her father, when only eight years of age. As a maiden, wife, mother, Christian and friend, Mrs. Laura L. Primm discharged every duty faithfully, and was beloved by all who knew her. She died at the resi-

144---LIEUT. CYRUS A. LEMEN.

dence of her husband's father, near Pinckneyville, March 5, 1885, and was buried at Atlanta, Ill., by the side of her little son, Ralph.

779—REV. JOHN WHITE PRIMM.

Rev. J. W. Primm, husband of Laura L. Primm, was of Huguenot descent, and was born November 17, 1848, near Centerville Station, St. Clair County, Illinois. In early life he united by conversion and baptism with the Pinckneyville Baptist Church. He felt that he had a call to the ministry, and by means acquired by school teaching and assisted somewhat by his father, he entered and finally completed a collegiate course at Shurtleff College, Upper Alton, Ill., graduating in 1874, and in 1877, he completed and graduated in the course of study at Newton Theological Institution, near Boston, Mass. In the meantime he frequently preached, and in 1875, a church on the coast of Maine, which he was supplying, experienced a wonderful revival.

With his splendid equipments in scholarship and naturally fine abilities for serving the great cause of the church successfully, Rev. J. W. Primm entered upon a wide field of usefulness, giving his pastoral services to many of the churches in Illinois, and for some time he was also pastor of the Baptist Church at Citra, Florida. In due time after the death of his first wife, Mrs. Laura L. Primm, he was united in marriage with Mrs. Mary E. Woolford, of Carrollton, Ill. In 1896, he removed to Upper Alton, where he now lives. His children are, Clara L., daughter of Laura L.; James K., Philip T. and Pauline, children of Mary E. His ministry has been characterized by a good degree of spiritual interest in the churches he has served.

273—REV. THEODORE ADOLPHUS LEMEN.

Rev. Theodore Adolphus Lemen, the fourth son of Sylvester Lemen and Susan K. Lemen, was born at the home of his parents near O'Fallon, Ill., on July 10, 1853. He was educated at Shurtleff College, Illinois, and then graduated at the law school of Rochester, N. Y. After graduation he removed to Colorado and practiced law at Leadville, and four years at Denver. Then, feeling called to the ministry, he abandoned the profession of the law and was ordained a Baptist minister. He was pastor of two Baptist churches, which were missions of the First Baptist Church of Denver. He is a man of marked ability, and has continued in the ministry doing great good; he is now a traveling evangelist.

He was married to Miss Ella Lapham in July, 1887, and four children were born to them, namely: Timothy, Dorathea (deceased), Dorinda, and an infant son.

270—MARY MAHULDAH LEMEN.

Mary Mahuldah Lemen, the second daughter of Sylvester Lemen and Susan K. Lemen, was born at their residence near O'Fallon, Ill. She received a liberal education and united with the Bethel Baptist Church, and was a faithful Christian. In a marked degree she possessed all the graces of person and character which justly command the esteem and admiration of all. Her death occurred at Denver, Colo., where she had previously lived for several years, on June 8, 1874, and her remains were brought back to St. Clair, Ill., and interred in the Bethel Cemetery.

73—SYLVESTER LEMEN AND SUSAN K. LEMEN (266).

Sylvester Lemen, second child and first son of Rev. James Lemen, Jr., and Mary Lemen, nee Pulliam, was born at his parents' home in Ridge Prairie, Ill., on November 5, 1816. In early life he acquired a liberal education and taught several terms of school. In childhood he united with the Bethel Baptist Church, and was ever a faithful and devoted Christian. At the home of his wife's parents, near Belleville, Ill., he was united in marriage with Miss Susan K. Shook, on March 16, 1838, and they settled on their farm near the present city of O'Fallon, Ill., where they built them a comfortable home and reared their family. There were nine children born to them in the following order: Harrison Augustus, Edward Clark, Katherine Adora, Mary Mahuldah, Lewis Erastus, Lucy Lenora, Theodore Adolphus, Sarah Ellen and Charles Truman Lemen, six of whom are yet living.

Sylvester Lemen was deeply devoted to his children's best interests, but like his pioneer ancestors, he maintained a strict family government to which his children all rendered a loving and willing obedience. By the active aid and loving devotion of his noble wife, they gave their children liberal educational advantages and a thorough moral and religious training, and altogether theirs was a singularly happy home. The parents always maintained family worship and were constant attendants at church. In the later years of their lives Sylvester and Susan Lemen became two of the constituent members in the O'Fallon Baptist Church, to which they had given several hundred dollars to assist in rearing a church edifice, but until that time their membership had been in Bethel Church.

Mr. Lemen was a man of large reading, was a good speaker, a fine singer of sacred music, very active and influential in assisting to build up churches and a liberal supporter of all good causes; he owned a good farm where he lived and was a successful and excellent farmer; he was a man of very genial, popular manners, and had every attribute of noble manhood, physically, morally and mentally. The people often tendered him the candidacy for high and responsible elective positions, but he declined them, though at one time he served under Abraham Lincoln's administration as marshal for his district in Illinois. A few years before his death, Mr. Lemen, in stepping from a car, broke one of his limbs, but recovered after a long term of intense suffering.

In every sense of the word, Mr. Lemen was one of "nature's noblemen,"—brave, generous and thoughtful; he was a friend to the poor, and a guardian of the helpless; in his dealings the golden rule was his criterion; honesty with him was not practiced "because it is the best policy," but because it was right. He was a Christian in all that the term suggests or implies.

But a few months previous to his death he and his wife removed to Belleville, where, after an illness of some days, he died on September 28, 1872. But he was not unprepared. When the last summons came he peacefully passed to that rest which awaits God's faithful children. And thus ended life's chapter with as kind a husband, as devoted a father, and as faithful a Christian as any whose life makes society and the world the better for living. His funeral services occurred at Bethel Church, attended by his family and a vast concourse of other relatives and friends, and after appropriate discourses commemorative of his life and labors, the remains were interred in Bethel Cemetery.

Susan K. Lemen was born at the home of her parents near Belleville, Ill, on January 16, 1813, and was married to Sylvester Lemen on March 16, 1838. In early life she united with the Baptist Church and was ever a faithful Christian. She received a common school education, and in a marked degree possessed all those attributes of character, mind and disposition which constitute a worthy and noble womanhood. She was a loving and faithful wife, a devoted mother and an ardent and active Christian. Her death occurred at Denver, Colo., on June 28, 1878. The remains were brought to Bethel Church, St. Clair County, Illinois, where, after appropriate funeral services attended by the family and a large concourse of relatives and friends, they were interred in Bethel Cemetery by the side of her husband.

Of their three children who are dead, Mary Mahuldah Lemen lived to the years of womanhood, and she will be mentioned elsewhere; Charles Truman was born August 12, 1857, and died January 12, 1859; and Sarah Ellen Lemen was born June 11, 1855; she was a lovely child, who, early in life, professed a faith in Christ and was baptized and united with the Bethel Baptist Church. She died February 29, 1868, and was buried by the side of her little brother, Charles Truman Lemen, in Bethel Church Cemetery.

79—ROBERT STOCKTON LEMEN.

Robert S. Lemen, a son of Rev. James Lemen, Jr., and Mary Lemen, his wife, was born at the parental

79—ROBERT S. LEMEN.

homestead in Ridge Prairie, Ill., on December 16, 1830.
In early boyhood he had acquired a good beginning
for a liberal education, and he completed his course
at Shurtleff College, Upper Alton, Ill., in June, 1857.
His first marriage was to Miss Mary Crowder. One
child was born to them, Jesse, who died in early infancy shortly after the death of its mother. Some
years later Mr. Lemen was married to Miss Sarah
Lancaster, from which union there were three children.
In the vicissitudes of fortune Mr. Lemen was farmer,
merchant and teacher, and he is now engaged in merchandising at Cairo, Ill., where he and his wife and
only surviving son, Ernst Lemen, now reside. The
latter is a machinist of high skill and a fine reputation in his calling. Of the other two children, Robert Elmer died in infancy, and Arthur lived to the
years of manhood, had a good practical education,
was married some years since to a most worthy young
lady, and but recently died in Cairo, where he had
lived for many years. He was a great but patient
sufferer in his last illness, and he was a devout Christian.

Mr. Lemen and his wife are members of the Baptist faith, having united with that church in early
life. Mr. Lemen is a forceful and excellent writer,
having written many valuable and interesting articles
for the papers and periodicals. He has also written
some poems of merit, one of which, called "The
Burial by Nightfall," was pronounced by the late
Rev. John M. Peck to be one of the finest gems of its
kind in the English language.

75—NANCY LEMEN LOCKWOOD.

Nancy Lemen Lockwood, a daughter of Rev. James Lemen, Jr., and wife, was born at her parents' home in Ridge Prairie, Ill., on May 7, 1821. She had a liberal education, and was a member of the Baptist faith. In early life she was married to Jessy Hart, and they settled on their farm near O'Fallon, Ill., where two children were born to them, Laura and Lewis Hart—Lewis dying in early childhood.

Jessy Hart died in 1849, and in due time his widow married Ebenezer Lockwood, formerly a merchant of Collinsville, and at a later period, of Carlyle, Ill. She died August 26, 1854.

Her daughter, Laura Hart, was born November 12, 1843; she was married to Joshua S. Bond, of Carlyle, Ill., and they settled on their farm near O'Fallon, where three children were born to them, namely: Benjamin, Jessie Lee and Laura Mae, the latter two dying in infancy. She died on May 11, 1865. Her son, Benjamin, is in the service of the railroads in the West, and her husband, Hon. Joshua S. Bond, a prominent attorney, is in the service of the government at Washington City, D. C.

78—JAMES PULLIAM LEMEN.

James Pulliam Lemen, seventh child and fourth son of Rev. James Lemen, Jr., and Mary Lemen, nee Pulliam, was born at the home of his parents in

Ridge Prairie, St. Clair County, Illinois, on September 16, 1828. In early life he united with Bethel Baptist Church, and has ever since been a faithful Christian and a liberal supporter of religious interests and other good causes. He acquired a liberal education, and for several years he devoted his time and talents to the high calling of teaching school in Illinois, and was pronounced by the best educators as one of the first teachers in the State. He was also a farmer in St. Clair, Ill., where he owned a farm; but he eventually removed to Hastings, Minn., and selling his farm in Illinois he invested his capital in lands and other property in that State, where he conducted farming, and at times engaged in merchandising in Hastings, his home city. He was united in marriage on October 28, 1862, to Miss Elizabeth B. Bowman, a daughter of the late Martin Bowman and Harriet Bowman, nee Christy, of Green County, Illinois, and they repaired to their home in Hastings where they now live. From this marriage union two children were born to them, namely, Christy S. Lemen, born on September 11, 1863, and Mary B. Lemen, born on July 11, 1865. Christy Lemen was married in March, 1896.

After settling in Hastings, Mr. Lemen became one of its leading citizens, and in every position in life he has been a man who discharged his duty faithfully. Honest, intelligent and naturally industrious, he has always commanded the esteem and confidence of all his acquaintances. For some years past he has

suffered from failing health which confines him
mostly at home.

309—MRS. LENORE LEMEN THORSEN.

Mrs. Lenore Lemen Thorsen, a daughter of Dr.
Moses P. Lemen and Philura J. Lemen, was born at
the home of her parents, in DuQuoin, Ill., on October 2, 1867. Her father was a son of the late Rev.
James Lemen, Jr., of St. Clair County, Illinois, and
her mother was a daughter of the late Merlin Jones,
Sr. and Mary Jones, a prominent and worthy pioneer
couple of Ridge Prairie, St. Clair County, Illinois,
three of whose sons were in the war for the Union;
namely, Merlin, Jr., Thomas and Charles, the latter
falling mortally wounded in the great battle at Chattanooga. Her father, Dr. Moses P. Lemen, died in
1870; and, at a little later period, her mother, with
the two children, Lenore and Charles Lemen, removed
temporarily to Texas, to regain her failing health,
but finally she settled with her children in Denver,
Colo. Her mother died in 1876, and Lenore and her
little brother were left orphans. But she was a
thoughtful, industrious, intelligent child, and learned
rapidly, and she finally acquired a liberal education,
having graduated at the East Denver High School in
1887. She engaged in school teaching in Colorado,
and became a successful and popular teacher. In a
marked degree she possesses all the graces, attrac-

tions and gentle attributes which constitute a noble womanhood, and she is universally esteemed by all her acquaintances.

On October 2, 1889, at Denver, Colo., she was united in marriage with Mr. P. L. Thorsen, a young and highly esteemed merchant; and they settled at Idaho Springs, Colo., and engaged in merchandising. But more recently they removed and settled at Cripple Creek, Colo., where they erected a fine and large building, and stocked it with goods; but building and all were destroyed by the great fire at that city, in April, 1896, and their losses amounted to many thousands of dollars—but with true courage they have erected another substantial building, and stocked it with a good line of goods, and they hope eventually to recover from the great losses of the destructive fire.

Her husband, Mr. P. L. Thorsen (834), was born April 3, 186'. He is intelligent, active and thoroughly qualified in every department of business and merchandising, and is highly esteemed for his generous qualities and excellent character by all his acquaintances; and their's is a very happy home. Since the above sketch was written Mr. Thorsen and his wife have removed, and now reside in Boulder, Colo. Having retired from merchandising, Mr. Thorsen has become the resident agent of the great H. J. Mayham Investment Co., with his office at 1936 Twelfth Street, in that city.

72—LUCINDA LEMEN COOK.

Lucinda Lemen Cook, daughter of Rev. James Lemon, Jr. and wife, was born in Ridge Prairie, Ill., December 25, 1814. United with the Bethel Baptist Church in early life. Married Captain Samuel Bowman in 1830, and settled on their farm near Carrollton, Ill., where their only child and son, John C. Bowman, was born in 1832. Captain Samuel Bowman was a soldier in the Black Hawk War, and in 1832, he fell, mortally wounded, while leading his company in battle against the Indians. After his death, his wife married John A. Cook, April 18, 1836. Mr. Cook was a member of the Baptist Church, a farmer by vocation and a liberal supporter of educational and religious interests. He and his wife settled on their farm, near Troy, Ill., where they accumulated a large estate. They reared a large family of children, all of whom, who reached their majority, were members or believers in the Baptist faith. Lucinda Cook died August 25, 1867, and her husband, John A. Cook, was killed by accident, by a runaway team, on July 15, 1869; both were buried in the family cemetery, near their old homestead. Of their children, only two survive, Miss Sarah Cook, who has been an invalid for many years, and Charles F. Cook, who owns a fine farm near Troy, Ill., but who resides in Edwardsville, Ill.

256—HON. CYRUS L. COOK.

256—HON. CYRUS LEMEN COOK.

Judge Cyrus L. Cook was born at Alton, Ill., on March 18, 1839. His father, John A. Cook, was a native of Virginia; his mother was a daughter of Rev. James Lemen, Jr., of St. Clair County, Illinois, one of the pioneer Baptist ministers of the State, who was also a member of the first Constitutional Convention, and noted for his services and efforts to make Illinois a free State. His parents were married April 18, 1836. While Judge Cook was yet an infant, his parents removed from Alton to a farm in Madison County, six miles south of Edwardsville, in Collinsville Township. He attended the common district school of the neighborhood, and at Troy. His parents were firm adherents of the Baptist faith, and one of his preceptors was Rev. Elihu Palmer, an eminent Baptist divine and teacher, and a brother of ex-Senator John M. Palmer. In the fall of 1856, he entered the preparatory department of Shurtleff College, at Upper Alton, and graduated there in the classical course, in June, 1862. He afterwards enlisted in Company D, 133d Illinois Volunteer Infantry (Captain John Carsten's Company), from which he was honorably discharged at the expiration of his term of service, near the close of the war. He taught school several terms, and then attended the law department of the University of Michigan, at Ann Arbor, including the lectures of Judges Cooley, Campbell and Walker, the two former of whom were at the time on the Supreme Bench of the State. He began the practice of law at Edwardsville, in 1869, was elected States Attorney of Madison County in 1876 on the Republican ticket, the county going for Tilden. At the end of his term he resumed the practice of law, and in 1886 was elected County Judge of Madison County, which office he filled very acceptably and creditably for four years, when a renomination was unanimously tendered him again by his party. His first vote was cast for Abraham Lincoln, and he has always been a pronounced Republican. He was appointed by Governor Fifer, in connection with Hon. Chas. Becker, of St. Clair County, and Rev. Father Ferland, of Kaskaskia, on the commission created by the Legislature to remove the pioneer dead from Kaskaskia, Ill., to purchase ground for a cemetery and erect monuments to their memory; a gratuitous task that was performed to the satisfaction of the State, and approved by Governor Altgeld, during whose term of office the work was completed. His ancestors on both sides served in the Revolutionary and Indian wars. His mother, at the time of her marriage to his father, was the widow of Captain Samuel Bowman, who fell while in command of his company in the final fight with the Indians under Black Hawk, in Illinois.

Cyrus L. Cook was an open-hearted, generous, honest man. In his profession, the law, he ranked up among the best. As a public speaker, he was unusually entertaining, witty at times, and at others, earnest and eloquent. He had pronounced literary tastes, and was well read in literature and history. As a public officer he was prompt, just and conscientious; one of the highest tributes to his legal abilities being that while County Judge, of all the appeals taken from his decisions none were reversed by the higher courts. He was never married, and leaves only one brother, Mr. Chas. F. Cook, of Edwardsville, Ill., and a sister, Miss Sarah Cook, who has been an invalid for years. Besides the above, he leaves a little niece, Miss Clara L. Primm, daughter of Rev. J. W. Primm, of Upper Alton, who were both present at the obsequies.

Judge Cook had recently been nominated for Congressman at Litchfield, by the Republican Congressional Convention of the Eighteenth District, to fill the vacancy caused by the death of Congressman-elect, Hon. F. Remann; and he was in Chicago in connection with his candidacy when he was stricken with heart failure, and died on October 11, 1895, at the Great Northern Hotel, in that city, attended by sympathetic friends and good medical aid. His sudden death produced a profound gloom of sadness, not only in his home city of Edwardsville and throughout the Eighteenth District, but nearly all of the great dailies of Chicago, on the following morning, contained his portrait and column articles of his life and labors.

By the kind hands of sorrowing friends his remains were brought to Edwardsville, where he lay in state in the parlors of the St. James Hotel, and was viewed by hundreds of people. On Sunday morning, October 13th, the body was removed by a guard of honor to the opera house, where, in the presence of a vast audience, Rev. Justus Bulkley, of Shurtleff College, Upper Alton, delivered an eloquent and appropriate funeral discourse; the Rev. Mr. Cooper, of Troy, also assisting in the services. When the final cortege moved to Woodland Cemetery, where the remains were buried, it was the largest funeral procession ever witnessed in Edwardsville. The last rites of burial were performed in the solemn and impressive rituals of the Grand Army and the Masonic fraternities, in both of which noble orders Judge Cook, during life, had been an honored and faithful member. Judge Cook's legal friends placed a high estimate on his learning and abilities as a lawyer, which is evidenced by the fact that the late Hon. Lyman Trumbull, only a short time before his own death, declared that Judge Cook scarcely had an equal in the Illinois legal bar for accuracy and reliability in difficult points of law. In his social characteristics, in a singular degree, he possessed the rare and happy disposition of making friends of all and enemies of none. But our friend has passed to his rest. Peace to his memory.

269—MRS. KATHERINE SUESS AND SONS.

Katherine Adorah Lemen Suess, first daughter of Sylvester Lemen and Susan K. Lemen, nee Shook, was born at her parents' farm residence near O'Fallon,

269—KATHERINE SUESS.   789—DR. HUGH L. TAYLOR

792—DR. CLYDE L. TAYLOR.   790—DR. RALPH L. TAYLOR·

Ill. In childhood she acquired a common school education, and finally completed a course in the classics and higher branches at Almira College at Greenville, Ill., having previously attended school at an academy in Salem, Ill., under the instructions of that noble Christian and noted lady teacher, Mrs. Mary Putnam Lemen. She united with the Bethel Baptist Church in early life and has ever since adorned her profession of religion with a blameless life and a noble Christian devotion. At her parents' home near O'Fallon, Ill., she was united in marriage on May 5, 1869, with Francis Marion Taylor, then proprietor and publisher of the *Belleville Advocate*, and they settled in Belleville, Ill. From this union there were four children, namely: Hugh Lemen Taylor, Ralph Lemen Taylor, Ford Lemen Taylor and Clyde Lemen Taylor, born in the order named. Ford, a beautiful and bright little boy, died at their Belleville home on May 20, 1878, and the other three are yet living.

The subject of this sketch possesses a happy individuality which always impresses one favorably. In a marked degree she has all the graces, attractions and attributes which constitute a noble womanhood, and from the moment of her pledges at the marriage altar she has been faithful to every obligation and to every trust which duty ever imposed. It was never the good fortune of any man to have a more faithful and devoted wife than her husband had—vigilant to every want of the family, true to every duty of her position, and faithful to every obligation as wife, mother, woman, Christian or friend—her husband was singularly fortunate in having, through her steady and constant attentions, every condition that ought to make home as nearly a reflection of Paradise as it is possible to attain in this life when both parties do their duty. There are no brighter, richer jewels in the diadem of noble womanhood than the holy duties of a wife well performed and the sacred duties of a mother well fulfilled; and that Mrs. Kate Lemen Suess was faithful in all of these is a sufficient measure of well-deserved praise.

˙ She became a widow in 1880 and shortly afterwards, with her three children, she removed from Belleville, Ill., and settled in Denver, Colo. She then had but little means left; but with an undaunted courage, active hands and a motherly devotion for her three little dependent children, never excelled, in time she secured a home. Through almost insurmountable difficulties she gave her two older sons, Hugh and Ralph, a liberal education, and Clyde, the younger son, is well advanced in his course and is now attending school. In proportion to her means Mrs. Kate Lemen Suess has always been a liberal and active supporter of religious interests and other good causes. Her sons are all dutiful, industrious and affectionate, and altogether, mother and children, constitute a very happy family.

˴ She was united in marriage to Major Henry Suess of Denver, Colo., in that city, on March 23, 1897.

785—ELSIE J. LEMEN.   271—DR. LEWIS E. LEMEN.
786—MARGARET LEMEN.   797—LEWIS LEMEN.

Major Suess was a gallant soldier and officer in the Union army during the war, and was a brave defender of the old flag in many a hard-fought battle. He is a man of large means and liberal culture, and he has a very substantial rating among the business men of Colorado and the West. He and his wife live at their residence at 1634 Downing avenue, Denver, Colo., and some of the members of the Major's family and Clyde Lemen Taylor live with them.

Hugh Lemen Taylor (789), the first son of Mrs. Kate Lemen Suess, completed a liberal education, comprising a thorough course in every department of the theory and practice of medicine. He traveled abroad for a short time visiting the chief capitals and countries of Europe, and is now a practicing physician in Denver, Colo., with a large and successful practice. In that city on April 14, 1897, he was united in marriage to Miss Sallie Bomberger, of Denver, formerly of Ohio, a young lady of excellent accomplishments, and they reside at their home at 1828 Marion street, Denver, Colo.

Ralph Lemen Taylor (790), the second son, also completed a thorough course of study including a full course in medicine. He practiced medicine for a short time in the City of Mexico (old Mexico), and is now a successful practitioner in the West, being in the service of some of the leading lines of railroad. Since the above was written Dr. Ralph L. Taylor has enlisted in the First Regiment, Colorado Volunteers, and in the capacity of a surgeon will accompany that regiment to the Philippine Islands.

The younger son, Clyde Lemen Taylor (792), with an otherwise liberal education, is now a medical student well advanced in his course.

793—MAJOR HENRY SUESS.

Henry Suess was born June 8, 1837, in Niederzwehren, near Hessen-Cassel, Germany, attended the public, and later, private schools at Cassel, and learning the saddler and harnessmakers' trade, came to America when seventeen years old. Worked at his trade in Romeo, and started in business on his own account at New Baltimore, Mich., in 1858. Moved to St. Louis, Mo., in 1859, again going into business at Concordia, Mo. When the late war broke out he joined the first troops as First Lieutenant of Company B., Lafayette Co. Home Guards, was taken prisoner at Lexington, Mo., returned home on parole, which parole not being respected by the enemy, he re-enlisted in the 7th Missouri Cavalry as private, serving until near the close of the war as Lieutenant and finally, as Major of same regiment, and with the latter rank was honorably mustered out of service at Warrensburg, Mo. He located at Sedalia, Mo., engaging in the saddlery business. In 1878 moved to Texas, where, at Houston, he took charge of the interests of a large manufacturing business of St.

305—NANCY C. LEMEN.

Louis, Mo. He removed to Denver, Colo., in 1881, and is yet acting in the same capacity for the St. Louis company.

He was married to Mrs. Kate Lemen Taylor, March 23, 1897, and they reside at 1634 Downing avenue. He has seven children, all grown—three sons and four daughters by former marriage.

271—DR. LEWIS ERASTUS LEMEN.

Dr. Lewis Erastus Lemen, a son of Sylvester and Susan K. Lemen, was born on April 1, 1849, at his parents' home in St. Clair County, Illinois. He attended school at the Ogle Creek school house and worked on his father's farm until sixteen years of age. He then took a three-years' course at Shurtleff College, after which he entered the St. Louis Medical College, graduating with the degree Doctor of Medicine in 1871.

Upon graduating he was appointed assistant physician to the St. Louis City Hospital, which position he filled for one year. After thorough training he entered the practice of his profession in the city of St. Louis.

In 1873, owing to failing health, he was compelled to seek the climate of Colorado. He first located at Georgetown in that State, where he practiced his profession until 1883, removing then to the city of Denver.

Upon his removal to Denver he was appointed surgeon to the Omaha & Grant Smelting and Refining Company, and upon the organization of the Globe Smelting and Refining Company, was honored with a similar appointment by them.   Dr. Lemen has held these positions continuously to the present time.

He also served as the division surgeon of the Union Pacific Railway for the past six years.   He is at present the consulting surgeon of the Union Pacific, Denver & Gulf Railway, also, consulting surgeon to St. Luke's Hospital.

On the reorganization of the staff of attending physicians and surgeons to St. Joseph's Hospital he was honored with the presidency of that body, as well as being selected as the attending surgeon for that institution.

In 1889 he was appointed by Governor Cooper as a member of the Board of Commissioners for the State Insane Asylum, serving continuously for six years, the last two as president of the board.

In 1893 he was appointed Health Commissioner of the city of Denver, serving one term of two years.

In May, 1896, he was elected a member of the Board of Education of School District No. 1, for the term of three years.

Dr. Lemen has always taken a great interest in all that pertains to his profession, and has been active in the advancement of medical education in the West—having for two years lectured in the Medical Department of the University of Denver; then occupied the

304—JESSICA M. STEBBINS.

30—MARY E. STEBBINS.

chair of surgery for one year in the Gross Medical College, and for the past four years has filled the chair of clinical surgery at the Medical School of the University of Colorado. In 1887 the honorary degree of A. M. was conferred upon Dr. Lemen by Shurtleff College.

Dr. Lemen is a member of the Denver and Arapahoe Medical Society, of the Colorado State Medical Society, of the American Medical Association, of the National Association of Railway Surgeons and of the American Academy of Railway Surgeons. He has served as president of the Denver Medical Association, and as vice-president of the American Academy of Railway Surgeons. He was elected president of the American Academy of Railway Surgeons at the meeting held in Chicago in 1896.

Dr. Lemen is a prominent member of the Masonic fraternity, having taken the thirty-second degree; he is also a Knight Templar and a Shriner.

Dr. Lemen was married to Miss Lizzie, daughter of Henry T. Mudd, of St. Louis, May 5, 1875. She died in 1876.

On April 12, 1882, he was married to Elsie, daughter of the Hon. Wm. H. James, of Denver. Mrs. Lemen was the first white girl born in the State of Colorado. Dr. Lemen and wife have two children, a daughter, Margaret, born January 23, 1888, and a son, Lewis, born May 8, 1890.

In physical development and the sturdy attributes of manhood, Dr. Lewis E. Lemen is a faithful reproduction of his pioneer ancestors. Above the medium in height, with every other proportion in harmony, and with a resolute temper, he is well equipped to quickly and successfully resent an injury, but he just as promptly forgives upon reasonable apology. With a genial, generous and happy disposition, a liberal education and a positive and effective individuality, he is naturally and deservedly popular, and the people of Colorado have repeatedly urged upon him the candidacy of several of the highest positions in their elective gift, but his faithful devotion to the vast circle of his patients and his high sense of duty to his profession prevented his acceptance. His professional reputation extends throughout the West, and his excellent mental and moral equipments for the great duties of his calling in every department of theory and practice, with the uniform success attending his labors, have justly placed him in the front ranks of his profession.

82—DR. MOSES PECK LEMEN.

Dr. Moses P. Lemen, a son of Rev. James Lemen, Jr. and Mary Lemen, his wife, was born at his parents' home in Ridge Prairie, Ill., on October 8, 1838. He acquired a good, practical education, and was married on October 25, 1859, to Miss Philura Jones, a daughter of Merlin Jones and Mary Jones, of Ridge Prairie, Ill. From this union there were three children born. In 1862 he completed his course

81—JOSEPH B. LEMEN.

at the St. Louis Medical College, and after serving
for some time as an assistant surgeon in the Union
army, he and his wife located at DuQuoin, Ill., where
he engaged in a large and successful practice. He
died at DuQuoin in May, 1870, aged about 32 years.
He and his wife were both members of the Baptist
Church, and to their latest hours they were devoted
Christians and liberal supporters of religious interests.
Shortly after the doctor's death his wife was over-
taken with chronic ill-health, and from that time on
was a great but patient sufferer until her death,
which occurred at Denver, Colo., in 1876. Of their
three children, Jesse died in infancy, Charles died in
early manhood, at Salt Lake City, Utah, and Lenore
is yet living. She graduated at the Denver High
School, and became a successful and popular teacher
in Colorado. On October 2, 1889, she was married
to Mr. P. L. Thorsen. They reside in Boulder, Colo.

8o—MRS. MARY ELIZABETH STEBBINS.

Mrs. Mary E Stebbins, a daughter of Rev. James
Lemen, Jr. and Mary Lemen, his wife, was born at
her parents' home in Ridge Prairie, Ill., on January
31, 1833. In early childhood she united with the
Baptist Church, and ever since has been a consistent
and faithful member of that faith. She acquired a
good, common school education, and in 1857 was
married to Columbus Stebbins, a successful journal-

ist and writer of Hastings, Minn. They settled in that city, and from this union three children were born. Mr. Stebbins was proprietor and editor of the Hastings *Independent*, which paper he finally changed into the Hastings *Gazette*. It was a good paper and exercised a large influence throughout the State. He died at Hastings, December 21, 1878. Of their three children, Ella died in childhood, Katie died when a young lady, after having graduated with high honors in the Hastings High School, and Jessica M. Stebbins is still living. She graduated in the High School of Hastings, and she and her mother now reside at Denver, Colo., where she is calculating clerk in the government mint at that city. The number of their residence is 1155 Downing avenue, Denver, Colo.

81—JOSEPH BOWLER LEMEN.

Joseph B. Lemen, a son of Rev. James Lemen, Jr. and Mary Lemen, his wife, was born at the home of his parents in Ridge Prairie, Ill., on August 6, 1836. He united with the Bethel Baptist Church in childhood; in early boyhood he acquired a liberal education, and taught school when eighteen years of age, having procured a certificate from the School Commissioner, covering the common school course and higher branches; he attended school at Shurtleff College, Upper Alton, Ill., where he graduated in June, 1857; he engaged in farming after his course

76–JACOB O. LEMEN.

of study, which also included a course in law and medicine.

He was married to Miss Nancy C. Scott, a daughter of Isaac and Elizabeth Scott, of Ridge Prairie, Ill., on November 23, 1864, at her parents' residence, the Rev. James Halliday officiating. But one child was born to them, a very promising little boy, Elmer Scott Lemen, who was born on August 31, 1865, and died on January 17, 1868, aged two years, four months and seventeen days.

The subject of this sketch followed the occupation of farming, but for quite a number of years he wrote editorial articles for the newspapers, though at present, on account of chronic ill health, he is unable to either write or labor. He and his wife reside at their home on their farm a few miles southeast of Collinsville, in St. Clair County, Illinois. Collinsville is their post-office address.

76—JACOB OGLE LEMEN.

Jacob O. Lemen, a son of Rev. James Lemen, Jr. and Mary Lemen, his wife, was born at the old homestead in Ridge Prairie, Ill., on November 23, 1823. He acquired a good education and became a successful teacher. He married Miss Martha Lancaster, a daughter of Levi Lancaster and wife, of Ridge Prairie, Ill., who was a young lady of good learning, having attended school at the Monticello Female College at Godfrey, Ill. Both were members of the Baptist Church and liberal in its support. They settled on their farm near O'Fallon, Ill. From this union several children were born. After some years they removed with their family to Hastings, Minn., where Mr. Lemen engaged for sometime in merchandising. He and his wife were among the first and leading members of the Hastings Baptist Church, and they contributed liberally to the sufferers who escaped from the great Indian massacre at New Ulm, in Minnesota.

Mr. Lemen died at Hastings on January 9, 1870. His wife, Mrs. Lemen, still resides there and is a leading member in the church and a most worthy Christian lady, greatly esteemed by all who know her. Of their children, Ninian was married and became a newspaper publisher and writer of noted ability. He died in early manhood. Alice married Mr. Burkholder, and they reared a very interesting family of daughters; the three oldest, Ethel, Edna and Viola are finely educated and very accomplished young ladies, and the other daughter, Hazel, is a bright little girl, and is now in the kindergarten school. Mr. Burkholder is connected with the newspapers in New York, and is a writer of good ability. The family reside at 716 Lafayette avenue, Brooklyn, N. Y. Of Mr. and Mrs. Lemen's other children, Amelia, now deceased, married Mr. Carr; William married an accomplished and excellent young lady, is an artist of considerable note, and they reside in Brooklyn, N. Y.; Charles also resides in New York, and the other children died in early childhood or infancy.

293—WILLIAM S. LEMEN.

293—WILLIAM S. LEMEN.

William S. Lemen is the youngest child of Jacob O. and Martha A. Lemen, he was born at Hastings, Minn., July 27, 1865. Mr. Lemen has a good education and a large endowment of natural ability; he is a good conversationalist and of a commanding personality. He has traveled extensively on American territory, and has been observing and of an enquiring mind, and is well posted on general subjects. Mr. Lemen is an artist of superior ability; he is located in New York City, where his ability is recognized in the circles of higher art. The art work of the "Lemen Family History" was done by him and attests to his skill.

Mr. Lemen has been twice married, first to Clara Remenschnider, of Trempler, Wis; of this union was born one child, Earl, who lived only four years and a few days, then passed to the shores of eternal blessedness; his second marriage was to Elizabeth B. Boettcher, of Brooklyn, N. Y. There have been no children born of this union.

227—MARY PUTNAM RAND-LEMEN.

(Taken from the *Christian Home*, of Council Bluffs, Ia., May 27, 1892.)

MY MOTHER.

Above we present a life-like portrait of Mother, taken about a year since. To-day, May 27, 1892, is the eighty-first anniversary of her birthday. She was full of life and vigor till the day of her final illness. Last fall she attended the National W. C. T. U. convention at Boston, and visited the scenes of her childhood. She was taken ill January 2, 1892, and peacefully passed to the Home beyond on the morning of the 12th of the same month. The 1st of January, just the day before she was taken ill, she wrote us this:

HER LAST LETTER.

NEOSHO, Mo., January 1, 1892.

MY DEAR SON:

A Happy New Year to you, and all the home workers.

My prayer is, that this may be your most prosperous year; that God may bless you in your basket and store, but more especially, physically; may your health be preserved, and this be the year that God will bless you with His presence and give you sweet communion with Himself.

Our Sabbath-school lessons are from the Prophets, during this quarter, and I trust they will do much good, causing the church to look into the future of our land.

The first Golden Text.is: "He shall have dominion also from sea to sea, and from the river unto the ends of the earth."—Ps. 72 : 8.

Did the Psalmist, in vision, see our land?

My prayer is that this may be the year when all shall awake to the great importance of saving our land from the ravages of intemperance.

227—MARY P. LEMEN.

With love to you all, I am yours for God, Home and Native Land.   Mother.

Her prayers are being wonderfully and graciously answered. The interest in the Home was never as great as now; never were as many cared for as now; never were as many homes found; never were receipts as good; never was our health as good as since that prayer was offered. She is consciously present with us, a blessed, ministering Spirit, praise be to our loving Father who is good, and whose mercy endureth forever.

Words of love and sympathy from friends have been abundant and cheering. And now they are taking practical shape in behalf of this work for which mother prayed night and day since it began, as will be seen by reference to the resolutions of Sheldon, Ia., W. C. T. U., given below. We quote from friends as follows:

The *St. Louis Daily Republic*, of January 17th, 1892, contained the following:

Mrs. Mary Putnam Rand-Lemen was one of the best-known women who ever lived in Illinois. She was a Christian lady and a renowned educator. She sprang from a noted ancestry. In 1669 two brothers, named Rand, came from England and settled in Massachusetts. Jonathan Rand, a descendant of one of these brothers, graduated at Dartmouth College in 1759, and was the first minister of the gospel ordained in Lyndborough, N. H. He married Sarah Goff, a daughter of General Goff, who fought in the French and Indian War. He was paid by the King of England in land, which still bears his name, in Hillsborough County, New Hampshire. They were the parents of four sons and two daughters, all of whom became distinguished in literary pursuits. Three of the sons became Baptist ministers. The youngest son, Nehemiah, married Miss Putnam, a descendant of General Putnam. They were the parents of nine children, one of whom was the deceased, Mary P. Rand-Lemen. She was born in New Boston, N. H., in 1811. In 1830 she was converted and joined the church of her ancestors. She graduated from the New Hampshire Female Seminary in 1834, and in the fall of the same year was sent by the Baptist Educational Society to Illinois as a teacher.

The *Marion County Republican*, of Salem, Ill., 1892, in the course of a long obituary notice, said:

On Wednesday of last week the sad news of Mother Lemen's death at Neosho, Mo., reached this place, where the best part of her life was spent. She was known and loved so well by all who live in this community that any words of ours will fail to express to their hearts the magnitude of her good qualities and her noble womanhood. When word came of her death, her picture, which has long hung in the school house building, was draped in mourning. Even the little children had a deferential reverence for the memory of the old teacher whose death was thereby announced.

The following resolutions by the organizations named, have been sent us:

MISSOURI DISTRICT W. C. T. U.

Once more has the W. C. T. U. of the Thirteenth District been called upon to mourn the departure of a beloved sister, Mrs. M. P. Rand-Lemen, of Neosho, who passed away Tuesday, January 12, 1892, aged 81 years.

Therefore, with sorrowing hearts, record we the fact, and—

Resolve: That in the death of Mother Lemen, the W. C. T. U. of the 13th District has lost a worthy member, an earnest advocate of its principles and one ever faithful in the discharge of duty in the various offices she had so honorably filled.

Resolved, that we cherish in loving remembrance the recollections of her kind aid, wise counsel and Christian influence.

Resolved, that we will strive to emulate the example of our worthy sister, pressing forward in our work with the same zeal and determination which were characteristic of her.

Resolved, that we tender loving sympathy to the family so sorrowfully bereft, and rejoice with them over the record of her "who so gloriously allured to brighter worlds and led the way."

MRS. MYRA B. CUSHING,
MISS GRACE S. ALLEN,
MRS. M. E. BARBER,
Committee.

NEOSHO, MO., W. C. T. U.

WHEREAS God in His all-wise providence has called our beloved sister and co-laborer in the temperance cause, Mrs. M. P. Rand-Lemen, from this scene of action, to her promised rest, therefore be it

Resolved, that we, as Christians, bow in submission to the will of the Divine Creator, "Who doeth all things well," and say, "Thy will be done."

Resolved, that we consecrate ourselves anew to His work, as she had done at the beginning of the year, and pray for greater zeal through 1892 than any year previous.

Resolved, that we tender our heartfelt sympathy to her bereaved family, and pray that our merciful and loving Savior may come to them in the person of His Holy Spirit and comfort their sorrowing hearts as no one else can.

MRS. SHIELDS,
MRS. RICHARDS,
MRS. NORTH,
Committee.

SENECA, MO., W. C. T. U.

We, the W. C. T. U., of Seneca, learn with much sadness that Mrs. M. P. Rand-Lemen, of Neosho, our Mother in Israel, and for many years a leader of the temperance work of Newton County, has been called by the great Ruler of the universe, to come up higher and from the battlements above view the progress of the good reform which was so dear to her heart.

541—DR. WILL BOSTICK.

We, a sorrowing band of sisters, would offer this tribute to her memory:

WHEREAS, It has pleased our Heavenly Father in His wise providence to take from us our friend and co-laborer in the temperance cause, Mrs. M. P. Rand-Lemen, therefore, be it

Resolved, that we recognize the will of Almighty God in the bereavement, and that we bow in submission to His Divine will.

Resolved, that we tender our heartfelt sympathy and love to the sorrowing friends who "sorrow not as those who have no hope."

> " Servant of God, well done,
> Thy glorious warfare's past;
> The battle's fought, the race is won
> And thou art crowned at last."

MRS. JULIA HALL, Pres't.

MRS. FANNIE MATHES, Sec'y.

SHELDON, IA., W. C. T. U.

SHELDON, IA., May 22, 1892.

In behalf of the Christian Home Orphanage, and as a fitting memorial of Mother Lemen, the W. C. T. U. of Sheldon, Ia., adopts the following:

WHEREAS, The Christian Home is caring constantly for an average of seventy homeless children, having received and found homes, in the past eight weeks, for forty-three; and

WHEREAS, the work of the Home is right along the line of our W. C. T. U. work, in that it is rescuing from lives of shame children made orphans by the rum fiend, and keeping them from swelling the ranks of drunkards; and

WHEREAS, the Home stands ready to receive from any State a homeless child recommended by the W. C. T. U of the locality where the child is; and

WHEREAS, Mother Lemon was a W. C. T. U. worker of acknowledged ability, a leader of the temperance work in Newton County, Missouri, for many years an earnest advocate of the W. C. T. U. principles, ever faithful in the discharge of her duties in the various offices she so honorably filled; therefore

Resolved, that we urge all W. C. T. U.'s, the world over, to join with us in an effort to have each Union raise at least $20 to make up a Memorial Fund, in memory of Mother Lemen, of $10,000, the amount needed to clear up all debts against the Home, buy additional ground and put up a hospital cottage, so much needed. And this let us do, "In His Name," and as a token of love and esteem for her whose memory is such an inspiration to her son in his life of self-denial and trust.

Resolved, that Sheldon, Ia., W. C. T. U. at once set to work to raise $20 for this purpose, desiring to be one of the 500 Unions necessary to raise the ten thousand dollars.

MRS. W. W. BROWN,
MRS. NELSON,
MRS. M. A. LABON,
MRS. R. ABORN,
MRS. S. M. LADD,
                    Committee.

180—EDWIN H. LEMEN.

Memorial services were held at a number of places. At Salem, Ill., where she spent many years of her life, elaborate services were held in the Baptist Church, Sunday evening, February 14, 1892. Of that service, the Salem *Democrat* said:

The memorial services in honor of Mrs. Mary P. Rand-Lemen, deceased, late of Neosho, Mo., and for years a resident of this place, held at the Baptist Church in this city, on last Sunday evening, was an event well worthy of notice. The church was filled to over-flowing with friends, eager to do honor to their friend and co-worker. Resolutions of respect, adopted by the church, and also by the W. C T. U., were read. Papers eulogizing her character as a teacher were read by Mrs. Webster, Mrs. Metcalf and Mr. S. S. Chance. Addresses, which teemed with words of praise and admiration for the heroic life of the deceased, were delivered by Judge Schæffer, G. R. Pace and Judge Kagy. It is fitting, in this age of equality before the law, that a *noble woman's life* and *character* should receive the honors due, as well as a man's.

"Gone to be with Jesus," to that bright land
   Where pain and sorrow nevermore can come;
Weary no more, she walks the shining strand,
   In God's celestial home.

541—DR. WILL BOSTICK.

Dr. Will Bostick was born in Holden, Johnson County, Missouri, December 10, 1876. He graduated from Holden High School at the age of fifteen years, and at once began to read medicine with Dr T. J. Simpson. After two years he entered the Kansas City Medical College, from which place he graduated in March, 1898. At an early age he was converted and united with the Methodist Episcopal Church.

His father, A. J. Bostick, is a native of Delaware, but moved to Collinsville, Ill., at about the age of twenty-four years. His mother, formerly E. F. Lemen, daughter of J. H. and Catharine Lemen, was born and grew to womanhood in Ridge Prairie, St. Clair County, Illinois. About six years after their marriage they moved to Holden, Mo., where they now reside.

1204—PROF. JAMES P. SLADE.

Prof. Slade, of St. Clair County, Illinois, has been an educator all his life. For twenty-five years he served as a teacher, city and county superintendent, to the satisfaction of all who knew him. His entire devotion to his profession and its interests is known from one end of the State to the other. He has been for years an active member of the State Teachers' Association, and has never failed to perform to the best of his ability every duty that was assigned him. He has labored unceasingly for a quarter of a century to promote the interests of education and of teachers, and his success has been no less marked than his honesty and devotion. Whatever qualities may be deemed essential to a proper

633—CYNTHIA C. LEMEN.

administration of the Department of Public Instruction, Mr. Slade possesses in an eminent degree. From his early youth he has been identified with our schools. He has filled every position under our school law from teacher of an ungraded country school to State Superintendent of Public Instruction. For fifteen years he taught in the Belleville public schools—eleven of them as principal of the High School. For ten years he was County Superintendent; six of these years devoting his whole time to the supervision of the county schools, and four of them, serving as Principal of the High School and as County Superintendent. For four years he was State Superintendent; for eight years he had charge of Almira College, and for four years he was Superintendent of Schools at East St. Louis, Ill. In all these fields he has been remarkably successful. It may be truly said of him that he never filled a position that he did not adorn. Not only the schools of our county, but those of the entire State, have been elevated in standard and rendered more efficient by his connection with them. He is in thorough sympathy with our public school system; he has a comprehensive appreciation of the possibilities of that system, and the requisite administrative ability to so order details that these possibilities may eventually be realized. He knows what to do and how to do it. He is an educator of recognized power throughout the confines of the State, and is favorably known among school men of national reputation.

180—EDWIN H. LEMEN.

Edwin H. Lemen, eldest child of Isaac and Caroline Lemen, nee Hogan, was born near Collinsville, Madison County, Illinois, November 9, 1844. Mr. Lemen was reared to the occupation of farming. He had received a liberal common school education while quite you ig, and having received a certificate, he taught school very acceptably at eighteen years of age. He afterwards attended school at Shurtleff College, and subsequently attended the course at the law department of Michigan University, at Ann Arbor, and received his diploma. Having thus thoroughly prepared himself for the practice of the law, he received his license and was admitted to the Illinois bar in 1868. He located in Pinckneyville, Ill., and for some two years in connection with his first practice of the law his time was partially occupied in school teaching and journalism. On September 24, 1871, at Bethel Baptist Church, the Rev. Dr. Post officiating, Mr. Lemen was united in marriage with the companion of his early childhood and youthful schoolmate, Miss Cynthia C. Begole, youngest child of Joshua and Mary Begole, of Ridge Prairie, St. Clair County. As a result of this union there were two children: the first, Maude Parepa, was born May 2, 1875; the second child, a son, born December 15, 1876, and died in infancy. Mr. Lemen and his wife purchased themselves a good farm adjoining Pinckneyville, a part of which is included in its incorporated limits.

634—MAUDE PAREPA LEMEN.

While Mr. Lemen's religion and politics were matters of deliberate reason and careful choice after the mature judgment of manhood, it so happened in these important matters there is no conflict between them and those of his ancestors for a century back. While his ancestors were in religion, Baptists, and in politics, Whigs, of the anti-slavery and Republican faith, so also was the subject of this sketch. He united with the Bethel Baptist Church in the winter of 1871, and uniformly contributed his influence for the support of his church, though not narrowly sectarian in his respect for and confidence in the other Christian churches. Mr. Lemen transferred his membership by letter from Bethel to the First Baptist Church at Pinckneyville, in which church he remained until his death. He was a prominent member and supporter, contributing to the church, as well as to other religious and eleemosynary purposes, such aid as his means would justify.

In the rational gradation of duty next perhaps to a man's religion, is his humanitarian impulses toward his race. For the aristocracy of men of shoddy wealth Mr. Lemen had no veneration, but the toilers of the country, whether in the department of mental activity or of manual labor, he held in perpetual esteem and honor; and with the latter his sympathy was not theoretical but experimental, as his labors in every department of farming duly qualified him to respect toil. The toilers of the age are the men who are bearing the banners of our civiliza-

tion upward and onward, and he respected them.   In
the application by the government of the great questions of political economy he favored such adjustments
as would reduce the burdens of taxation on the laboring masses, while at the same time protecting them
from the too overpowering competition of the products of foreign labor.

An unbending conscience, a resolute will and a
discerning judgment form a combination which is the
augury of success.   Possessed of this triple alliance
of subjective forces in a large measure, the subject
of this sketch pressed to the front ranks of the legal
profession. The possession of those intellectual forces
which made it possible for him to deliver a speech
before a jury or an audience with such marked effect
and impassioned feeling as generally characterized
his efforts, justly won for him the popular good will
and esteem which such qualities merit.   As a writer
of merit and force he was recognized by the journal-
ists throughout the State, and through this avenue
the line of success and distinction was opened to him
if he had elected to accept it.

MR. AND MRS. EDWARD GARETSON.

Sardenia, Ohio, was the birthplace of my father,
Robert W. Purcell.   He was a true Union man, but
on account of failing health he could not serve his
country; he instilled into his children strong Repub-
licanism from childhood.   During his life he held

559—DR. EDWARD GARETSON.

offices of trust, and was a leader of all good works. He was a member of the Methodist Church from childhood, and was always a noble helper in the cause of Christ. In the year of 1877, at the age of 48 years, he departed from his earthly home. Father had been previously married before he wed my mother, and had two children, one girl and a boy, Sarah and William Purcell—William is now deceased. In Johnson County, Kansas, near Kansas City father met and in a short time married my mother, Harriett Daugherty, a widow of means with a family of five children, three girls and two boys—Marium, Mary, Lucy, Edward and James Daugherty. My mother is a Shawnee Indian by birth; her parents were residents of Ohio until their removal from that State to the Indian reservation in Kansas, in 1838. Mother was left an orphan at the age of six years. She was first married quite young to Lewis Daugherty, then to my father, Robert Purcell. There were eight children born to them, making in family fifteen children, of whom six are now living, two half-sisters and three full-brothers; Charles H. Wesley, Abraham Lincoln Purcell and myself, all are married. Brothers are extensive farmers and Republican politicians, who command the highest respect and esteem of all who know them. Mother united with the Methodist Church in early life and has been a devout Christian. She now lives near Adair, Indian Territory.

In 1886, I met, loved and married Edward Garetson, now deceased. Our married life was one of true happiness, our five children came to bless our home, four of whom are now living. He was a true, devoted husband and father, with a true, noble Christian heart. Through his professional life all with whom he met were made his friends forever. We located our home in the Indian Territory in 1886; the doctor attended to his profession and, at the same time, opened up a farm of 900 acres. After remaining for four years we moved to Poplar Bluff, Mo., residing there two years; we then moved to Adair, Indian Territory, where we are now living in a nice home with all conveniences, and in comfortable circumstances. My age is 33 years; I united with the Presbyterian Church in 1895. My whole heart's trust is in the Divine Savior. As a Christian mother I shall ever strive to teach my dear children to put their trust in, and to love Him who died for us all, and to lead the precious lives entrusted to me into His kingdom. One cannot place before the public eye or cast upon the altar of public criticism a sacred joy or sorrow; the gaze must be veiled by a tear of sympathy, or be shared by true hearts in whose tender responsive love we wear the diadem of earthly happiness.

150—CAPT. JAMES L. GARETSON.

Capt. James L. Garetson was born on the banks of the Mississippi, twenty-eight miles below St. Louis, Mo., in Monroe County, Illinois, March 19, 1826.

150 - CAPT. JAMES L. GARETSON.   553—SARAH A. GARETSON.

His father, John Garetson, was also born in Monroe County, Illinois, in 1800; and his mother, whose maiden name was Catharine Lemen, was born in St. Clair County, Illinois, 1808. His grand-parents were all born in Virginia, and settled in Illinois in 1784. His father died before he was three years old, and from that time until 1844 he lived with his uncle, Benjamin Scott. October 15, 1844, he married Margaret McFarland, who died November 12, 1845. June 15, 1846, he volunteered to go to the Mexican War, and was mustered into the service of the United States, June 17th, as a member of Company G, 2nd Regiment, Illinois Infantry Volunteers, and was discharged therefrom June 17, 1847. After the war he returned to Monroe County, Illinois, where, in April, 1848, he married Sarah A. Harlow.

In 1858 he moved to Odin, Marion County, Illinois, where he successfully engaged in the hotel business. In 1857, he was appointed postmaster at Odin, by President Buchanan, and held the position continuously until July, 1870, when he resigned, but was not relieved until the next summer. His sons ran the office while he was in the War of the Rebellion. He did not determine to take part in the Civil War until he met and talked with his old Mexican War captain, J. K. Lemen, when his patriotism became thoroughly aroused and he recruited a company of which he became captain. It was attached to the 62d Illinois Infantry as Company G. After serving about three years he returned to his home at Odin and engaged in the mercantile business.

In October, 1870, he moved with his family to Butler County, Missouri, and settled near Harvill, where he remained until 1888, when he moved to Poplar Bluff.

Captain Garetson cast his first Presidential vote for Gen. Zach. Taylor. He voted for "Honest old Abe" Lincoln twice, and during his life, from his first vote, supported the nominees of the Republican party. He was the first Republican treasurer in Butler County.

561—MR. ROBERT L. GARETSON.

Mr. Robert Lemen Garetson, the subject of our sketch, was born at Odin, Ill., November 30, 1866. At the age of five years his parents moved with him to Butler County, Missouri; when he was fifteen years old he obtained a position with B. Duncan & Co. of Poplar Bluff, Mo.; he served this firm faithfully and efficiently for three years; at the expiration of which he severed his connections with them to enter the Bryant & Stratton Business College of St. Louis, Mo., where he took a thorough business course. After leaving college he again engaged with B. Duncan & Co. for a short time. In about one year from the time he completed his business course he bought a half interest in the general

561—MR. ROBERT L. GARETSON

merchandise business of his father's at Harville, Mo. Soon after this he and his father moved their stock of goods to Poplar Bluff where they conducted a thriving business for seven years, when misfortune overtook them, and their store building with all its contents was burned to the ground. About the middle of November, 1893, immediately after the loss by fire, Mr. Garetson, undaunted by misfortune, went to St. Louis and bought a complete stock of general merchandise, which he shipped to Fisk, a saw-mill town, about eleven miles east of Poplar Bluff, and started in business again by himself. This under-taking has proven very satisfactory to the present time.

In December, 1889, Mr. Garetson married Miss Bertha Ball, of Ann Arbor, Mich., who was a beauti-ful and accomplished lady; she was a graduate of the Burlington College, Iowa. The result of this union was one daughter, Nellie, born December, 1890. In December, 1890, Mrs. Bertha Garetson was called from the joys and pleasures of a happy home and loving friends to that upper and better land, leaving to the husband and father their bud of promise, now developed into a rugged, healthy and bright school girl.

At the age of twenty Mr. Garetson professed a hope in Christ, and united with the Baptist Church, of which he is a prominent member, being earnest and consistent in his Christian life.

558—FRANK A. GARETSON.

F. A. Garetson, son of James and Sarah A. Garetson, is a prominent and successful lumber merchant of Poplar Bluff, Mo. He was born in Odin, Ill., February 18th, 1860, where he lived until 1870, when his parents moved with him to the wilds of Missouri. There they settled on a farm 85 miles from any railroad, and within a mile of the site where Harvill afterwards was built. About two years later James L. Garetson, the father of F. A. Garetson, started a store where Harvill now stands, the Iron Mountain Railroad having just been built, and with his son John did a thriving business, leaving the subject of our sketch and two brothers, Ben. and Ed., to till the farm. His school education was limited, consisting of four terms of four months each. When he was twenty-one years old he started into the lumber business, contracting with the I. M. R. R. to furnish wood, ties and piling for the company. At the age of twenty-three he and his brother Ben. bought out the mercantile business; in about two years his brother Ben. died, when he associated with him his father; together they took up the lumber business again and run it in connection with the mercantile business until 1885, when he sold out his interest. About this time, September 4th, 1884, Mr. Garetson was married to a most estimable young lady of Union, Ill., Miss Julia L. Metz; there have been five children born of this union: Sarah E., Ray A., Frank A., Jr., Julia L. and Sylvains H. In 1885

1073—JULIA L. GARETSON.
565—FRANK A. GARETSON.

1071—RAY A. GARETSON
1072—FRANK A., JR.
1074—SYLVAINS H. GARETSON.

1070—SARAH E. GARETSON.
1069—JULIA L. GARETSON.

Mr. and Mrs. Garetson united with the Baptist Church and were baptized. They are staunch supporters of that faith, and are liberal contributors to the cause. About the year 1886, Mr. Garetson moved to Poplar Bluff, where he associated himself with a Mr. A. H. Greason, and again went into the timber and lumber business; in 1892 James L. Garetson was taken into the partnership and the company was incorporated with a capital of $30,000. This firm is still in existence and doing a thriving business; they have a branch office at St. Louis, under the supervision of James L. Garetson, who is also secretary of the firm. The subject of our sketch is president, and A. H. Greason, vice-president. This firm has extensive timber claims on the St. Francis River, and operate numerous saw mills, also a large and well equipped panel and planing mill, which turns out millions of feet of box lumber annually.

70.—WILLIAM KINNEY LEMEN.

William Kinney Lemen, a son of Rev. Joseph Lemen and Polly K. Lemen, his wife, was born at the home of his parents in Ridge Prairie, St. Clair County, Ill., on October 3d, 1828. He acquired a common school education, and in early life united with the Baptist Church. By an accident in 1852 one of his lower limbs was broken, and although it healed, it was always a source of inconvenience to him, and at times, of more or less pain. On March 27th, 1856, he united in marriage with Miss Lieuann Edwards, from which union four children were born, namely: John E. and Ella, living, and two died in infancy. The death of his first wife occurred on July 13th, 1865, and he was united in marriage with her sister, Miss Mary A. Edwards, on July 29th, 1866.

Through industry and good management, as a farmer and trader, Mr. Lemen accumulated large property interests, holding at the time of his death a large and splendidly appointed farm in Ridge Prairie, St. Clair County, on which the family resided, and, also, a large farm near Troy, in Madison County, Illinois. He was a good neighbor, exceedingly kind and sympathetic in cases of affliction and bereavement, and a good citizen; and though never seeking official preferment, he was often school director, served often on local juries, and one term on the Federal Grand Jury at Springfield, Ill. Was a supporter of the church and other good causes; kind and affectionate as a husband, and as a father, indulgent, always providing abundantly for the wants of his family. In politics he was a Democrat, though never a rank partisan; and in later years he said he made a habit of looking more at the fitness and qualifications of candidates than he did at their party affiliations. He lived and died in the faith of the Baptist Church, expressing, particularly in his last days, an abiding confidence in his final acceptance, and a hope that reached beyond the confines of the grave. In his

70—WILLIAM K. LEMEN.

last illness, which was protracted, he suffered with one form of Bright's disease, complicated with sympathetic heart trouble, which eventually baffled the best medical skill, and in the early afternoon of October 6th, 1897, at his home, without a struggle, he passed to his rest, aged sixty-nine years and three days. On October 8th, at the residence, in the presence of his family and a vast concourse of other relatives and friends, the funeral services were conducted by Rev. J. B. Webb, after which the cortege moved to Edward's Cemetery in Madison County, where his remains were interred.

Of the children, John E. Lemen (247), a successful and prominent farmer, united in marriage with Miss Luella, an accomplished daughter of Mr. and Mrs. Hiram Pierce, of Shiloh Valley, Ill., and they reside at their farm residence in Ridge Prairie. The daughter, Miss Ella (249), a young lady of rare accomplishments and culture, was united in marriage with Mr. James C. Harvey, a gentleman highly esteemed throughout St. Louis and vicinity for his business traits and sterling integrity, and they reside in that city.

Mrs. Mary A. Lemen, the widow, is an excellent Christian lady, as was also her sister, the late Lieuann Edwards-Lemen. She is residing temporarily in the city of St. Louis, but will probably live a part of her time at the homestead residence in Ridge Prairie, Ill.

214--CAPT. WILLIAM K. MURPHY.

Sarah Lemen was the oldest child of the Rev. Joseph and Polly Lemen, nee Kinney. She was born November 2, 1809, at the old homestead near Bethel Church, St. Clair County, Illinois, of which she became a member at an early age. She was married September 2, 1834, to Richard G. Murphy, a native of Smith County, Tennessee, who came with his father's family and settled in Perry County, Illinois, in 1818. They lived upon a farm five miles south of Pinckneyville until she died, October 28, 1846. The issue of said marriage were five children: William K. Murphy, born July 20, 1835; Mary A. Murphy, born June 8, 1837; Joseph L. Murphy, born December 30, 1838; Benton P. Murphy, born April 12, 1841, and Geo. W. Murphy, born May 19, 1843.

Captain Wm. K. Murphy was married to Miss Penina Ozburn, April 18, 1860, at Pinckneyville, Ill.; Mary A. was married to D. A. Huntsman at Shakopee, Minn.; Joseph L. was married to Emma L. Carter at Pinckneyville, Ill.; Benton P. was married to Cora Sullivan at Pinckneyville, Ill., and Geo. W. was married to Anna F. Cole at Shakopee, Minn.

W. K., J. L., B. P. and Geo. W. are, at this writing, living in Perry County, Illinois. Mary A. died April 26, 1868, and was buried at Shakopee, Minn.

W. K. Murphy has two children living, Hawkin O. Murphy and Sarah V. Crawford, wife of Joseph

214—CAPT. WILLIAM K. MURPHY.

Crawford. The latter couple have one child, Wm. K. Crawford, aged six years.

Mary A. Huntsman, nee Murphy, left, surviving her, five children, to-wit: Cora, who married Charles Stanchfield; Sarah, who married Wm. Fitzer, both of whom are now deceased, but left surviving a little boy named Harry; Richard H. Huntsman, who resides at Pinckneyville, Ill., and Mary L., who married Geo. W. Stewart, a lawyer, and they reside at St. Cloud, Minn., and Bertha F. Huntsman, who is a teacher in one of the public schools of Duluth, Minn.

Jos. L. has no children. Benton P. has four children living, to-wit: May, Nellie, Virginia and Sidney, and one dead, Frankie Lemen—all girls. Geo. W. has no children.

Richard G. Murphy was Orderly Sergeant in Captain Adair's company in the Black Hawk War. In 1832 he was elected to the Eighth General Assembly of the State of Illinois as a member of the House from Randolph and Perry counties and again elected to the Ninth General Assembly in 1834, and again in 1836 to the Tenth General Assembly, in 1838 to the Eleventh General Assembly and again in 1840 to the Twelfth General Assembly, and again in 1850 to the Seventeenth General Assembly. He was Chairman of the Railroad Committee of the House which reported the bill that incorporated the Illinois Central Railroad Company and provided that 7 per cent. of the gross earnings should go to the State; a splendid measure which has already paid the State many millions of dollars. He was appointed Agent for the Sioux Indians by President Polk and again appointed by President Pierce, and during the Administration of the latter he moved his family to Shakopee, Minn., in 1854. He was elected to the State Senate of Minnesota and made president of that body during the pendency of the admission of the State into the Union. He died January 10, 1875, aged 74 years. Abraham Lincoln was also a member of the Ninth, Tenth, Eleventh and Twelfth General Assemblies of Illinois.

Captain W. K. Murphy was born July 20, 1835, in the Four-Mile Prairie, six miles south of Pinckney-ville, Ill. His education was limited to the log school-house and subscription schools of the neighborhood, with the exception of a few months that he attended school at Sparta, Ill., under B. G. Roots, a noted educator in those days in Southern Illinois.

At the age of eighteen his father put him into the business of buying and selling cattle, and during that and the three following years he bought and drove through by land from Perry County, Ill., to St. Paul, Minn., over 1600 head of cattle, making four trips there with cattle on horseback and one trip alone from there back to the starting point in Illinois. At this time there were but few white people north of the Iowa line and they were confined to the old Indian trading posts along the Mississippi River, such as Red Wing, Wabasha and Winona, at which places there were bands of the Sioux Indians, but at that time they were peaceably disposed and not inclined to seriously question the right of the "pale face" to invade the happy hunting grounds of their fathers, as they did a few years later.

The subject of this sketch then engaged in steamboating and for two years was an officer on the steamboat called the "Time and Tide," plying the upper Mississippi and Minnesota rivers, making occasional trips between St. Louis and St. Paul. He commenced as Second Clerk, but during the latter part of the season was in command of the boat. The hard lines that the steamboating got into in the fall of 1858, owing to the hard times in the northwest, was so discouraging that he quit the river and came back to his former home in Illinois, and commenced reading law in the spring of 1859 with Wm. H. McKee in Pinckneyville. He was admitted to the bar in the fall of that year and was taken in as a full partner in the practice under the firm name of McKee & Murphy. The health of Mr. McKee having broken down he gave up the practice in the fall of 1860, and Murphy continued the practice alone until August, 1862, when he entered the army as Captain of Company H, 110th Regiment Illinois Volunteers. Owing to ill health contracted by the exposure incident to the hardships of army life, he resigned in the spring of 1863, after having taken part in the battle of Stone River, one of the hardest fought and most destructive engagements of the war.

Returning home he resumed the practice of law and in the November election in 1864 was elected to the lower house of the State Legislature, and was again elected in 1866 and to the State Senate in 1872, and represented his district as Senator in the Twenty-eighth and Twenty-ninth General Assemblies. He was again elected to the lower house in 1880, making in all six years' service in the House and four years in the Senate. He was a delegate to every Democratic State convention for a quarter of a century, and, with a colleague, represented his district in three National Conventions.

Captain Murphy conducted the fight in the Committee on Resolutions in the State Convention at Springfield by which Grover Cleveland received the vote of Illinois in the National Convention at Chicago in 1892, in which he was also a delegate and took an active and conspicuous part.

He was appointed Collector of Internal Revenue for the Cairo District by President Cleveland in 1893, and has held the position for over four years. He was nominated by his party for Congress in 1882 and made the race against an average majority of 2000, which he reduced to 381, carrying his own county that was largely Republican by 462 majority, and the adjoining county of Jackson, that had for years been a stand-off, by 422 majority. He has always taken an active part in politics, and until the election of 1896 always acted with the majority of his party, but in the election of that year he supported Palmer and

1045—DR. JOHN VOISIN.   527—JOSIE VOISIN.
    1046—VERNA VOISIN.   1047—ADA VOISIN.

Buckner, and canvassed southern Illinois against the Bryan platform ticket and in favor of sound money.

He was for many years Master in Chancery of Perry County and continued to practice law until 1894, when he retired from practice. While he remained in practice, he and his partners had their full share of the best of the business in the courts of Perry County.

He has been at the head as manager of the bank of Murphy, Wall & Co. since it was organized in 1874, and is also President of the First National Bank of Murphysboro, Ill., and also of the Murphysboro Savings Bank and of the Murphysboro Waterworks, Electric and Gas Light Company.

Mary L. Huntsman (nee Murphy) was born and educated in Southern Illinois, except one year that she attended the Female Seminary in Gallatin, Tenn. She received most of her education at Salem, Ill., where she went to school for several years, and at all schools she attended she stood at the head of her classes. She received a very good education and was regarded by all who knew her as a very bright and intellectual woman. She was a loving wife, kind and affectionate mother, a good neighbor and a devoted Christian. She died in the prime of life, beloved by all who knew her.

Lieutenant Joseph L. Murphy received a common school education. He went into the Union army in August, 1862, as Sergeant-Major of the 110th Regi-

ment Illinois Volunteers. He was afterward elected
Second Lieutenant and then First Lieutenant, and
took part in all the engagements from and including
Stone River, Chattanooga, Atlanta and "Sherman's
March to the Sea," and was honorably discharged
after the surrender of General Lee at Appomatox.

He has been several times elected Mayor of the
city of Pinckneyville and served one term as a member of the Legislature of Illinois. His business has
been that of merchant and dealer in grain and lumber.

Benton P. Murphy served four years as County
Commissioner in Grant County, South Dakota, during
his eight years' residence there. He is now a lumber dealer in Pinckneyville.

Geo. W. Murphy never took any active part in
political matters, but is a plain farmer, who has the
respect and confidence of all who know him. Most
of his life has been spent in Minnesota and South
Dakota. He now lives in Pinckneyville, Ill.

527—MRS. JOSIE VOISIN.

The subject of our sketch was born in St. Clair
County, Illinois, December 7, 1869. She is the second daughter of Lieutenant Cyrus A. and Caroline
E. Lemen. She received a common school education,
and was instructed in instrumental music. At an
early age she was converted to Christ, and united
with the Bethel Baptist Church, of which she is now

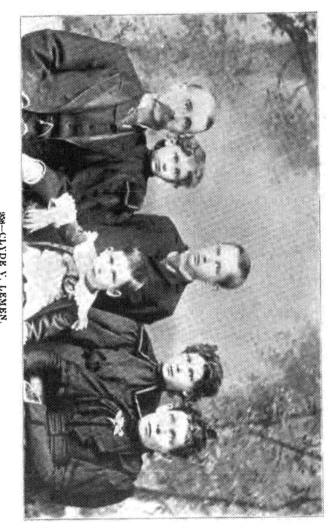

960—CARRIE M. LEMEN.   958—CLYDE V. LEMEN.   959—EDITH I. LEMEN.
397—PROF. LEWIS LEMEN.   361—WILLIAM T. LEMEN.   367—MARY V. LEMEN.

a member. While she resided with her parents, within the bounds of the church, she was a faithful laborer in the Sabbath-school and a consistent and enthusiastic helper in all Christian efforts.

On June 1, 1892, she was married to Dr. John Voisin, of St. Clair County, Illinois. Dr. Voisin took a literary course at McKendree College, Lebanon, Illinois, afterwards took a medical course at the St. Louis Medical College, then a post-graduate course at the Marion-Sims College of Medicine. After graduating from the latter he located in the city of St. Louis, and is at present practicing his profession with success. He is also proprietor of a fine pharmacy on the corner of Park Avenue and Broadway.

The home of Dr. and Mrs. Voisin is blessed with two little daughters, the eldest, Verna, born April 21, 1893, and the youngest, Ada Grace, born April 18, 1895.

110—JOSIAH D. LEMEN.

The subject of our sketch was born May 19, 1830, at New Design, Monroe County, Illinois, on a farm adjoining the old James Lemen homestead. He was the youngest son of Rev. Josiah and Rebecca Lemen, nee Huff, and as such, inherited his father's farm, that being the custom in those days.

On October 16, 1851, he was married to Susan A. Bales, a devout Christian, and a member of the New Design Baptist Church. She was a descendant of a rich Southern planter. Of his children by this marriage—William, Albert and Jennie are yet living, Henry and two sisters dying in infancy. Lewis, the eldest son, died November 4, 1897.

After her death, which occurred December 7, 1863, he was married to Bridget A. Reilly, September 8, 1864. The issue of his second marriage being Laura A., Mary B. and James H. living, two little daughters being called away in early life.

397—PROF. LEWIS LEMEN.

Prof. Lewis Lemen was born July 30, 1852, at New Design, Monroe County, Illinois. He was the eldest son of Josiah D. and Susan A. Lemen, nee Bales. His boyhood days were spent on the old homestead, at New Design, and he received his education at Portland school in that vicinity, a school noted for the number of persons who afterward became teachers.

He was married to Miss Mary V. Tolin, May 19, 1881. To them were born four children: Clyde V., Edith I., Carrie M. and William T. Shortly after his marriage he professed religion during a service held in the old New Design church. Although Mr. Lemen engaged in farming a few years, he was better known as a teacher, having taught fifteen terms, seven of which were at his home school, Portland. At the time of his death he was employed as a teacher in the public school of Columbia, Ill.; he was an earn-

398—PROF. WILLIAM LEMEN. 963—HULDA E. LEMEN. 962—LOUISA E. LEMEN.

est, hardworking, conscientious teacher, often feeling that he would like to do even more for his pupils than duty required. His life in the school-room as everywhere else, was one of purity and manliness—a fitting example for his pupils to follow. He was of a happy turn of mind, enjoyed the society of his friends immensely, possessed an abundance of good humor, was a reliable companion, firm in his convictions of right, and faithful to every trust.

He died at his home in Columbia, Monroe County, Illinois, November 4, 1897, and was buried at the old New Design cemetery. Rev. C. W. Alexander, of Red Bud made appropriate remarks from the 23d Psalm, after which the members of the A. O. U. W. and M. W. A. conducted solemn and impressive burial services at the grave.

398—PROF. WILLIAM LEMEN.

Prof. William Lemen, the subject of this sketch, is a lineal descendant, in the fourth generation, of the old and stalwart pioneer family, originating with Rev. James Lemen, Sr., from Virginia, and who settled with his family, in 1786, in New Design, Ill., as one of the vanguard who built the first church in Illinois, and who were the main factors in shaping the destiny and history of Illinois, was born on October 25, 1853, on the old homestead, the second son of Mr. Josiah Lemen and Susan A. Lemen, nee Bales, whose family came from the South. The issue resulting from this union were: Lewis Lemen, a teacher of merit, now deceased; William Lemen, the subject of this sketch; Albert Lemen, now residing at Lincoln, Neb., and holding a prominent government position, and one sister, Jennie Lemen, married to Martin Gundlach, and now living in Madison County, Illinois. After the death of their mother, Josiah Lemen, their father, was again married. The result of this second marriage were: Laura A., a member of a holy order at Seattle, Wash.; Mary B. Carlton, living in St. Louis, Mo., and James H. Lemen, a teacher in Monroe County, Illinois, besides several more children, who died in infancy.

The boyhood days of Prof. Lemen were spent at home, and when of the proper age he attended Portland school, which has produced many prominent teachers. Although attending his school only for short terms and without any other educational advantages, he, encouraged by the direction and guidance of his father, and endowed with inborn ability, indomitable zeal, energy and perseverance, added to and completed through home study his store of information and knowledge, so as to fit himself for the responsible and highly important position of a teacher. After he left school his time was divided between farm work and private study until 1874, when he took charge for the first time of a public school. The premature death of his father in 1875 ended his career as instructor of children for

THIS IS THE OLD HOMESTEAD OF REV. JOSIAH LEMEN. NOW OWNED AND OCCUPIED BY HIS GRANDSON, WILLIAM LEMEN.

the time, and he was called home to take control of the farm and family affairs. The work entailed upon him thereby did not occupy all his time, so in 1876 he again resumed his educational work and continued in it to 1879, when the management of the home place demanded his undivided attention. From this time on he confined himself altogether to these duties.

April 26, 1881, he was joined in the holy bonds of matrimony to Miss Louisa E. Briegel, the daughter of a prominent farmer of the neighborhood, whose natal day was September 28, 1859. As a result of this union there are two children—a son, born and died October 24, 1883, and Hulda E. Lemen, born October 27, 1884, an intellectual young lady, who, through her bodily and mental qualities and the attainments acquired with the aid of a cultured and refined education, is the pride and sunshine of this happy household.

Being of an intensive domestic disposition Mr. Lemen enjoyed the quiet of his cozy home in company of his wife and only daughter for thirteen years, engaged solely in the pursuit of farming, when his qualifications as a teacher being fully recognized, he was again called upon to take charge of a public school in his neighborhood; entering upon his duties on December 5, 1892, and holding this position to the present day to the full satisfaction of all parties.

The results achieved by Mr. Lemen show conclusively what amount of work, both physically and mentally, a man of ability and energy can perform.

Being of a splendid physique the care and toil of a large farm he considers not too hard a tax upon his constitution, and deems the same not sufficient to exhaust his energy, but finds satisfaction in teaching at the same time, performing both tasks so well that a man with inferior talents and qualifications could hardly expect to experience like good results in either of these alone by putting all his power and attention to the single one.

The home farm is situated in New Design, Ill., one mile north of Burksville, and contains many acres of fertile ground. Besides the arduous work to be performed on a large farm and the expense of intellectual force in choosing and applying the methods of performing such work, Mr. Lemen is operating a threshing machine during the fall months and doing all a wise housekeeper can do towards increasing his revenues and acquiring a competency for his beloved family. He is a first-class manager, and stands high in the esteem of the very best people of his section. Being of a highly cultured and refined mind, a fine conversationalist; of sound and good judgment in all matters of public and private interest, his advice is always favorably received and sought for. Although the minds of Professor Lemen and his most esteemed wife are always centered about their home, and they are not seeking distinction, as society people, their company is much sought after and socially they are considered the peers of any one. In political affairs the Professor, up to within a few.

407—PROF. JAMES H. LEMEN.

years, has been an ardent Republican, but becoming dissatisfied with the acts of both predominant parties he affiliated himself with the Populist party.

Although his ancestors were generally members of the Baptist Church, Mr. Lemen has not shown, publicly, a preference for any denomination, but he has proved by his honest and upright life and fair dealings with his fellowmen that the Christian spirit of his forefathers lives within him.

407—PROF. JAMES H. LEMEN.

Prof. James H. Lemen. The simple record of an honorable life is the best monument that can be reared to any citizen, and we shall therefore not attempt to enlarge upon the history of the gentleman above-named, who is a successful teacher of Monroe County, Illinois.

Our subject was born at New Design, Monroe County, Illinois, Nov. 8, 1871. He received his primary education in the district schools of his native county, which he attended through the winter seasons, while in the summer months he aided in the labors of the field. He remained upon the farm until nineteen years of age, when he entered the State Normal at Carbondale, there pursuing his studies for one year. At the age of twenty he began teaching in the district schools, and has thus been employed for six years.

His parents, Josiah and Bridget A. (Reilly) Lemen, were highly respected citizens, the former being born in Illinois and the latter in Virginia, near Harper's Ferry. In every duty of life Josiah was thoroughly conscientious—a kind father, true husband, a loyal citizen. Orphaned at the age of four, our subject made his home with his brother William, who carries forward to a successful completion whatever he undertakes, and has therefore won a prominent place in the community of leading farmers and teachers of this county.

In politics James is a stalwart Republican, and an active member of the Modern Woodmen of America. He is a man whose many excellencies of character have gained him high regard throughout the community.

153—GEORGE C. McKINLEY.

George C. McKinley, a pioneer of Solano County, but who has been living in Tulare County for some years past, died at his home near Visalia, in 1896, of Bright's disease. The body was interred at Dixon, where the funeral services were held in the Baptist Church, under the auspices of Silveyville Lodge F. & A. M., of which he was a member. George C. McKinley was born in Madison County, Illinois, July 2, 1832. In 1840 he moved with his parents to Missouri and there commenced his studies, which he finished in Gonzales County, Texas, whither he went

549—MRS. OLIVE STOCKETT.

in 1845. In 1852 he emigrated to Los Angeles County, California, along with his father and mother, but as there was much trouble in that district in respect to land titles, at the end of seven months they left for Sacramento. At Sacramento he was employed in the nursery and vegetable garden of Paul Hamilton, where he continued for three years. In 1855 Mr. McKinley made another trip to the southern counties of the State in quest of land, but finding the former stumbling block still prevailing he remained but a short time and then returned to Sacramento, from whence he made for Lynchburg, near Groville, and for two months pursued mining, and finally returned to Sacramento. On October 6, 1856, he and his father settled on the knoll south of Dixon, where the cemetery is now located. They there pitched their tent, which was soon followed by the construction of a dwelling house. Mr. McKinley's father was an unfortunate passenger on board the steamer Washoe when she blew up near Rio Vista on September 4, 1864, when he received injuries which resulted in his death at Sacramento, September 21, 1864. His mother died a few years since. In September, 1871, Mr. McKinley was elected County Recorder, an office which he held for two years. He married, December 17, 1860, Miss Emeline Benton, who was born in Joe Davies County, Illinois, September 28, 1842, by whom he had William B., Charlotte, George, Robert L., Sidney S., Paulina, and Lucino D.

549—MRS. OLIVE STOCKETT.

Olive Oatman, only daughter of Charles Russell Oatman, M. D., and Josephine Clifton Lemen, was born April 16, 1872, at O'Fallon, St. Clair County, Illinois. She was so named after the Olive Oatman—a cousin—who at twelve years of age was captured by the Apache Indians at the time of the massacre of her parents and most of the family, as they were traveling overland to California in March, 1851, and who spent five years in captivity among the Apache and Mohave Indians in what is now Arizona Territory.

In April, 1875, she moved with her parents to Collinsville, Madison County, Illinois, and there received her primary education and grew up to womanhood.

In feature and manner she strongly resembled her father, being short in stature, well proportioned and with a beautiful face and figure—a fair brunette of a Spanish type, with dark blue eyes, black lashes and brows and a wealth of dark brownish-black hair.

Her bright, sunny disposition, gentleness and kindness of manner caused her to be loved and admired everywhere. To all she was the same, the poor especially finding in her a friend who ever had a willing ear, a ready hand, kind words and deeds to soothe and relieve their troubles and distresses.

Quite early in life she displayed a decided talent for music, which was given every opportunity for development. She advanced rapidly under the direc-

147—JOSEPHINE C. OATMAN. 548—DR. CHARLES R. OATMAN.
55)—DR. LOUIS J. OATMAN. 47—JAMES H. LEMEN. 549—OLIVE OATMAN STOCKETT.
552—DR. CHRISTOPHER L. OATMAN 551—DR. CHARLES L. OATMAN.

tion of Profs. Robyn & Son, of St. Louis, Mo., and while still quite young was recognized a genius. The ease of touch, gracefulness of manner and precision with which she rendered the most difficult compositions of the masters was wonderful, during the rendition of which she would become so absorbed as to be seemingly oblivious to her surroundings. Her love of music—instrumental and vocal—was so great that it became the ruling passion of her life.

On October 11, 1894, at the home of her parents, she was united in marriage to Thomas Richard Stockett, Jr., of St. Louis, Mo., by the Rev. J. G. Wright, of Christ's Episcopal Church, Collinsville, a sister of the groom and a brother of the bride acting as bridesmaid and groomsman. After a month's trip through Canada and the Eastern States, she returned with her husband to her new home in St. Louis.

On November 11, 1895, she became the mother of a son, Lewis Oatman Stockett. Nature, however, was unable to withstand the ordeal, and with the crown of motherhood, so new and becoming, she departed this life on the morning of Thanksgiving Day, November 28, 1895. Services were held at her St. Louis home on November 30, 1895, by the Rev. J. G. Wright, and at Collinsville by the Rev. A. S. Leonard. The outpouring of relatives and friends at the latter place eloquently attested the great love and esteem in which she was held by those who had

known her from infancy. Interment took place the
same day in Bethel Cemetery, near Collinsville.

> The odor of a fragrant flower doth last
> Long after outward loveliness is gone;
> So when a beauteous life seems spent and past,
> The sweetness of its influence liveth on.

548—DR. CHARLES R. OATMAN.

Charles Russell Oatman, M. D., was born Octo-
ber 5, 1846, at Belleville, St. Clair County, Illinois.
He was the second child and eldest son of Daniel
Lay-Field Oatman, M. D., and Mary Louise Cham-
berland, who had moved to Belleville from Penn-
sylvania in 1844. His father was a native of the
Province of Alsace, France, now Germany, and was of
French and Prussian parentage.

The death of his mother in June, 1852, followed
by that of his father in September, 1852, left the
subject of our sketch an orphan before he was six
years of age, and he (with his elder sister and
younger brother), was placed under the guardianship
of Felix Scott, of Shiloh Valley, St. Clair County,
Illinois. Here he remained working on the farm of
Mr. Scott, and receiving his primary education in
the schools of Lebanon and Belleville, until the
breaking out of the Civil War. A sense of duty to
his country aroused the soldier in him—his grandfather having fought under the great Napoleon—and
though not yet sixteen years of age, he on August

59—GIDEON S. LEMEN.

9, 1862, enlisted as a musician in Co. H., 117th Regiment of Illinois Infantry Volunteers, under Capt. Robert A. Halbert, his superior officer being Col. R. D. Moore, Colonel of the 117th Illinois, and Genl. A. J. Smith, Commander of the 16th Army Corps.

His service in the army extended to the close of the war, covering a period of three years, during which time he served in the capacity of a drummer boy—and at one time acting as drum major—and suffered all the hardships and privations incident to an active soldier's life, and although present at many hard-fought battles, and on the march continually, was not wounded or taken prisoner.

He was under Sherman in his "March to the Sea," from Vicksburg to Meridian, Miss., and with his regiment in Meridian, Miss.; Red River, La.; Tupelo, Miss.; Oxford, Miss.; Missouri and Nashville campaigns during 1864; and the campaign against Mobile, Ala., in March and April, 1865, and took an active part in the storming and capture of Fort Blakely; at the latter place, just prior to the close of the war, and was the last engagement he took part in.

He was mustered out at Camp Butler, near Springfield, Illinois, on August 5, 1865. Just prior to his being mustered out at Camp Butler he was taken sick with typhoid fever, and lay in camp for two months after the regiment had disbanded. Surgeon Jennings remaining with him.

He returned to the farm of Felix Scott, in Shiloh Valley, and began the reading of medicine, in the evenings, under the direction of James L. Perryman, M. D., of Belleville (who had been a student under his father), and attended the St. Louis Medical College during the years 1868, 1869 and 1870.

He began the practice of medicine in O'Fallon, St. Clair County, Illinois, and on June 18, 1871, married Josephine Clifton Lemen, daughter of James H. Lemen and Catherine Burn Lemen, nee Chilton, of Bethel, St. Clair County, at the Bethel Church.

In April, 1875, he moved to Collinsville, Madison County, Illinois, where he has continued to reside, building up a large and lucrative practice, as well as taking an active part in the affairs of that city and county. In politics he is an ardent Republican, and at various times has held the offices of Alderman, Mayor, Member and President of the Board of Education, and Trustee of the School District. The City Hall was built in 1885, during his term as Mayor, and largely through his instrumentality.

He has always taken an active interest in the advancement of his chosen profession, and was a member of the faculty of the Marion-Sims Medical College, of St. Louis, as Examining Physician on Physical Diagnosis during the session of 1891-92. In October, 1892, he entered the faculty of the Barnes' Medical College, of St. Louis, occupying the chair of Professor of Proctology, and has taken an active in-

531—DON M. LEMEN.   700—RALPH A. LEMEN.

terest in building up the college, both as a stock-holder and member of the faculty.

His family consists of one daughter, Olive, and three sons, James Louis, Charles Lay-Field, and Christopher Lorenzo.

550—DR. JAMES LOUIS OATMAN.

Dr. James L. Oatman was born at O'Fallon, Illinois, December 13, 1873. He graduated, as valedictorian, at Public High School, of Collinsville, in 1890. After finishing his public school education he entered Marion-Sims College of Medicine, City of St. Louis, and graduated from there in the year 1893. After leaving the medical college he was tendered the position of Assistant Physician to the City Hospital of St. Louis, Mo., which he accepted. After serving there one year he accepted a position as Assistant Physician to St. Louis Insane Asylum. After serving at the Insane Asylum for two years and six months, he was appointed Assistant Superintendent of the Female Hospital, City of St. Louis, by Dr. Max. Starkloff, Health Commissioner, which position he is at present filling.

551—DR. CHARLES LAY-FIELD OATMAN.

Dr. Chas. L. Oatman was born at Collinsville, Illinois, November 22, 1875. Attending the Collinsville Public High School to within one year of graduating, he was sent to Schurtleff College, of Upper Alton, Illinois, to complete his primary studies. After completing his primary education at Shurtleff he attended Hayward's Business College, of St. Louis, Mo., for one year. Chas. L. entered Barnes' Medical College in the fall of 1893, graduating in the spring of 1896. After graduating, he was appointed Assistant Physician to the Female Hospital, which position he held until the summer of 1897, when he gave up his position to go into business with his father, Chas. R. Oatman, of Collinsville, Ill.

552—DR. CHRISTOPHER LORENZO OATMAN.

Dr. Christopher L. Oatman was born at Collinsville, graduating in the spring of 1894, as valedictorian. In the year 1896 he began the study of medicine, matriculating at Barnes' Medical College, St. Louis, Mo., where he is at present attending, being in his junior year. After completing his studies in medicine he intends taking up the study of dentistry.

538—MRS. KATIE B. SEAMAN.

Mrs. Katie B. Seaman, nee Bostick, was born near Collinsville, Illinois, August 24, 1876. In November of the same year her parents moved with her to Holden, Missouri, where she received a good com-

209—MRS. SARAH LEMEN.

mon school education. Mrs. Seaman is the fourth
daughter of A. J. and E. F. Bostick.

1050—JONATHAN SEAMAN.

Mr. Jonathan Seaman was born in Lebanon,
Illinois, August 22, 1867. His parents moved from
Lebanon to Greenville while he was quite young,
August, 1879; he received his education at Greenville, Illinois, where he resided with his parents until
1892, when they moved to Loveland, Colorado. At
Loveland Mr. Seaman, associated with his father,
engaged in the dry goods and clothing business, with
good success.

Mr. Seaman was united in marriage to Miss Katie
Bostick, of Holden, Missouri, June 19, 1895.

933—MRS. HULDA BETTEX.

Mrs. Hulda Bettex, nee Haeberle, was the third
child of Rev. Louis F. Haeberle and Flora, nee
Bock, his wife. She was born in St. Louis, Mo.,
March 23, 1870. She was a quick and faithful
student, graduating from Lindenwood College in 1888.
After her graduation she went abroad with her parents for several months. In 1892 she was married
to Rev. Edward F. Bettex, a former resident of
Stuttgart Wurthem, Germany. Her husband was

born in Ludwigsburg, Wurthem, in 1865. He was educated principally in Germany, taking a theological course at the Eden Theological College, near St. Louis, in this country. After completing his theological course he was ordained as a German Evangelical minister. As minister and wife they first labored in Nebraska, then successively in Ohio and Kentucky, and now in St. Louis, having charge of the same parish where Rev. Haeberle, Mrs. Bettex' father labored for almost seventeen years. Mrs. Bettex' family is prominent in professional circles; and she is a highly educated and kind and sympathetic lady, being a great support to her husband in his work among his parishioners. The issue of this union is a lovely little girl, five years old, and an infant son, born in 1896.

59—GIDEON SCANLAND LEMEN.

Gideon S. Lemen was born March 18, 1827, and died December 6, 1889. He was a son of Robert, who was a son of James, Sr. Mr. Lemen was married to Miss Susan McMahan in early manhood, and one son, Thomas, was born to them, who died in infancy. Mrs. Lemen survived the son only a short time. January 23, 1851, he married Miss Sarah Begole, daughter of Joshua and Mary Begole, Rev. W. F. Boyakin officiating. Of this union two sons, Joshua and Frank Begole, and one daughter, Mary Laurene, were born.

699—LYDIA A. LEMEN.

702—EDITH E. LEMEN.

At the time of Mr. Lemen's marriage to Miss Begole he was living with his father, who had promised that if he would stay with, and take care of him in old age that he would heir the homestead. He lived with his father about one year after his second marriage, when his father, for some unknown reason, changed his mind, and Mr. Lemen and his wife had to find another home. They bought eighty acres of land in Madison County, Illinois, about two and a half miles east of Collinsville, to which, by strict economy and unceasing energy and great industry, they added to until they acquired over 200 acres of valuable land, with comforts and conveniences to make a pleasant and desirable home.

Mr. Lemen professed faith in Christ early in life and united with the Bethel Baptist Church, where he retained his membership until his death. He lived an active, earnest and consistent Christian life. Rev. W. R. Andereck wrote of him as follows: "During all my pastorate of nearly nine years, I found him a true friend and wise counselor. He was truly one of the pillars of the church, and almost invariably at his post. The pastor had in him a loyal helper in every good work. Many words of encouragement have I received from him. In his hospitable home the preacher was always sure of a glad welcome." Mr. Lemen acquired, in the pioneer schools of his youth, the elements of a good common school education, and this, supplemented by useful reading in later life, made him a man of large and practical information.

He was a cheerful giver to the cause of Christ, dealing of his goods with a liberal hand to the poor; conscientious in the discharge of all public and private duties, he left behind a precious memory and bright example for younger members of the church and community. A visit to his happy home, rendered doubly pleasant by the cheerful piety which pervaded it, was a refreshment to mind and body. He served Old Bethel in various divisions of church work, and for many years prior to his death acted as her treasurer.

209—MRS. SARAH LEMEN.

Mrs. Sarah Lemen, nee Begole, was born in St. Clair County, Illinois, October 24, 1826. She was united in marriage with Gideon S. Lemen, of St. Clair County, Illinois, January 23, 1851. Of this union there were born three children, Joshua, Franklin B. and Mary Laurene. Mrs. Sarah Lemen professed a hope in Christ, and was baptized February, 1841. She united with the Bethel Baptist Church, where she labored faithfully for fifty-six years—over a half century—for the Master, living an earnest and devoted Christian life. She was a kind, loving and self-sacrificing wife and mother. She was an obliging neighbor, sympathizing with and helping those who suffered affliction. She was helpful and encouraging to those starting in life, and ever ready to lend a

701—AMOS W. LEMEN.

helping hand to the needy. She fell asleep in Jesus, Thursday morning, March 18, 1897, being seventy years, four months and twenty-four days old.

> " We miss thee from our home, mother,
>   We miss thee from thy place;
> A shadow o'er our life is cast,
>   We miss the sunshine of thy face.
>
> We miss thy kind and willing hand,
>   Thy fond and earnest care;
> Our home is dark without thee,
>   We miss thee everywhere."

Mrs. Lemen was of a large and respected family, being a daughter of Joshua and Mary Begole. One sister, Cynthia C., and two brothers, Franklin and Francis, also married into the Lemen family. The Begole family are of French descent, emigrating from France during the close of the seventeenth century. They were Huguenots, and were expelled from the realm as a result of the revocation of the celebrated edict of Nantes about the year 1685, whence they settled in America.

211—FRANK B. LEMEN.

Frank B. Lemen, a farmer and stock breeder, was born December 11, 1853, near Collinsville, Ill., where he still resides on his paternal estate. His father was Gideon S. Lemen, son of Robert, son of James, Sr., and his mother was Sarah Lemen, nee

Begole, daughter of Squire Joshua Begole, of St. Clair
County, Illinois.   Mr. Lemen's school education
ended with a high school course at Collinsville, Ill.,
where, during the last year, he assisted the principal
in school work.   Poor health deprived him of a collegiate course.   However, his education did not end
with his school days, but he is still a close and persistent reader, and has collected a well-chosen library.
He has contributed largely to the press, and his
articles, especially those on swine and poultry, have
done much to encourage better breeding.   Mr. Lemen
has belonged for years to the Illinois Association of
Expert Judges of Swine, from which association he
holds a certificate of expert judging.

He professed faith in Christ when twelve years of
age, and has ever since been earnest and devout in
his services for the Master, giving largely of his time
and means for the advancement of religion.   He has
superintended a Sunday-school at Bethel for about
twenty years, and has been deacon and financial secretary of that historic church for years.   He has a
thorough knowledge of both vocal and instrumental
music; he teaches both and has assisted with the
music at Bethel for twenty-five years.

On December 29, 1875, Mr. Lemen was united in
marriage with Miss Lydia A. Coleman, of Ridge
Prairie, Ill.   Mrs. Lydia Lemen (699) is the eldest
daughter of Richard E. and Lucy Coleman, she was
born in Randolph County, Illinois, September 7, 1855.
At the age of seven years she was brought by her

703—CLEDA L. LEMEN.

parents to St. Clair County, Illinois, where she resided until her marriage to Mr. Lemen. Mrs. Lemen received a good common school education. At the age of eighteen she professed a hope in Christ, and would have united with the Bethel Baptist Church, as she had strong convictions that the ordinance of baptism should be observed by immersion in order to a full compliance with the command of Christ. Her parents were of the Methodist persuasion and objected to her uniting with the Baptists, the result was that she delayed joining a church until after her marriage, when she united with the Bethel Baptist Church. She has been a faithful, consistent Christian, sympathetic, earnest and enthusiastic in all her church relations; she is a faithful worker in the Sabbath-school, always found at her post, with words of cheer and encouragement.

Of this union there have been born four children —two boys and two girls—of these the boys are both older than the girls, Ralph A. being the firstborn, and Amos W. the second in order, they have a good common school education, and both have taken instruction in music; Ralph is proficient on several kinds of instruments, while Amos is not as much inclined toward music. The daughters, Edith E., the older, and Cleda L. are yet in school; both are apt scholars and well advanced for their ages. Edith is under the tutorage of Prof. F. Pesold, professor of music, McKendree College, Lebanon, Ill.

212—MRS. MARY LAURENE HADLEY.

Mary Laurene Hadley, nee Lemen, was the youngest child of Gideon S. and Sarah Lemen. She was born July 21, 1855, and died July 30, 1887. She was married to Mr. Charles C. Hadley, February 21, 1883. Of this union one child was born—Gideon Clifton, April 28, 1884.

In her tenth year Mrs. Hadley professed faith in Christ, and became a member of Bethel Baptist Church. She was baptized by Elder Deppe, who was then pastor of the church. It is certainly a comfortable reflection to know that more than two-thirds of her short life was spent in the service of the Master, and that she adorned the Christian profession, all who knew her intimately will gladly testify. There were none more faithful and devoted than she to the church in its services and various departments of Christian labor. She was always found at her post ready to speak and work in the Master's service. She lived a consistent Christian, and died in the faith. Up to the time of her death she was actively engaged in Christian work as organist and teacher in the Sabbath-school.

208—PROF. CLARENCE JOSIAH LEMEN.

The subject of this sketch was the only child of the marriage of Josiah Lemen, son of Robert Lemen,

208—PROF. CLARENCE J. LEMEN.

Sr., son of James Lemen, Sr., the original Lemen, who immigrated to Illinois from Virginia just after the Revolutionary War; to Mary Laurene Gay, daughter of Eliza H. Gay, who was a daughter of Levi Lawrence, descendant of Henry Lawrence, who emigrated from Wisset, England in 1635 to Charlestown, Mass. Henry Lawrence was a direct descendant of one Robert Lawrence of Lancashire, England, who attended Richard Coeur de Lion in his crusade to the Holy Land. He was knighted for bravery at the siege of Acre, and was known as Sir Robert of Ashton.

C. J. Lemen was born in Madison County, Illinois, within a mile of Collinsville in a log house, then situated · on what is now known as the D. D. Collins farm. His father died in his infancy and he was reared in the family of his grandmother on his mother's side, who had married Mathew Rippey, a lumber merchant of St. Louis. His education was acquired in the public schools of that city, entering the High School in his fourteenth year. He taught school a couple of years before the war, and while studying law in Burlington, Ia., enlisted in Company G, Twenty-fifth Iowa, as a private. His first service was in and around Vicksburg during the winter of '62 and '63. Was in the first attack on Haynes' Bluff, and also at the taking of Arkansas Post and the surrender of Vicksburg, after which event the army returned to Memphis and marched overland to the relief of Rosencrans at Chattanooga, getting there in time to take part in Hooker's battle among the clouds and the battle of Missionary Ridge.

He was all through the Atlanta campaign and marched with Sherman to the sea. At Beaufort, S. C., he was left with Fifteenth Army Corps headquarters, and about the close of the war accepted a commission as First Lieutenant and Adjutant of the One Hundred and Twenty-eighth U. S. C. T., Colonel, afterwards Brigadier-General, C. C. Howard, commanding, after eighteen months service his regiment being disbanded. He was honorably discharged from the service and returned to his home in St. Louis, having spent over four years in the service of his country. Since that time his energies have been mostly devoted to teaching, wherein he has attained a reasonable degree of success, having been superintendent and principal of schools in the southern part of the State of Illinois, and for about fifteen years has been known to the educational fraternity over the State. In 1886 he moved to Kentucky and was principal of Union Academy at Morganfield, Ky., and in conducting a private school has spent his time making for himself and family a good living and using his best endeavors to make out of his pupils good men and women. His pupils are scattered all over the country and bear witness to his thorough training.

He has written considerably for various publications, and is considered a good descriptive writer, he has at various times delivered before the G. A. R., of which he is a charter member of M. K. Lawler

Post, Shawneetown, Ill., their memorial address on Decoration Day. He is a member of the Presbyterian Church.

He was married to Sarah Catherine Smith April 2, 1868, who died January 30, 1890, and is buried at Morganfield, Ky. They had born to them three children: Mary L., Mabel C. and Wm. C. S. Lemen.

His forefathers on both his father's and mother's side took honorable part in the Revolutionary War, of which fact due chronicle has been made in his family history (addenda).

GENEALOGICAL.

CHAPTER XIV.

FIRST GENERATION.

In gathering data for these tables we found that the Lemen name is spelled in several ways, brothers, in some instances, spelling it differently. In order to systematize the work we have adopted the method that is followed by the largest number of the connection. The name is variously spelled as follows: Lemen, Lemon, Leman, Lehman and Leaman.

1—**ROBERT LEMEN**. Born in Scotland. Ship carpenter.
2—**WILLIAM LEMEN**. Born in Scotland.
3—**JAMES**. Born in Scotland.
6—**THREE SISTERS**. Born in Scotland.

SECOND GENERATION.

1—ROBERT LEMEN.

7—MARY ANDERSON. Born in Scotland. After marriage they emigrated from Scotland and settled in North Ireland, 1656. There were children of this union, two of whom we have been able to trace. They are:

8—Nicholas. Born in Ireland; was one of the older children, and was a ship builder and navigator. He died 1728.

9—Thomas. Born in Ireland. Was the younger son.

THIRD GENERATION.

8—NICHOLAS LEMEN.

10—NANCY McKANE. Born in Scotland. They were married, 1685. They had four sons and three daughters Three of the sons immigrated to America in the year 1708. All three were mariners and ship builders, and were:

11—James. Born in Ireland.

12—Robert. Born in Ireland.

13—Nicholas. Born in Ireland.

16—Three Daughters.

FOURTH GENERATION.

11—JAMES LEMEN.

17—JANE BURNS   Born in Virginia. They were married, 1714. Their children were:

18—John. Born in Virginia, June 4, 1715. Died 1776.

19—Robert. Born in Virginia, August 3, 1716.

20—Nicholas. Born in Virginia 1725.

21—Thomas. Born on the sea, June 20, 1730.

23—Two Daughters.

28—Five children who died in early life.

FIFTH GENERATION.

20—NICHOLAS LEMEN.

29—CHRISTIAN ————. They were married in Virginia in 1747. Their children were all born in Virginia, and were:

30—John. Born December 14, 1749.

31—Robert. Born November 6, 1750.

32—Nancy. Born March 4, 1754.

33—Mary. Born January 7, 1756.

34—Thomas. Born February 4, 1758.

35—James. Born November 20, 1760. Died January 8, 1823.

SIXTH GENERATION.

35—JAMES LEMEN.
36—CATHARINE OGLE. Born in Virginia.
They were married, 1782. Their children
were:

37—Robert. Born in Berkley County, Virginia,
September 25, 1783. Died August 24, 1860.
Weaver and farmer.

38—Joseph. Born in Berkley County, Virginia,
September 8, 1785. Died June 28, 1861. Baptist minister.

39—James. Born at New Design, Ill., October 8,
1787. Died February 8, 1870. Baptist minister.

40—Nancy. Born at New Design, Ill., 1789.

41—William. Born at New Design, Ill., May 3,
1793. Died November 2, 1858. Baptist Minister.

42—Josiah. Born at New Design, Ill., August 15,
1794. Died July 10, 1867. Baptist minister.

43—Catharine. Born at New Design, Ill., 1795.

44—Moses. Born at New Design, Ill., 1797.
Baptist minister.

37—ROBERT LEMEN.
45—HESTER TOLIN. Born January 4, 1789.
They were married July 2, 1805. Their chil-

dren were all born in St. Clair County, Illinois, and were:

46—Milton. Born April 1, 1806. Died August 29, 1828. Farmer.

47—James H. Born April 20, 1807. Died September 12, 1872. Farmer.

48—Catharine. Born November 28, 1808. Died November 4, 1878.

49—John Tolin. Born January 28, 1810. Died December 23, 1875. Farmer and mine operator.

50—Joseph. Born October 12, 1811. Farmer.

51—Emma. Born January 22, 1813.

52—Isaac. Born February 2, 1815. Died January 31, 1874. Farmer.

53—Miriam. Born January 23, 1817. Died June 30, 1840.

54—Robert. Born May 12, 1818. Died May 24, 1818.

55—Hester. Born July 7, 1819. Died ——.

56—Moses. Born June 8, 1821. Died January 11, 1840.

57—Josiah. Born January 23, 1823. Died August 30, 1844. Farmer.

58—William. Born January 6, 1825. Died June 11, 1844. Farmer.

59—Gideon. Born March 18, 1827. Died December 6, 1889. Farmer.

60—Rachel. Born December 29, 1830. Died August 7, 1840.

38—JOSEPH LEMEN.

61—**MARY KINNEY.** Born November 24, 1792. Died June 1, 1863. They were married, 1809. Their children were all born in St. Clair County, Illinois, and were:

62—Sarah. Born November 2, 1809. Died October 28, 1846.

63—James. Born November 29, 1811. Died November 4, 1884. Stock trader.

64—Benjamin. Born September 28, 1813. Died May 10, 1865. Merchant and gold miner.

65—Joseph. Born January 25, 1817. Died 1895. Farmer.

66—Isaac W. Born January 26, 1819. Died May 6, 1895. Farmer and trader.

67—Polly. Born January 1, 1821. Died March 8, 1873.

68—Robert C. Born January 20, 1823. Died February 21, 1892. Farmer.

69—Eliza L. Born May 18, 1825.

70—William K. Born October 3, 1828. Died October 6, 1897. Farmer.

39—JAMES LEMEN.

71—**MARY PULLIAM.** Born in Richmond, Va., April 27, 1794. Died February 23, 1876. They were married December 8, 1813. Their children were all born in Ridge Prairie, Ill., and were:

72—Lucinda. Born December 25, 1814. Died August 25, 1867.

73—Sylvester. Born November 5, 1816. Died September 28, 1872. Farmer.

74—Catharine. Born November 26, 1818. Died March 3, 1860.

75—Nancy. Born May 7, 1821. Died August 20, 1854.

76—Jacob O. Born November 23. 1823. Died January 9, 1870. Farmer and merchant, Hastings, Minn.

77—John C. Born February 24, 1826. Died October 14, 1844. Farmer, Collinsville, Ill.

78—James P. Born September 16, 1828. Farmer and merchant. Hastings, Minn.

79—Robert S. Born December 16, 1830. Merchant, Cairo, Ill.

80—Mary E. Born January 31, 1833. 1155 Downing Avenue, Denver, Colo.

81—Joseph B. Born August 6, 1836. Farmer, Collinsville, Ill.

82—Moses P. Born October 6, 1838. Died May 17, 1870. Physician, Du Quoin, Ill.

_____

40—NANCY LEMEN.

83—JOHN TOLIN. Born at New Design, Ill. Their children were all born at New Design, Ill., and were:

84—Sally.

85—Elizabeth.

86—Charles.

87—Luster.

88—Susan.

89—Brocket.

90—Emeline.

91—James.

41—WILLIAM LEMEN.

92—POLLY MILLER. Born on the South Branch of the Potomac, in Virginia, December 11, 1793. Married October 10, 1810 Their children were all born in Monroe County, Illinois, they were:

93—Susan. Born July 4, 1811. Died January 26, 1884.

94—Delilah. Born at New Design, Ill., September 2, 1813.

95—Katy. Born at New Design, Ill., November 24, 1815. Died September 10, 1816.

96—Polly. Born September 4, 1817. Died March 1, 1895.

97—Adaline. Lived twelve years.

98—Elizabeth.

99—Lemuel. Died in infancy.

100—William. Born April 1, 1829. Died May 5, 1868.

101—Lloyd. Born October 12, 1832. Died June 27, 1871.

42—JOSIAH LEMEN.

102—REBEKAH HUFF. Born at Red Stone, Old Fort, October 15, 1795. Died March 26, 1858. They were married August 31, 1815. Their children were:

103—John Lewis. Born at New Design, Ill., June 23, 1816. Died February 1, 1861. Politician.

104—Elizabeth. Born March 11, 1818. Died January 13, 1844.

105—James Clark. Born February 3, 1820. Died November 11, 1821.

106—Robert. Born February 11, 1822. Died October 3, 1822.

107—Noah. Born October 27, 1823. Died March 8, 1844.

108—Catharine. Born November 21, 1825. Died April 28, 1862.

109—Harvey S. Born October 23, 1827. Lincoln, Neb.

110—Josiah D. Born May 19, 1830. Died September 27, 1875.

111—Jemima. Born November 18, 1833. Died March 13, 1859.

112—Sidney. Born February 20, 1836. Died March 14, 1836.

43—CATHARINE LEMEN.

113—JOSEPH KINNEY. Born in Ridge Prairie, Ill., October 15, 1779. Died January 31, 1846.

They were married March 2, 1817. Their children were:

114—Samuel. Born at New Design, Ill., March 3, 1818. Farmer.

115—John Clark. Born at New Design, Ill., September 28, 1820. Died May 22, 1864. Farmer.

116—James L. Born at New Design, Ill., December 29, 1823. Died March 11, 1886. Farmer.

117—William. Born at New Design, Ill., March 6, 1826, Died March 8, 1898. Farmer.

118—Mary. Born at New Design, Ill., February 10, 1832. Died July 15, 1879.

119—Julia. Born at New Design, Ill., 1836. Died February 13, 1856.

120—Maria L. Born at New Design, Ill., January 30, 1838. Died December 5, 1893.

121—Catharine. Born at New Design, Ill.

44—MOSES LEMEN.

122—SALLY HULL. They were married February 24, 1817. Their children were:

123—Hull. Born in Monroe County, Illinois, January 13, 1818. Died October, 1892. Baptist minister.

124—Lewese. Born at New Design, Ill., September, 1820. Died September, 1887.

125—Amira. Born at New Design, Ill., January 17, 1823. Died June 12, 1894.

44—MOSES LEMEN.

126—SARAH ANN VARNUM. Born at Belfast, Me.,
August 16, 1804. Died December 11, 1880.
Weaver. They were married February 14,
1825. Their children were:

127—Caroline. Born at New Design, Ill., 1825.
Died 1833.

128—Sally. Born at New Design, Ill., 1827. Died
in 1827.

129—Byron. Born in Monroe County, Illinois, November 5, 1829. Died May, 1861. Carpenter.

130—Laura Ann. Born at New Design, Ill., December, 1831. Died August, 1832.

131—Moses F., Jr. Born at New Design, Ill., January, 1834. Died June, 1855. Farmer.

132—Judson. Born at Kane, Ill., September, 1836.
Died September, 1867. Carpenter.

133—James N. Born at Kane, Ill., August, 1838.
Died July 1, 1863. Farmer.

134—Sarah Ann. Born at Kane, Ill., April 14,
1840. Black Rock, Ark.

135—Mary C. Born at Kane, Ill., October 11,
1843. Eureka, Kan.

SEVENTH GENERATION.

47—JAMES H. LEMEN.

136—CATHARINE B. CHILTON. Born at Lebanon, Ill., June 2, 1809. Died September 19, 1878. They were married May 15, 1828. Their children were all born in Ridge Prairie, Ill., and were:

137—Elizabeth. Born February 22, 1829. Died September, 1893.

138—Caroline. Born November 3, 1831. Died December 14, 1834.

139—Infant. Born May 11, 1833. Died June 22, 1833.

140—Infant. Born April 20, 1834. Died April 1834.

141—Mary Ann. Born May 29, 1835, Died September 12, 1864.

142—Hester Jane. Born July 12, 1837. Died December 21, 1858.

143—Catharine. Born May 21, 1839. Died August 22, 1840.

144—Cyrus Augustus. Born June 22, 1841. Died March, 1894. Farmer and soldier.

145—Emily F. Born February 19, 1844.

146—Adaline. Born August 22, 1846.

147—Josephine Clifton. Born July 7, 1849.

148—Henry Clay. Born January 8, 1851. Died June 24, 1853.

48—CATHARINE LEMEN.

149—JOHN GARETSON. Born in Monroe County, Illinois, 1800. Died 1829. Farmer. They were married in 1825. Their children were:

150—James L. Born in Monroe County, Illinois, March 19, 1826. Died May 1, 1845. Farmer and merchant. Poplar Bluff, Mo.

151—Eliza. Born in St. Clair County, Illinois, September 4, 1827.

48—CATHARINE GARETSON, nee LEMEN.

152—WILLIAM BERRY McKINLEY. Born in Monroe County, Kentucky, July 12, 1804. Died September 21, 1864. Farmer. Dixon, California. Their children were:

153—George C. Born in Madison County, Illinois, July 2, 1832. Died July 4, 1892.

154—Hester. Born in Madison County, Illinois, April 19, 1834.

155—Agnes. Born at Alton, Ill., November 7, 1837. Deceased.

156—Ann. Born in Buchanan County, Missouri, July 17, 1842. Deceased.

157—Robert L. Born at Clinton, Mo., May 22, 1844.

158—Catharine. Born in Calhoun County, Texas, December 21, 1848. Deceased.

49—JOHN TOLIN LEMEN.

159—PATIENCE WILDERMAN. Born near Belleville, Ill., October 14, 1814. They were married August 30, 1832. Their children were:

160—George C. Born in St. Clair County, Illinois, December 13, 1833. Died October 30, 1857. Farmer.

161—Robert W. Born in St. Clair County, Illinois, November 15, 1835. Farmer and coal operator. Freeburg, Ill.

50—JOSEPH LEMEN.

162—CAROLINE M. MORNEY. Born near Belleville, Ill., October 7, 1821. They were married 1840. Their children were:

163—Virginia. Born in St. Clair County, Illinois, November 25, 1840. Died May 22, 1875.

164—Miriam. Born in Madison County, Illinois, September 14, 1842.

165—Nancy.

166—Infant.

167—Guy M.

168—Albert.

169—Katherine.

170—Elanor N. Born September 27, 1855.

51—EMMA LEMEN.

171—JOSEPH BEEDLE. Born July 29, 1808. They were married January 24, 1831. Their children were:

172—Fransis. Born December 12, 1831. Died April 25, 1865.

173—Catharine. Born January 31, 1834. Died
January 12, 1896.

174—Hester. Born March 30, 1836.

175—James. Born September 20, 1838.

176—Sarah. Born October 12, 1841.

177—Rebecca. Born January 22, 1844.

178—Amanda. Born May 7, 1846.

52—ISAAC LEMEN.

179—CAROLINE E. HOGAN. Born in St. Clair
County, Illinois, November 2, 1821. They
were married January 19, 1842. Their children were:

180—Edwin H. Born November 9, 1844. Died
May 14, 1888. Lawyer. Pinckneyville, Ill.

181—Hester A. Born March 14, 1847. Died June
26, 1849.

182—Frederick. Born January 15, 1849. Farmer.
Collinsville, Ill.

183—Clara S. Born December 21, 1851. O'Fallon, Ill.

184—Oscar. Born March 27, 1854. Farmer. Collinsville, Ill.

185—Lillie H. Born May 29, 1856. School-
teacher, Ewing, Ill.

186—Fanny. Born April 24, 1859. Died July 29,
1859.

53—MIRIAM LEMEN.

187—JOHN PRICE. Born in Garrard County, Kentucky, February 21, 1807. Died November

19, 1893. Farmer. They were married 1835.
Their children were:

188—Edwin. Born near Jefferson City, Mo., December 13, 1836.

189—Hulda. Born in Coles County, Missouri,
October 19, 1838.

190—Robert. Born in Johnson County, Missouri,
June 29, 1840.

55—HESTER LEMEN.

191—**BENJAMIN F. BOWLER.** Born October 10,
1817. They were married January 12, 1837,
by the Rev. James Lemen, Jr. Their children were all born in St. Clair County, Illinois, and were:

192—George W. Born January 8, 1838. Farmer.
Collinsville, Ill.

193—John L. Born January 26, 1839.

194—Nancy. Born December 6, 1840.

195—Ellen. Born December 14, 1842.

196—Robert L. Born October 17, 1844.

197—Peter A. Born October 20, 1845.

198—Harriet E. Born August 30, 1847.

199—Hester Ann. Born October 13, 1849.

200—Susan. Born June 8, 1850.

201—Mary E. Born February 28, 1852.

202—Adelaide. Born December 28, 1853.

203—B. Franklin. Born April 28, 1855.

204—James B. Born October 17, 1856.

205—Julia. Born May 12, 1858.

206—Infant Daughter. Born March 24, 1861.

57—JOSIAH LEMEN.

207—**MARY LAURENE GAY.** Born in Madison County, Illinois, October 7, 1825. They were married March 21, 1842. They had one child:

208—Clarence Josiah. Born in Madison County, Illinois, January 9, 1843. School teacher. Morganfield, Ky.

59—GIDEON LEMEN.

209—**SARAH BEGOLE.** Born in St. Clair County, Illinois, October 24, 1826. Died March 18, 1897. They were married January 23, 1851. Their children were all born in Madison County, Illinois, and were:

210—Joshua Robert. Born January 28, 1852. Died September 28, 1853.

211—Franklin Begole. Born December 11, 1853. Farmer and stock breeder. Collinsville, Ill.

212—Mary Laurene. Born July 21, 1855. Died July 30, 1887. Grocery and dry goods merchant.

62—SARAH LEMEN.

213—**RICHARD G. MURPHY.** Born in Smith County, Tennessee, January 4, 1801. Farmer and ten years a legislator. They were married in 1834. Their children were:

214—William K. Born July 20, 1835.

215—Mary A. Born June 8, 1837.

216—Joseph L. Born December 30, 1838.

217—Benton P. Born April 12, 1841.

218—Geo. W. Born May 19, 1843.

63—JAMES LEMEN.

219—ROXANA KINGSTON. Born January 1, 1822. Died May 10, 1887. They were married June 17, 1847. Their children were:

220—Maria E. Born in Madison County, Illinois, June 26, 1848. Cairo, Ill.

221—Catharine. Born April 16, 1850. 519 N. Spring Avenue, St. Louis, Mo.

222—Ida Roxana. Born December 5, 1853. St. Louis, Mo.

223—William C. Born July 19, 1855. St. Louis, Mo.

224—Joseph E. Born February 27, 1858.

225—Olive M. Born March 13, 1861. Died March 24, 1864.

226—Nellie E. Born June 2, 1867.

64—BENJAMIN F. LEMEN.

227—MARY PUTNAM RAND. Born at Lake Champlain, N. Y., May 27, 1811. Died January 12, 1892. School teacher. They were married April 28, 1842. Their children were;

228—Ella K. Born at Salem, Ill., April 8, 1843. Temperance lecturer. Vincennes, Ind.

229—Putnam. Born at Salem, Ill., July 19, 1845. Died September 13, 1847.

230—Joseph Goff. Born at Salem, Ill., February 20, 1848. Baptist minister and manager of the Christian Home, Council Bluffs, Ia.

231—Lydia Gertrude. Born at Salem, Ill., January 3, 1851. Public speaker. Neosho, Mo.

65—JOSEPH LEMEN.

232—NANCY JACKSON. They had one child.

233—George.

66—ISAAC W. LEMEN.

234—LOUISE SHOOK. Born in St. Clair County, Illinois, 1820. Died March 27, 1853. They were married December 27, 1846. Their children were:

235—Catherine Fredonia. Born in St. Clair County, Illinois, June 12, 1848.

236—James. Born in St. Clair County, Illinois, June 8, 1852. Died 1857.

66—ISAAC W. LEMEN.

237—CAROLINE S. KINGSTON. Born near Lebanon, Ill., October 15, 1828. They were married June 5, 1860. They had one child:

238—Julius D. Born in Madison County, Illinois, March 5, 1862. Farmer.

68—ROBERT C. LEMEN.

239—ELIZA JOHNSON. Born near Lebanon, Wilson County, Tenn., July 1, 1826. Removed to Waterloo, Ill. They were married March 12, 1849. Their children were:

240—Joseph Robert. Born in Madison County, Illinois, June 5, 1853. Physician, 3223 Lucas Avenue, St. Louis, Mo.

241—Olivia E. Born near Collinsville, Ill., January 6, 1856. Missionary. Safford, Ariz.

69—ELIZA LEMEN.

242—DAVID WILLOCK. Their children were:

243—William.

244—Mary.

245—James. Born in St. Clair County, Illinois, 1855.

70—WILLIAM K. LEMEN.

246—LIEUANN EDWARDS. Born at Troy, Ill., December 12, 1836. Died July 15, 1865. They were married March 27, 1856. Their children were all born in Ridge Prairie, and were:

347—John E. Born June 6, 1857. Farmer and stock breeder. Collinsville, Ill.

248—Sarah C. Born March 19, 1859. Died March 25, 1861.

249—Ella A. Born June 24, 1861. 4145 Cook Avenue, St. Louis, Mo.

250—Jessie. Born November 24, 1862. Died September 4, 1864.

70—WILLIAM LEMEN.

251—MARY A. EDWARDS. Born at Troy, Ill., October 30, 1841. They were married July 29, 1866. They had no children.

72—LUCINDA LEMEN.

252—SAMUEL BOWMAN. Captain Bowman fell mortally wounded while leading his company in battle against the Indians in the Black Hawk war. They were married in 1830. They had one child.

253—John C. Born in 1832.

72—LUCINDA LEMEN-BOWMAN.

254—JOHN A. COOK. Farmer. They were married April 18, 1836. Their children were:

255—James T. Born at Alton, Ill., February 10, 1837. Died August 23, 1839.

256—Cyrus L. Born at Alton, Ill., March 18, 1839. Died October 11, 1895. Attorney at law. Edwardsville, Ill. He graduated at Shurtliff College, 1862.

257—Joseph O. Born near Troy, Ill., January 15, 1841. Died December 17, 1845.

258—Minnie C. Born near Troy, Ill., September 8, 1842. Graduated at Almira College, June 20, 1862. Died August 14, 1862.

258½—Harriet. Born near Troy, Ill., March 20, 1844. Graduated at Almira College, Illinois, June 20, 1864. Died July 29, 1874.

259—Sarah P.—Born near Troy, Ill., March 18, 1847. She graduated at Almira College, Illinois, June 20, 1866.

260—Susan A. Born near Troy, Ill., October 25, 1848. Died July 6, 1849.

261—Isabella. Born near Troy, Ill., March 9, 1851. Died March 25, 1853.

262—Laura L. Born near Troy, Ill., August 29, 1853. Died March 10, 1885.

263—Robert. Born near Troy, Ill., July 24, 1855. Died September 26, 1855.

264—Infant Daughter. Born January 26, 1850.

265—Charles F. Born near Troy, Ill., September 21, 1857. Graduate of State University of Illinois, 1880. Edwardsville, Ill.

73—SYLVESTER LEMEN.

266—SUSAN SHOOK. Born in St. Clair County, Illinois, January 16, 1813. Died June 28, 1878. They were married March 16, 1838. Their children were all born in St. Clair County, Illinois, and were:

267—Harrison A. Born September 26, 1840. Physician, 1646 Grand Avenue, Denver, Colo.

268—Edward C. Born July 20, 1842. Physician, Upper Alton, Illinois.

269—Katherine. Born September 22, 1845.

270—Mary M. Born December 25, 1847. Died June 8, 1874.

271—Lewis E. Born April 1, 1849. Physician, 1605 Pennsylvania Avenue, Denver, Colo.

272—Lucy. Born January 7, 1851. Baptist.

273—Theodore A. Born July 10. 1853. Baptist Minister.

274—Sarah Ellen. Born June 11, 1855. Died February 29, 1868.

275—Charles T. Born August 12, 1857. Died January 12, 1859.

74—KATHERINE LEMEN.

276—JAMES B. LYON. Born in Kentucky May 11, 1811. They were married March 25, 1841. Their children were:

277—Mary M. Born in St. Clair County, Illinois, March 16, 1842. Died May 14, 1880.

278—James W. Born in St. Clair County, Illinois, January 10, 1845. Died September 24, 1870.

279—John T. Born in St. Clair County, Illinois, November 25, 1847. Died August 22, 1869.

280—Nancy Josephine. Born in St. Clair County, Illinois, August 27, 1855. Died February 28, 1853.

281—Lucy I. Born in St. Clair County, Illinois, August 6, 1853. Died August 26, 1854.

282—Louis Albert. Born in St. Clair County, Illinois, September 16, 1855. Milling and farming. Shorter, Ala.

75—NANCY LEMEN.

283—JESSE HART. They had two children.

284—Laura and Lewis.

76—JACOB O. LEMEN.

285—MARTHA A. LANCASTER. Born in St. Clair County, Illinois, September, 1824. Hastings, Minn. They were married April 2, 1845. Their children were:

286—Alice E. Born in St. Clair County, Illinois, April 11, 1847. 716 Lafayette Avenue, Brooklyn, N. Y.

287—Amelia N. Born in St. Clair County, Illinois, March 30, 1849. Died September 24, 1891.

288—Ninian E. Born in St. Clair County, Illinois, January 9, 1852. Died December, 1876. Editor.

289—Nancy Maria. Born August 7, 1854. Died January, 1857.

290—James Levi. Born November 4, 1856. Died June 11, 1867.

291—Catharine. Born March 3, 1860. Died March 15, 1860.

292—Charles Collins. Born in St. Clair County, Illinois, January 21, 1861. Telegraph Operator, Chicago Board of Trade.

293—William S. Born in Hastings, Minn., July 27, 1865. Artist, 51 Winthrop street, Brooklyn, N. Y.

78—JAMES P. LEMEN.

294—ELIZABETH B. BOWMAN. Born in Greene County, Illinois. They were married October 28, 1862. Their children were:

295—Christy S. Born at Hastings, Minn., September 11, 1863. Farmer.

296—Mary B. Born at Hastings, Minn., July 11, 1865.

79—ROBERT S. LEMEN.

297—SARAH M. LANCASTER. Born May 20, 1840. They were married at Hastings, Minn., 1864. Their children were:

298—Arthur S. Born January 6, 1865. Died August 29, 1896.

299—Lemuel Ernest. Born October 22, 1868. He is in the Medical Department of the University of Nashville, Tenn.

300—Robert Elmer E. Born January 7, 1885. Died March 19, 1885.

80—MARY E. LEMEN.

301—C. STEBBINS. Born in Cincinnati, O., April 30, 1825. Died December 21, 1878. Newspaper man for twenty-eight years. They were married November 2, 1858. Their children were:

302—Mary E. Born at Hastings, Minn., September 30, 1859. Died May 31, 1871.

303—Katie L. Born at Hastings, Minn., December 2, 1867. Died November 7, 1884.

304—Jessica M. Born at Hastings, Minn., January 30, 1874. Calculating Clerk in United States Mint, Denver, Colo.

81—JOSEPH B. LEMEN.

305—**NANCY C. SCOTT.** Born in Ridge Prairie, Ill., March 27, 1841. They were married November 23, 1864. They had one child:

306—Elmer Scott. Born in Ridge Prairie, Ill., August 31, 1865. Died January 17, 1868.

82—MOSES P. LEMEN.

307—**PHILURA JONES.** Born in St. Clair County, Illinois, May, 1844. Died January 31, 1876. They were married October 25, 1859. Their children were:

308—Jessie. Born in St. Clair County, Illinois, 1860 Died 1870.

309—Lenora. Born at Du Quoin, Illinois, October 2, 1866.

310—Charles P. Born at Du Quoin, Illinois, May 27, 1869. Died February 15, 1891.

84—SALLY TOLIN.

311—**JOSEPH W. HILTON.** Born in Maine, June 17, 1809. Died October 2, 1880. Farmer. They were married November 24, 1828. Their children were:

312—Lemuel. Born at New Design, Ill., March 20, 1831. Farmer, Livermore, Cal.

313—Gilbert. Born at New Design, Ill., December 17, 1832. Hotel clerk, Livermore, Cal.

314—Francis. Born at New Design, Ill., December 30, 1835. Died September 1852.

315—Sidney B. Born in New Design, Ill., November 4, 1837. Liveryman, Waterloo, Ill.

316—Martha. Born at New Design, Ill., March, 1842.

317—Eliza. Born at New Design, Ill., May 1, 1844.

318—Sylvester. Born at New Design, Ill., April 24, 1846. County officer, Chester, Ill.

319—Joseph. Born at New Design, Ill., August 14, 1848. Died August 9, 1862.

85—ELIZABETH TOLIN.

320—DANIEL HILTON.

Their children not known.

86—CHARLES TOLIN.

321—WEALTHY RADER. Their children were:

322—Hestran.

323—Harvey.

324—Rhoda.

325—Hazeltine.

326—Commodore.

327—John.

87—KUSTER TOLIN.

328—LOUISA BOLES.

Their children not known.

88—SUSAN TOLIN.
329—LOUIS BARKER. They were married in 1847.
Their children not known.

89—BRACKET TOLIN.
330—SARAH ROWEL. They were married in 1850.
Their children not known.

90—EMELINE TOLIN.
331—LOUIS BARKER. They were married in 1850.
Their children not known.

91—JAMES TOLIN.
332—LALLIE CAREY. Their children not known.

92—SUSAN LEMEN.
333—CLAYBORN MODGLIN. Their children were:
334—Lemuel.
335—Polly.
336—Rhoda.
337—Nancy.
338—Catharine.

93—SUSAN LEMEN.
339—WILLIAM FISHER. They had one child:
340—Isabel.

94—DELILAH LEMEN.
341—LLOYD BOSTWICK. Their children were:
342—Eliza.
343—James.

344—William.
345—Harriet E.
346—John.

96—POLLY K. LEMEN.
347—**GABRIEL S. JONES.** Born in Adair County, Ky., May 10, 1821. Blacksmith. They were married January 21, 1841. Their children were:
348—Harriet E. Born in Randolph County, Ill., April 6, 1842.
349—Catherine B. Born in Randolph County, Ill., March 15, 1844. Died February 1, 1848.
350—Mary E. Born in Randolph County, Ill., February 16, 1846.
351—Edward W. Born in Randolph County, Ill., July 27, 1848. Died September 2, 1856.
352—William F. Born in Randolph County, Ill., June 21, 1851. Died November 11, 1889.
353—Charley L. Born at Newton, Ill., April 26, 1854. Died April 16, 1872,
354—Fannie K. Born at Newton, Ill., February 11, 1857.
355—Lydia L. Born at Newton, Ill., December 18, 1859.

98—ELIZABETH LEMEN.
356—**JOHN C. BROWN.** Their children were:
357—Gabriel.
358—Mary E.

100—WILLIAM LEMEN.

359—**MARY C. SHELL.** Born July 31, 1828. Died December 21, 1894. They were married 1847. Their children were:

360—John B. Born June 25, 1848. Contractor and Builder. Canton, Mo.

361—Mary E. Born January 28, 1851.

362—James L. Born July 30, 1853. Died May 10, 1882.

363—William. Born 1856. Died 1862.

364—Dora. Died in infancy.

365—Robbie. Died in infancy.

366—Winnie. Died in infancy.

367—Martha. Died in infancy.

101—LLOYD LEMEN.

368—**DEMYRA WINTER,** nee Fisher. Born February 14, 1822. Died January 4, 1882. Baptist. They were married March 25, 1849. Their children were:

369—Leander. Born January 25, 1850. Stone Mason. Baptist.

370—James. Born December 22, 1852. Farmer. Baptist.

371—Amos.

372—Mary F. Born November 11, 1856. Baptist.

373—Eliza Jane. Born September 28, 1859. Christian.

374—Alonzo.

375—Laura B.

376—Lyman T. Born January 1, 1867. Farmer. Baptist.

103—JOHN L. LEMEN.

377—MARTHA C. JONES. Born at Georgetown, Ill., August 21, 1821. Died November 25, 1871. They were married June 3, 1841. Their children were:

378—Elizabeth R. Born at Benton, Ill., December 31, 1842.

379—Mary J. Born at New Design, Ill., October 23, 1845. Died July 26, 1847.

380—Noah. Born December 16, 1847. New Design, Ill. Farmer.

381—Emma. Born at New Design, Ill., March, 29, 1850.

382—John L. Born at New Design, Ill., November 7, 1852. Farmer. Pinckneyville, Ill.

383—Mattie. Born at Du Quoin, Ill., August 23, 1856. Died January 9, 1888.

104—ELIZABETH LEMEN.

384—ABRAHAM CLARK. Children not known.

108—CATHERINE LEMEN.

385—DR. FREDERICK B. BOCK. Born in Germany, May 19, 1809. Died November 26,

1884. Physician. Waterloo, Ill. They
were married 1840. Their children were:

386—Flora. Born in Monroe County, Ill., November 23, 1841. Eden Seminary, St. Louis,
Mo.

387—Philomena. Born in Monroe County, Ill.,
April, 1842.

388—Theresia. Born in Waterloo, Ill., June, 1844.

389—Armenius F. Born in Monroe County, Ill.,
October 19, 1846. Physician, 1107 N. Grand
Ave., St. Louis, Mo.

390—America. Born in Monroe County, Ill.,
December, 1847. Died 1882.

391—Cora. Born in Monroe County, Ill., February, 1850. Died 1880.

109—HARVEY S. LEMEN.

392—JANE M. BROWN. Born at Utica, Mich.,
September 17, 1840. They were married
July 12, 1860. Their children were:

393—Alice M. Born at Du Quoin, Ill., April 9,
1862.

394—Fred. Born at Du Quoin, Ill., January 5,
1864. Wall Paper Store, Grand Island, Neb.

395—Bessie. Born at Du Quoin, Ill., August 24,
1869.

110—JOSIAH D. LEMEN.

396—SUSAN A. BALES. Born in Illinois, February 8, 1834. Died December 7, 1863. They

were married October 16, 1851. Their children were;

397—Lewis. Born July 30, 1852. Died September 10, 1897. School Teacher.

398—Willliam. Born October 25, 1853. Farming and School Teaching. New Design, Ill.

399—Albert. Born April 11, 1856.

400—Henry. Born February 4, 1859. Died September 3, 1859.

401—Jennie. Born August 20, 1860.

402—Infant. Born August 7, 1862. Deceased.

403—Infant. Born November 27, 1863. Died December 3, 1863.

110—JOSIAH D. LEMEN.

404—BRIDGET A. REILLEY. Born near Harper's Ferry, Va., July 11, 1841. Died February 6, 1875. They were married September 8, 1864. Their children were:

405—Laura A. Born June 6, 1865.

406—Mary B. Born April 11, 1869.

407—James H. Born November 9, 1871.

408—Infant daughter. Born and died January 15, 1867.

111—JEMIMA LEMEN.

409—ALFERSON CARY. Born at New Design, Ill., July 18, 1828. Died July 27, 1895. Farmer. They were married October 1, 1850. They had no children.

114—SAMUEL KINNEY.
410—MARY CHANDLER.　Their children were:
411—Joe.
412—Mary.

114—SAMUEL KINNEY.
413—ANNA DENNIS.　They had no children.

115—JOHN C. KINNEY.
414—FRANCIS CAVANAUGH.　Their children were:
415—James H.
416—Emeline.

116—JAMES L. KINNEY.
417—EDITH ROW.　Their children were:
418—Covis.
419—Senator.
420—Brack.
421—Julia.
422—Minnie.
423—Lillie.
424—George.

117—WILLIAM KINNEY.
425—LUTE HARLOW.　Their children were:
426—Dealie.
427—Millard.
428—Don.

429—Catherine.
430—Eliza.
431—Louis.

117—WILLIAM KINNEY.
432—ELIZA MOFFITT. Their children were:
433—Lon.
434—Jessie.
435—Archie.
436—Nettie.

118—MARY KINNEY.
437—JOSEPH McMURTNEY. Their children were:
438—Loring.
439—William.
440—James.
441—Nellie.

119—JULIA KINNEY.
442—GID MAYCHILD. Their children were:
443—Claude.
444—May.

120—MARIA L. KINNEY.
445—TIMOTHY DENNISS SLATTERY. Born in Lansing, N. Y., July 16, 1832. They were married January 28, 1856. Their children were all born at Harrisonville, Ill.
446—Julia Ellen. Born December 13, 1857. 1213 Grand Ave., East St. Louis, Ill

447—Joseph E. Born December 23, 1859. Fireman, East St. Louis, Ill.

448—Catherine. Born April 1, 1861. Died August 26, 1861.

449—William. Born October 16, 1862. Died October 17, 1862.

450—James. Born January 7, 1864. Died January 14, 1864,

451—Charles A. Born January 19, 1867. R. R. Conductor, East St. Louis, Ill.

452—Annie May. Born June 9, 1869. Died December 5, 1893.

453—Mary M. Born February 21, 1872. Schoolteacher, East St. Louis, Ill.

454—Clara F. Born September 17, 1874.

121—CATHERINE KINNEY.
455—JOHN SHIPLEY. Their children were:
456—James.
457—Orlando.
458—Maria.
459—Clara.
460—Louis.
461—Elick.
462—John.
463—Nettie.

123—HULL LEMEN.
464—MARTHA TOMKINS. Their children were:
465—James R.

466—Moses.
467—Laura A.
468—Irene.
469—Myron.
470—Hull Jr.
471—Hannah S.

123—HULL LEMEN.
472—FANNIE GOLDSMITH. Their children were:
473—Frederick.
474—Lilly.
475—Cora.

124—LEWESE LEMEN.
476—BENJAMIN M. KING. Their children were:
477—Susan E.
478—Frances H.
479—Edward R.

124—LEWESE KING, nee LEMEN.
480—IRVIN CARY. Their children were;
481—Lemen.
482—Myron.

125—AMIRA LEMEN.
483—CAPTAIN LUCIAN KING. Born near Syracuse, N. Y., June 11, 1817. Died June 6, 1879. Captain in the war of the Rebellion. Farmer

Kane, Ill. They were married January 14, 1841. Their children were all born near Kane, Ill., and were:

484—Harriet. Born July 4, 1842. Died August 9, 1888.

485—Frederick. Born March 20, 1845. Died November 30, 1846.

485—Maria L. Born November 29, 1847.

486—Sarah C. Born January 17, 1854. Died November 11, 1855.

487—Emma. Born January 22, 1857.

488—Adell. Born January 16, 1860.

489—Sudie. Born May 13, 1862. Died October 1, 1884.

127—BYRON LEMEN.
490—PRUDENCE INMAN. Their children were:
491—James W.
492—Clark.
493—Alva L.

131—MOSES F. LEMEN.
494—BERTHA AMES. They had one child:
495—Amira A.

132—JUDSON LEMEN.
496—FANNIE MURPHY. They had no children.

132—JUDSON LEMEN.

497—MARY DOSHIA EBERLINE. Born in Monroe County, Ill., December 10, 1837. They were married 1858. Their children were:

498—Chester F. Born at Lemen Mound, Walshville, Ill., April 28, 1860. Contractor and Builder, Litchfield, Ill.

499—Seigel. Born at Walshville, Ill., 1862. Died 1872.

500—Annie J. Born at Columbia, Kans., March 3, 1865. Salem, Ill.

501—Katie. Born in Montgomery County, Kans., March, 1866. Nokomis, Ill.

502—James.

503—Adonariam.

JAMES N. LEMEN.

504—MARY GASTON. Their children were

505—Myron.

506—James R.

134—SARAH ANN LEMEN.

507—JAMES H. KINGSTON. Born in Moro, Ill., January 15, 1838. Farmer, Black Rock, Ark. Married April 28, 1859. Their children were:

508—William F. Born at Walshville, Ill., July 29, 1860. Died April 11, 1895. Printer.

509—John Moses. Born at Walshville, Ill., January 24, 1862. Died September 15, 1877.

510—George E. Born at Columbia, Kans., July 20, 1872. Died November 21, 1872.

511—Maud. Born at Elk City, Kans., October 6, 1874. Died June 9, 1876.

135—MARY C. LEMEN.

512—WILLIAM T. DOUGHERTY. Born in Lawrence County, Ind., March 8, 1833. Died March, 17, 1870. Carpenter and Cabinetmaker. Married March 7, 1859. Their children were:

513—Wilmington. Born in Montgomery County, Ill., July 26, 1860. Died August 3, 1860.

514—Lemen. Born in Montgomery County, Ill., October 13, 1862. Printer, Eureka, Kans.

515—James U. Born in Montgomery County, Ill., April 5, 1865. Died December 21, 1871.

516—Bertha Ann. Born in Cherokee County, Kans., November 30, 1868. Teacher, Elk City, Kans.

EIGHTH GENERATION.

137—ELIZABETH LEMEN.

517—WILLIAM M. COVENTRY. Born July 29, 1816. They were married January 18, 1848. Their children were:

518—Sarah C. Born September 18, 1849. Died November 11, 1854.

519—Mary Elizabeth. Born September 4, 1851. Died September 28, 1897.

520.—Charles W. Born September 19, 1854. Died June 6, 1876.

521—James Henry. Born January 5, 1857. Died February 14, 1888.

142—HESTER JANE LEMEN.

522—FRANK EDWARDS. They were married January 1, 1857. They had one child.

523—Sarah C. Born near Troy, Ill., July 31, 1858.

144—LIEUT. CYRUS A. LEMEN.

524—CAROLINE E. MYERS. Born in Collinsville, Ill., July 14, 1846. They were married April 23, 1864. Their children were all born in St. Clair County, Ill., and were:

525—Clarence E. Born in St. Clair County, Ill., July 20, 1865. Farmer.

526—Jennie E. Born November 4, 1867. Died March 28, 1886.

527—Josie C. Born December 7, 1869.

528—Charles O. Born March 17, 1872. Died October 23, 1878.

529—Cora. Born August 28, 1874. Died July 24, 1889.

530—Emma. Born January 25, 1877. Collins ville, Ill.

531—Don M. Born August 16, 1880.

532—Raymond. Born December 21, 1883.

533—Mary Grace. Born April 29, 1891.

145—EMMA F. LEMEN.

534—A. J. BOSTICK. Born in Kent County, Del., November 15, 1834. Furniture and Undertaking, Holden, Mo. They were married November 15, 1864. Their children were:

535—Minnie. Born in Madison County, Ill., October 1, 1865. Died September 8, 1884.

536—Jessie. Born in Ridge Prairie, Ill., November 12, 1866.

537—Fannie. Born in Ridge Prairie, Ill., August 5, 1868. Died October 17, 1870.

538—Katie. Born in Ridge Prairie, Ill., August 24, 1870.

539—Addie. Born at Holden, Mo., September 20, 1872.

540—Frank. Born at Holden, Mo., October 18, 1874.

541—Willie. Born at Holden, Mo., December 10, 1876.

542—Harvey. Born at Holden, Mo., April 29, 1879. Died July 14, 1880.

146—ADALINE H. LEMEN.

543—AUGUSTUS D. BEEDLE. Born in St. Clair County, Ill., January 27, 1842. Real Estate and Insurance Agency, 3604 Baltimore Ave., Kansas City, Mo. They were married January 31, 1866. Their children were:

544—Mary C. Born in St. Clair County, Ill., January 1, 1867.

545—Leona L. Born in St. Clair County, Ill., March 19, 1868.

546—Gordon A. Born in Kansas City, Mo., September 25, 1870. Physician, 3604 Baltimore Ave.

547—Claude T. Born in Kansas City, Mo., September 8, 1872. Gent's Furnishing Goods.

147—JOSEPHINE CLIFTON LEMEN.

548—DR. CHAS. R. OATMAN. Born in Belleville, Ill., October 5, 1846. Physician and Surgeon, Collinsville, Ill. They were married June 18, 1871. Their children were:

549—Olive. Born at O'Fallon, Ill., April 16, 1872. Died November 28, 1895. Musician.

550—Louis J. Born at O'Fallon, Ill., December 13, 1873. Physician, St. Louis, Mo.

551—Charles Lay Field. Born at Collinsville, Ill., November 22, 1876. Physician and Surgeon, Collinsville, Ill.

552—Christopher Lorenzo. Born at Collinsville, Ill., September 7, 1878. Medical Student.

150—JAMES L. GARETSON.

553—SARAH A. HARLOW. Born in Monroe County, Ill., May 12, 1830. They were married April 19, 1848. Their children were:

554—Katharine G. Born in Monroe County, Ill., June 30, 1849. Kansas City, Mo.

555—John W. Born in Monroe County, Ill., April 9, 1851. Real Estate Broker, Wentworth, Mo.

556—James S. Born at Monroe City, Ill., September, 1852. Lumber Manufacturer and Dealer, Kirkwood, Mo.

557—Benjamin S. Born in Monroe City, Ill., July 24, 1858. Merchant, Poplar Bluffs, Mo.

558—Frank A. Born in Odin, Ill., February 18. 1860. President, Garetson & Greason Lumber Co., Poplar Bluffs, Mo.

559—George Edward. Born at Odin, Ill., May 9, 1861. Died August 25, 1893. Doctor, Farmer and Stock Raising, Adair, Indian Territory.

560—Nellie II. Born at Odin, Ill., April 9, 1865. Died December 26, 1889.

561—Robert L. Born at Odin, Ill., September, 1866. Merchant, Fink, Mo.

562—Maggie R. Born at Odin, Ill., August 9, 1868. Poplar Bluff, Mo.

151—ELIZA GARETSON.

563—JOHN FEEBACK. Only one child known:

564—J. G.

153—GEORGE C. McKINLEY.

565—EMELINE BENTON. Born in Illinois, 1842. Died August 8, 1881. They were married December 17, 1860. Their children were:

566—William B. Born in California, October 4, 1862. Tailor, Bakerfield, Cal.

567—Addison B. Born in California, August 25, 1864. Clerk, at Auburn, Cal.

568—Charlotte. Born in California, October 3, 1866. Died 1867.

569—George G. Born in California, 1868. Clerk, Bakersfield, Cal.

570—Robert L. Born in California, 1870. Lawyer, Bakersfield, Cal.

571—Sidney S. Born in California, August 9, 1872. Ice Dealer, Bakersfield, Cal.

572—Pauline. Born in California, 1874. Bakersfield, Cal.

573—Lucius D. Born in California, 1876. Student, Visalia, Cal.

154—HESTER McKINLEY.

574—W. A DASHIELL. Born in Sacramento County, Md., May 6, 1825. Liquor Dealer, 1821 Q Street, Sacramento, Cal. They were married December 24, 1854. Their children were all born in Solano County, Cal., and were:

575—Matilda. Born January 31, 1855. 904 N Street, Sacramento, Cal.

576—Catherine. Born August 7, 1857. Dixon, Cal.

577—Charlotte. Born April 1, 1859. Dixon, Cal.

578—Agnes. Born October 13, 1862. Courtland, Cal.

579—George B. Born September 21, 1864. Butcher, Sacramento, Cal.

580—Edward E. Born August 20, 1860. Died February 16, 1880.

581—Frederick S. Born June 1, 1866. Painter, 1821 Q Street, Sacramento, Cal.

582—Anne. Born July 6, 1868. Auburn, Cal.

583—Benjamin T. Born May 20, 1870.

584—Hester. Born September 1, 1872. 121 J Street, Sacramento, Cal.

585—Robert R. Born July 17, 1874. Luther, 1821 Q Street, Sacramento, Cal.

586—Jessie. Born July 2, 1876. 1821 Q Street, Sacramento, Cal.

160—GEORGE C. LEMEN.

587—MARIA GRIFFEN. Born in St. Clair County, Illinois. They were married April 2, 1856. They had one child:

588—George C., Jr. Born in St. Clair County, Illinois, January 15, 1858. Farmer.

161—ROBERT W. LEMEN.

589—BARBARY E. STOOKEY. Born in St. Clair County, Illinois, July 10, 1838. They were married December 9, 1856. They had one child:

590—Walter W. Born in St. Clair County, Illinois, March 13, 1859. Railroading, E. St. Louis, Ill.

175—VIRGINIA LEMEN.

591—WILLIAM D. LITTLE. Born at Hagerstown, Md., August 29, 1839. Commission Merchant National Stock Yards, E. St. Louis, Ill. They were married May 13, 1860. Their children were:

592—Akin Platte. Born in St. Clair County, Illinois, February 5, 1862. Inspector of dockage at National Stock Yards. 428 N. Ninth St., E. St. Louis, Ill.

593—Samuel H. Born in St. Clair County, Illinois, September 30, 1863. Commission Merchant National Stock Yards, E. St. Louis, Ill.

594—Susan C. Born in St. Clair County, Illinois, January 25, 1865. Died January 7, 1887.

595—Edith L. Born September 29, 1866. Died
    March 10, 1875.
596—William L. Born April 19, 1868. Commis-
    sion Merchant.
597—Emma C. Born February 28, 1870.
598—Virginia M. Born February 21, 1872.
599—Ida May. Born May 13, 1873.
600—Grace. Born May 22, 1875. Died July 16,
    1876.

164—MIRIAM LEMEN.
601—HENRY ALTMAN. Born in Collinsville, Ill.,
    January 20, 1840. Dealer in Coal and Sand,
    Collinsville, Ill. They were married Decem-
    ber 22, 1864. Their children were all born in
    Collinsville, Ill., and were:
602—Harry P. Born December 5, 1867. Engi-
    neer.
603—Percy C. Born December 4, 1868. Died
    August 22, 1895.
604—Joseph W. Born September 20, 1871. Team-
    ster.
605—Cora E. Born April 6, 1875. School-teacher,
    Collinsville, Ill.

165—NANCY LEMEN.
606—HOWEL PROSSER. They had one child:
607—Earl.

167—GUY M. LEMEN.

608—MARY PETERS. They had one child:

609—Platt. Born at Greenup, Ill. Died October 10, 1897.

168—ALBERT LEMEN.

610—MELISSA BEEDLE. Born in St. Clair County, Illinois. Their children were:

611—Maud.

612—Roy.

613—Albert.

169—KATHERINE LEMEN.

614—JACOB MOORE. Born in Madison County Illinois. Their children were:

615—Charley.

616—Miriam.

617—Mary.

618—Victor.

170—ELANOR N. LEMEN.

619—EDWARD WIGGINS. They were married January 22, 1873. Their children were:

620—Anna Grace. Born January 2, 1874.

621—Gideon L. Born August 1, 1876.

622—Mary E. Born June 17, 1881.

623—Victor L. Born November 19, 1884.

172—CATHARINE BEEDLE.

624—JAMES LOUIS HUFMAN. Married January 22, 1851. Died April 7, 1894. Their children were:

625—Joseph S. Born October 2, 1853.

626—Angelina. Born August 7, 1858.

627—Hester. Born March 17, 1860.

628—James L. Born November 16, 1861. Died April 7, 1894.

629—Alonzo S. Born September 4, 1863.

630—Emma. Born October 15, 1867.

173—JAMES BEEDLE.
631—(His Wife.)
They had one child:
632—Charley.

180—EDWIN H. LEMEN.
633—CYNTHIA C. BEGOLE. They were married September 24, 1871. Their children were:
634—Maude Pareppa. Born in Perry County, Illinois, March 2, 1875.
635—Infant. Born December 15, 1876. Died in infancy.

182—FREDERICK LEMEN.
636—ANNIE J. VUJTECK. Born in Collinsville, Ill., June 8, 1882. They were married December 7, 1892. Their children were:
637—Edwin Dale. Born in Ridge Prairie, Ill., September 9, 1893. Died June 2, 1896.
638—Frederick Guy. Born in Ridge Prairie, Ill., July 27, 1895.

183—CLARA L. LEMEN.

639—FRANCIS N. BEGOLE. Born in Ridge Prairie, Ill., December 8, 1838. Farmer, O'Fallon, Ill. They were married March 2, 1887. Their children were:

640—Charles Elmer. Born in Ridge Prairie, Ill., January 16, 1889.

641—Mary Ethel. Born in Ridge Prairie, Ill., September 25, 1890.

642—Elbert L. Born in St. Clair County, Illinois, March 11, 1893.

184—OSCAR LEMEN.

643—RUTH L. PIGGOTT. Born in Ridge Prairie, Ill., November 26, 1854. Their children were:

644—Hubert S. Born in St. Louis, Mo., October 20, 1875. Farmer, Collinsville, Ill.

645—Alice May. Born in Ridge Prairie, Ill., June 27, 1878.

646—Nellie C. Born in Madison County, Illinois, January 5, 1883.

647—Stella C. Born in Madison County, Illinois, August 9, 1884.

648—Charley T. Born in Madison County, Illinois, June 9, 1887.

649—Russell II. Born in Madison County, Illinois, January 12, 1890. Died March 26, 1890.

185—LILLIE H. LEMEN.

650—REV. A. J. LEAVITT. They had one child:

651—Frederick.

188—EDWIN M. PRICE.

652—MARY A. EWERS. Born in St. Clair County, Illinois, May 20, 1847. They were married November 18, 1862. Lexington, Okla. Their children were:

653—Albert A. Born in St. Clair County, Illinois, November 30, 1863. Died May 1, 1883.

654—Mary Agnes. Born in St. Clair County, Illinois, March 23, 1866. Dressmaker, Creston, Wash.

655—Henry. Born in St. Clair County, Illinois, March 9, 1869. Gold and silver mining.

656—Ann E. Born at Holy Cross, Kans., August 31, 1874. Milling business, Halder, Wis.

657—Emma G. Born at Holy Cross, Kans., October 21, 1876.

658—John E. Born at Holy Cross, Kans., August 15, 1879.

659—Edward. Born at Holy Cross, Kans., January 6, 1882.

660—Robert Lee. Born at Holy Cross, Kans., December 31, 1884.

661—Mary A. Born at Holy Cross, Kans., October 26, 1886.

189—HULDA PRICE.

662—BENJAMIN F. BEGOLE. Born in St. Clair County, Illinois, November 30, 1828. Farmer, O'Fallon, Ill. They were married January 18, 1858. Their children were:

663—Mary T.   Born in St. Clair County, Illinois, March 31, 1860.

664—Ida P.   Born in St. Clair County, Illinois, August 18, 1861.

665—John F.   Born in St. Clair County, Illinois, December 18, 1862.   Farmer.

666—Cyrus E.   Born in St. Clair County, Illinois, April 24, 1867.   Miner.

667—Bessie B.   Born in St. Clair County, Illinois, January 15, 1876.

668—Ford E. W.   Born in St. Clair County, Illinois, January 17, 1880.

190—ROBERT PRICE.

669—MARY FOREMAN.   Born in St. Clair County, Illinois.   They had one child:

670—Ida.   Born near Belleville, Ill., January 12, 1862.   Died 1896.

192—GEORGE W. BOWLER.

671—HARRIET E. SIMPSON.   Born near Bethel Church, St. Clair County, Illinois, August 16, 1838.   Farming, near Collinsville, Ill.   They were married February 10, 1859.   Their children were:

672—Ella.   Born in Ridge Prairie, Ill., February 14, 1860.

673—Thomas J.   Born in St. Clair County, Illinois, September 25, 1863.   Died August 25, 1864.

195—ELLEN BOWLER.

674—SAMUEL H. BEEDLE. They were married December 13, 1866. Their children were:

675—Stella E. Deceased.

676—Horrace.

677—Hubert. Physician.

678—Nellie. Deceased.

679—Samuel.

197—PETER A. BOWLER.

680—ALMIRA H. SIMPSON. Born in St. Clair County, Illinois. They were married December 20, 1870. They had one child:

681—E. Lee. Born in St. Clair County, Illinois, November 19, 1873. Horse trainer, Jerseyville, Ill.

197—PETER A. BOWLER.

682—BARBARA SHORT. Born in St. Clair County, Illinois, July 16, 1850. They were married January 6, 1876. They had one child:

623—William Pitts. Born in St. Clair County, Illinois, September 10, 1877.

199—ANN BOWLER.

684—DANIEL H. EVANS. They were married January 20, 1880. They had no children.

200—SUSAN C. BOWLER.

685—ANDREW B. SMILEY. Born in Ridge Prairie, Ill., December 8, 1846. Retired, 514 South

Jackson Street, Belleville, Ill. They were
married December 17, 1872. They have one
child

686—Frank B. Born in Ridge Prairie, Ill., June
27, 1875. Student Lake Forrest University.

202—ADELAIDE BOWLER.

687—JAMES MATTHEWS. Born near Collinsville,
Ill. They were married December 4, 1879.
Their children were:

688—Florence. Born in Collinsville, Ill., March 1,
1880.

689—Fern. Born in Collinsville, Ill., April 15,
1883.

203—B. F. BOWLER.

690—CARRIE PEERS. Born at Hudson, Wis., December 10, 1859. They were married January 17, 1883. Their children are:

691—Rilla. Born at Collinsville, Ill., January 5,
1884. Student.

692—Alida. Born at Moro, Ill., November 29,
1887. Student.

205—JULIA BOWLER.

693—HENRY S. SIMMONS. They were married
September 23, 1879. They had one child:

694—Maud. Born November 2, 1880.

208—CLARENCE J. LEMEN.

695—SARAH CATHARINE SMITH. Born in New
York State, March 21, 1846. Died January
30, 1890. They were married April 2, 1868.
Their children were:

696—William C. Born in Madison County, Illinois, December 19, 1873. Civil engineering,
2858 Henrietta Street, St. Louis, Mo.

697—Mabel C. Born in Madison County, Illinois,
June 10, 1871. Morganfield, Ky.

698—Mary L. Born in St. Clair County, Illinois,
December 26, 1868. School-teacher, Morganfield, Ky.

211—FRANKLIN BEGOLE LEMEN.

699—LYDIA A. COLEMAN. Born in Randolph
County, Illinois, September 7, 1855. They
were married December 29, 1875. Their
children were all born in Madison County,
Illinois, and were:

700—Ralph A. Born December 3, 1876. Farmer.

701—Amos W. Born January 12, 1878. Farmer.

702—Edith E. Born December 30, 1883. Musician.

703—Cleda L. Born August 2, 1890. Student.

212—MARY L. LEMEN.

704—CHAS. W. HADLEY. They were married February 21, 1883. They had one child:

705—Gideon C. Born in Collinsville, Ill., April
28, 1884. Student.

214—WM. K. MURPHY.

706—PENINA OZBURN. They were married April 18, 1860.

707—Hawkins Ozburn.

708—Sarah Verrina.

709—William K.

710—Infant.

215—MARY MURPHY.

716—RICHARD HUNTSMAN. They were married June, 1860. Their children were:

712—Anna Cora.

713--Sarah Gertrude. Deceased.

814—Francis Bertha.

715—Richard Harry.

716—Mary Louise.

216—JOSEPH MURPHY.

717—EMMA L. CARTER. They had no children.

217—BENTON P. MURPHY.

718—CORA SULLIVAN. Their children are:

719—Mae Florence.

720—Nellie Adele.

721—Franklin Lemen. Deceased.

722—Virginia Louise.

723—Sydney Irene.

218—GEORGE W. MURPHY.

724—ANNA COLE. They had no children.

220—MARIA LEMEN.

725—EBENEZER A. BURNETTE. Proprietor of the Cairo *Bulletin*, Cairo, Ill. They had no children.

221—CATHARINE LEMEN.

726—WILLIAM A. DRIPS. Has been with the Missouri Pacific Railroad for eighteen years. They have no children.

222—IDA R. LEMEN.

727—GILES W. BEATTI. Has been with the Missouri, Kansas & Texas Railroad sixteen years. Their children were:

728—Pauline E.

729—Nellie B.

730—Abby.

731—Edith.

223—WILLIAM C. LEMEN.

732—(His Wife.)

They have two children:

733—Eva C.

734—Burnett.

224—JOSEPH E. LEMEN.

735—DORA M.

They had no children.

238—JULIUS D. LEMEN.

762—LUCY BELLE WILLOUGHBY. Born near Collinsville, Ills., September 24, 1867. They were married June 19th, 1884. Their children were:

763—Henry Gerke. Born in Madison County Ill., July 29, 1889.

764—Hazel Grace. Born in Ridge Prairie, Ill., November 11, 1891.

765—Joseph J. Born in Ridge Prairie, Ill., December 23, 1893.

766—Mary G. Born in Ridge Prairie, Ill., August 7, 1896.

240—JOSEPH ROBERT LEMEN.

767—IDA MAY CHICK. Born in Kansas City, Mo., July 5, 1855. They were married March 12, 1884. Their children were:

768—Eugene C. Born in St. Louis, Mo., December 15, 1885.

769—Joseph R. Jr.—Born in St. Louis, Mo., August 20, 1890.

241—OLIVIA LEMEN.

770—REV. FRANK W. DOWNS. Born in Ohio, February 7, 1853. M. E. Minister, Safford, Ariz. They were married September 17, 1885. They have one child:

771—Robert Francis. Born in Safford, Ariz., November 1, 1896.

245—JAMES WILLOCK.

772—EVA ELLISON. They were married in 1872. They had one child:

773—Dorotha.

247—JOHN E. LEMEN.

774—ELLA PIERCE. Born in Belleville, Ill., March 28, 1856. They have no children.

249—ELLA A. LEMEN.

775—JAMES C. HARVEY. Born in Xenia, Ohio, May 10, 1858. Wholesale Grocer, 4145 Cook Avenue, St. Louis, Mo. They were married July 24, 1884. They have no children.

253—JOHN C. BOWMAN.

776—VIRGINIA COUCH. Born in Waterloo, Ill., They were married 1852. They had no children.

253—JOHN C. BOWMAN.

777—(His Wife.) They had one child.

778—Fannie.

262—LAURA L. COOK.

779—JOHN W. PRIMM. Minister, Upper Alton, Ill. They were married January 2, 1878. Their children were:

780—Ralph Cook. Born September 21, 1879. Died November 23, 1880.

781—Clara L. Born April 17, 1883.

267—HARRISON A. LEMEN.

782—VIRGINIA M. THOMAS. Born in Lebanon, St. Clair County, Ill., May 11, 1840. They were married May 16, 1867. They had one child:

783—Thomas Watson. Born at Olney, Richland County, Ill., August 26, 1868. Died October 4, 1876.

268—EDWARD C. LEMEN.

784—SUSAN P. JACKSON. Born at Upper Alton, Ill., September 26, 1847. They were married June 9, 1868. Their children were:

785—Cora May. Born at O'Fallon, Ill., December 21, 1869, Died January 5, 1870.

786—Harry R. Born at Upper Alton, Ill., March 21, 1871. Physician, Upper Alton, Ill.

787—Mamie T. Born at Upper Alton, Ill., August 9, 1878. Student.

267—KATHERINE LEMEN.

788—FRANCIS M. TAYLOR. Publisher of *Belleville Advocate*, Ill. They were married May 5, 1869. Their children were:

789—Hugh L. Born at Belleville, Ill., February 21, 1870. Physician, Denver, Colo.

790—Ralph L. Born in Belleville, Ill., October 15, 1871. Physician, City of Mexico, Mex.

791—Ford L. Born in Belleville, Ill., October 16, 1874. Died May 20, 1878.

792—Clyde L. Born at Belleville, Ill., March 7, 1876. Medical Student.

269—KATHERINE TAYLOR, *nee* LEMEN.

793—HENRY SUESS. Born in Niederzwehren, near Hessen-Cassel, Germany, June 8, 1857. They were married March 23, 1897. They have no children.

271—LEWIS E. LEMEN.

794—LIZZIE MUDD. Born in St. Louis, Mo. Died, 1876. They were married May 5, 1875. They had no children.

271—LEWIS E. LEMEN.

795—ELSIE JAMES. She was the first white girl born in the State of Colorado. They were married April 12, 1882. Their children are:

796—Margaret. Born at Denver, Colorado, Jan. 23, 1888.

797—Lewis. Born at Denver, Colorado, May 8, 1890.

272—LUCY LEMEN.

798—WILLIAM GOULD SHEDD. Born in Chicago, Ill., September 18, 1849. Silver Mining, 1055 Corona Street, Denver, Colo. They were married July 10, 1883. Their children were:

799—William Gould, Jr. Born at Los Angeles, Cal., May 23, 1884. Student. Baptist.

800—Edward J. Born in Denver, Colo., September 25, 1885. Baptist.

801—Charles L. Born in Leadville, Colo., January 31, 1887. Baptist.

273—THEODORE A. LEMEN.

802—ELLA LAPHAM. They were married in 1887. Their children were:

803—Timothy.

804—Dorothy. Deceased.

805—Dorinda.

277—MARY M. LYON.

806—H. O. MOWERS. Born in Cherry Valley, N.Y. October 7, 1829. Doctor and Dentist. They were married November 24, 1863. Their children were:

807—William H. Born at Hastings, Minn. September 11 1864.

282—LEWIS LYON.

808—CARRIE LANHAM TUTTLE. Born in Macon County, Ala., November 29, 1859. They were married October 10, 1878. Shorter, Alabama. Their children are:

809—Louis Amos. Born at Cross Keys, Ala., July 7, 1883. Student.

810—James B. Born at Cross Keys, Ala., January 7, 1888.

811—Mary Marguerete. Born at Cross Keys, Ala., July, 1889.

284—LAURA HART.

812—JOSHUA S. BOND. Born in Carlyle, Ill., September, 1839. Clerk in the Surveyor-General's office, No. 6 Gothic Place, Denver, Colo. They were married October, 1860. Their children were:

813—Jessie L. Born in O'Fallon, Ill., November 1861. Died, November, 1864.

814—Ben. Born in Carlyle, Ill., August 1863. Inspector, 509 Olive St., St. Louis, Mo.

815—Laura May. Born in O'Fallon, Ill., April 1865. Died April, 1865.

286—ALICE E. LEMEN.

816—C. C. BURKHOLDER. Born in Ohio, March, 21, 1848. Journalist. 716 Lafayette Ave., Brooklyn, N. Y. They were married January 1874. Their children were:

817—Ethel. Born in Chicago, Ill., December 3, 1874. Violinist.

818—Edna. Born in Chicago, Ill., December 24, 1876. School-teacher.

819—Viola. Born in Brooklyn, N. Y., February 5, 1881. Musician. 716 Lafayette Ave.

820—Hazel. Born in Brooklyn, N. Y., July 13, 1890.

287—AMELIA LEMEN.

821—ALMON CARR. Of Dexter, Maine. They were married January 1879. They had no children.

288—NINIAN E. LEMEN.

822—LOU BRYANT. Of Kasson, Minn. They were married 1874. They had one child.

823—Edward B. Born December, 1875. Died September, 1896.

292—CHARLES C. LEMEN.

824—BERTHA ABSHER. Of Emma, Ill. They were married 1893. They had three children:

825—Pauline. Born January, 1894.

826—Alice. Born August, 1895.

827—Infant. Born June, 1897.

293—WILLIAM S. LEMEN.

828—CLARA REMENSCHNIDER. Born Trempeleau, Wis., September, 1866. Died October 29, 1891. They were married June 22, 1886. They had one child:

829—Earl. Born at Minneapolis, Minn., May 20, 1887. Died May 27, 1891.

293—WILLIAM S. LEMEN.

830—ELIZABETH B. BOETTCHER. Born at Brooklyn, N. Y., May 31, 1866. They were married May 29, 1894. They have no children.

295—CHRISTY S. LEMEN.

831—(His Wife.) Their children not known.

296—MARY B. LEMEN.
832—(Her Husband.) They have no children.

298—ARTHUR S. LEMEN.
833—KATIE B. HAWKINS. They were married
November 19, 1890. They had no children.

309—LENORE LEMEN.
834—P. L. THORSEN. Born at Porsgrund, Norway,
April 3, 1863. Denver, Colo. They were
married October 2, 1889.

312—LEMUEL HILTON.
835—(His Wife.) Their children not known.

313—GILBERT HILTON.
836—(His Wife.) Their children not known.

315—SIDNEY B. HILTON.
837—LOU HANLEY. Their children not known.

318—SYLVESTER HILTON.
838—LOUISE J. COCHRAN. Born at Evansville,
Ills., October 4, 1849. They were married
February 11, 1874. Their children were:
839—Mollie. Born at Chester, Ill., December 1,
1874.
840—Emma L. Born at Chester, Ill., April 20,
1878.

841—Sarah A. Born at Chester, Ill., April 27, 1882. Died July 15, 1882.

842—Jessie M. Born at Chester, Ill., April 7, 1887. Died June 19, 1887.

843—Minnie E. Born at Chester, Ill., July 3, 1891.

326—COMMODORE TOLIN.

844—PHILLIPINE C. HESTERBERG. Born in Europe, November 9, 1850. They were married September 24, 1871. Their children were all born at New Design, Ill., and were:

845—Mary Sophia. Born August 23, 1872.

846—Weltha P. Born November 6, 1873. Farmer.

847—Anna C. Born August 4, 1875. Died October 6, 1875.

848—Theodore H. Born October 29, 1876. Died December 10, 1876.

849—Rhoda A. Born October 17, 1877.

850—Charles L. Born November 24, 1879.

851—Anna A. Born March 27, 1881.

852—Lorena L. Born January 1, 1884.

853 }
854 } Alma and Emma.—Born December 18, 1888.

855—Ida L. Born July 20, 1891.

348—HARRIET ELIZABETH JONES.

856—JOHN W. C. HARRIS. Born October 6, 1840. Farmer. They were married September 7, 1865. Their children were:

857—Claude L.   Born in Olney, Ill., September 8,
1866.   Traveling Salesmen.

858—Marshall S.   Born in Olney, October 1, 1869.

859—Etta B.   Born in Olney, Ill., August 28, 1871.

860—Charlie L.   Born in Olney, Ill., August 25,
1873.

861—Elsie L.   Born in Olney, Ill., February 8, 1875.

862—William E.   Born August 27, 1876.

863—Mary E.   Born January 30, 1879.   Died February 9, 1881.

864—Infant.   Born in Olney, Ill., August 15, 1880.
Died September 2, 1880.

865—Ralph W.   Born in Olney, Ill., March 11, 1883.

352—WILLIAM F. JONES.

866—ELLEN A. WARREN.   Born in New Haven,
Conn., 1846.   They were married December
24, 1872.   Their children were:

867—Charles L.   Born in Olney, Ills., September
3, 1874.   In third year at Ohio Musical College.

868—Joseph E.   Born at Olney, Ill., December 13,
1873.   Engineer.

869—Frank H.   Born at Olney, Ill., October 5, 1878.

870—Fannie A.   Born at Olney, Ill., February 13,
1882.

360—JOHN B. LEMEN.

871—HATTIE B. HOUSE.   Born at Indianapolis,
Ind., January 1, 1854.   They were married

January 2, 1869. They are Southern Methodists. Their children are:

872—Minnie B. Born November 14, 1871.

873—Laura L. Born August 8, 1873.

874—Dim Wid. Born October 8, 1875.

875—Johnnie. Born January 5, 1878. Died March 4, 1878.

361—MARY E. LEMEN.

876—DAVE ROLL. Their children were:

877—Wiley.

878—Ellsworth.

369—LEANDER LEMEN.

879—MATTIE NALL. They were married November 4, 1877. Their children were:

880—Cora. Born November 4, 1878.

881—John T. Born August 24, 1882.

882—Verda V. Born November 11, 1884.

883—Claude. Born February 18, 1890.

884—Lloyd. Born July 9, 1892.

885—James. Born October 2, 1895.

370—JAMES LEMEN.

886—ANNIE B. WELCH. Born January 16, 1859. They were married September 19, 1875. They are Baptists. Their children are:

887—William. Born April 4, 1877. Died April 6, 1877.

888—Laura B. Born April 17, 1878.
889—Walter. Born April 14, 1881.
890—Oliver. Born February 25, 1888.

372—MARY F. LEMEN.

891—JAMES F. NALL. Born January 1, 1854. Farmer. Baptist. They were married August 4, 1877. Their children were:

892—Nora. Born October 12, 1878.
893—Minnie. Born August 11, 1880.
894—Willie A. Born September 20, 1883.
895—Charles E. Born April 20, 1887.
896—Pearl E. Born February 10, 1889.
897—Gladys. Born January 17, 1891.
898—McKinley. Born June 25, 1896.
899—Nellie L. Born December 3, 1897.

373—ELIZA JANE LEMEN.

900—GEORGE E. NALL. Born April 4, 1856. Farmer. Christian. They were married February 14, 1880. Their children were:

901—Amos E. Born June 28, 1881. Died August 28, 1885.
902—Maude L. Born July 28, 1884.
903—Olin S. Born November 22, 1890. Died November 24, 1890.
904—Clarence W. Born April 1, 1892.
905—Thomas. Died in infancy.

375—LAURA B. LEMEN.

906—ISAAC HARPER. They were married March 17, 1891.

376—LYMAN T. LEMEN.

907—MARY A. CLOW. Born June 10, 1873. They were married December 24, 1888. Their children were:

908—Elsie V. Born August 23, 1890.

909—Nora E. Born March 17, 1892.

378—ELIZABETH R. LEMEN.

910—THOMAS J. LAYMAN. Born in Franklin County, Ill., January 8, 1838. Died January 15, 1892. Lawyer, Benton, Ill. They were married May 14, 1868. Their children were all born at Benton, Ill., and were:

911—John C. Born May 8, 1869.

912—Mattie B. Born December 31, 1871.

913—Carrie. Born March 8, 1874. School-teacher.

914—Thomas J. Born November 27, 1878. Student.

380—NOAH LEMEN.

915—MAGGIE M. STOCKWELL. They were married March 7, 1872. Their children were:

916—Guy L.

917—Charlie.

918—Lulu M.

919—Mamie A.

381—EMMA LEMEN.

920—FRANCIS M. MILLER. Born in St. Clair County, Ills., May 2, 1842. Died April 19, 1875. Merchant, Du Quoin, Ill. Their children were:

921—Isaac N. Born at Du Quoin Ill., August 31, 1870. Merchant.

922—Harry C. Born at Du Quoin, Ill., September 21, 1873. Merchant.

382—JOHN L. LEMEN.

923—ZOE E. WILSON. Born at Pinckneyville, Ill., November 28, 1853. They were married September 2, 1883. Their children were:

924—Emma V. Born at Pinckneyville, Ill., June 11, 1884.

925—John L., Jr. Born at Pinckneyville, Ill., July 26, 1886.

383—MATTIE LEMEN.

926—JAMES R. WHITE. Born in Fayette County, Penn., December 14, 1848. Died June 13, 1893. Merchant, Du Quoin, Ill. They were married March 2, 1881. Their children were:

927—Walter E. Born at Du Quoin, Ill., January 2, 1882.

928—Mary E. Born at Du Quoin, Ill., October 11, 1883.

929—Laura M. Born at Du Quoin, Ill., February 2, 1885.

386—FLORA BOCK.

930—LOUIS F. HAEBERLE. Born at Fourndan, Wuerttemburg, Germany, May 26, 1838. Professor at Eden College, St. Louis, Mo. They were married October 7, 1862. Their children were: -

931—Frederick S. Born at St. Louis, Mo., August 1, 1866. Physician, 1913 St. Louis Avenue.

932—Selma. Born in St. Louis, Mo., November 21, 1867.

933—Hulda. Born in St. Louis, Mo., March 23, 1870.

934—Armin Theophilus. Born in St. Louis, January 23, 1874. Prof. of Modern Languages at St. Charles College, Mo.

387—PHILOMENA BOCK.

935—M. J. SCHRODER Of Du Quoin, Ill. They had one child:

936—Rutherford.

388—THERESIA BOCK.

937—SAMUEL E. EVANS. Born in St. Clair County, Ills., March 17, 1843. They were married November 25, 1897. Illinois Central Coal and Salt Co., St. John, Ill. They have no children.

389—ARMENIUS F. BOCK

938—EMMA L. BECKMAN. Born in St. Louis, Mo., January 28, 1856. They were married September 8, 1875. Their children were:

939—Bertha E. Born in St. Louis, Mo., December 12, 1877.

940—Elsa C. Born in St. Louis, Mo., September 14, 1880.

941—Frederick L. Born in St. Louis, Mo., December 25, 1887.

942—Alice F. Born in St. Louis, Mo., May 19, 1891.

391—CORA BOCK.

943—DR. M. C. CARR. Their children were:

944—Earl.

945—Flora.

946—Berde.

393—ALICE M. LEMEN.

948—F. L. ROSE. Born at McConnelsville, Ohio, October 3, 1858. Attorney-at-Law, 124 South 13th Street, Lincoln, Neb. They were married May 18, 1882. Their children were:

949—Harvey.

950—Jennie.

394—FRED LEMEN.

951—DELLA MITCHELL. Born in Wood County, Ohio, May 30, 1873. They were married May 11, 1892. Their children were:

952—Marjorie. Born at Grand Island, Neb., December 28, 1894.

953—Dorothea.

395—BESSIE LEMEN.

954—H. G. WENTZ. Born at Pana, Ill., December 6, 1865. Book-keeper, Lincoln, Neb. They were married October 14, 1891. Their children were:

955—Harry.

956—Lawrence.

397—LEWIS LEMEN.

957—MARY V. TOLIN. Born at New Design, Ill., May 31, 1855. They were married May 19, 1881. Their children were:

958—Clyde V. Born at New Design, Ill., August 5, 1882.

959—Edith I. Born at New Design, Ill., August 16, 1884.

960—Carrie May. Born at Lincoln, Neb., October 10, 1888.

961—William T. Born at New Design, Ill., September 8, 1891.

398—WILLIAM LEMEN.

962—LOUISA E. BRIEGEL. B rn at New Design, Ill., September 28, 1859. They were married April 26, 1881. Burksville, Ill. They have one child:

963—Hulda E. Born at New Design, Ill., October 27, 1884. Student.

452—ANNIE MAY SLATTERY.

964—GEORGE SMELTZER. Born at Muscatine, Iowa, February 22, 1865. They were married December 10, 1890. Their children were:

965—Valeria M. W. Born at E. St. Louis, Ill., April 28, 1891.

966—Victor S. Born November 27, 1893. Died January 8, 1894.

467—LAURA A. LEMEN.

967—JESSIE B. JOHNSON. Born in Monroe County, Ill., November 22, 1839. They were married August 6, 1863. Their children were:

968—Cleome I. Born in Johnson County, Ill., September 26, 1867.

969—Duillia L. Born in Jackson County, Ill., February 19, 1870.

970—Agnes D. Born in Jackson County, Ill., June 24, 1873. Died April 3, 1880.

971—Jessie R. Born in Jackson County, Ill., April 25, 1879.

972—Lenny D. Born in Jackson County, Ill.,
May 29, 1883. Died August 13, 1896.

973—Herthia H. Born in Jackson County, Ill.,
February 2, 1885.

470—HULL LEMEN JR.

974—LAURA E. BENTLEY. Born at Hillsboro,
Ind., May, 1869. They were married in 1886.
Their children were:

975—James G. Born in Cass County, Mo., January, 1888.

976—Lizzie C. Born in Bates County, Mo., June,
1890.

977—Susan V. Born in Vermillion County, Ill.,
October, 1892.

978—Dora I. Born in Warren County, Ind., April,
1895.

471—HANNAH S. LEMEN.

979—HENRY J. KILLION. Born January 28, 1844.
They were married September 16, 1880. Their
children were

980—Dora S. Born November 10, 1881.

981—Harry L. Born December 23, 1883.

982—Stella O. Born September 27, 1886. Died
October 20, 1887.

983—Vinnie L. Born December 23, 1889.

984—Fred L. Born October 2, 1892. Died April
20, 1893.

985—Clara L. Born December 12, 1893. **Died** December 13, 1893.

986—Shelly L. Born February 4, 1896.

484—HARRIET KING.

987—**HENRY L. PARKER.** Born at Romney, Va., December 22, 1826. Died July 26, 1883. Farmer, Kane, Ill. They were married October 13, 1867. Their children were:

988—E. Florence. Born at Kane, Ill., August 8, 1868.

989—Myra May. Born at Kane, Ill., August 26, 1871.

990—Hattie G. Born at Kane, Ill., November 5, 1875. Died March 30, 1884.

485—MARIA L. KING.

991—**THEODORE JONES.** Born in Grant County, Wis., July 3, 1840. Farmer, Kane, Ill. They were married February 16, 1865. Their children were:

992—Lucian King. Born in Greene County, Ill., June 27, 1870. School-teacher.

993—Effie May. Born March 20, 1874.

994—Adele. Born in Sedgwick County, Kan., September 18, 1876. School-teacher.

995—Fred. Born April 7, 1879.

996—Myra. Born in Greene County, Ill., July 22, 1883.

487—EMMA KING.

997—CHARLES E. NEELEY. Born at Glasgow, Mo.
January 28, 1851. Banker, Arkadelphia, Ark.
They were married August 25, 1874. Their
children were:

998—Lotta K. Born at Kane, Ill., May 21, 1878.
Pupil at Forest Park University, St. Louis, Mo.

488—ADELL KING.

999—FRANK McCLURE. Born at Carlinville, Ill.,
September 28, 1856. Banker at Arkadelphia,
Ark. They were married September 9, 1879.
Their children were:

1000—Charles K. Born at Kane, Ill., September
12, 1881. Student at Baptist Colllege, Arkadelphia, Ark.

1001—Florence. Born at Kane, Ill., April 11, 1884,
Student at Baptist College.

1002—Sudie L. Born at Kane, Ill., June 19, 1887.
Student at Baptist College.

489—SUDIE KING.

1003—GEORGE MARSH. They were married August
27, 1884.

498—CHESTER F. LEMEN.

1004—MARTHA ANN LOGSDON. Born at Walshville, Ill., January, 1860. Died December 10,

1886. They were married October 11, 1882.
Their children were:

1005—Gertie M. Born at Walshville, Ill., February
22, 1885. Litchfield.

1006—Infant.

1007—Infant.

498—CHESTER F. LEMEN.

1008—ESTHER A. WINSPEARE. Born at Hands-
worth, Staffordshire, England, December 5,
1867. They were married June 14, 1892.
Their children were:

1009—Dorothy N. Born at Superior, Wis., March
31, 1893.

1010—Chester K. Born at Litchfield, Ill., September
15, 1897.

500—ANNIE J. LEMEN.

1011—JOHN C. WIBEL. Born at Quincy, Ill., May
20, 1858. Printer. Salem, Ill. They were
married June 3, 1882. Their children were:

1012—May. Born at Nokomis, Ill., September 13,
1883.

1013—Blanche. Born at Salem, Ill., January 9, 1885.

1014—Luella. Born at Salem, Ill., January 10, 1888.

1015—Hattie. Born at Salem, Ill., December 7,
1890.

1016—Charlie. Born at Salem, Ill., May 3, 1896.

501—KATIE LEMEN.

1017—JOHN C. SCHAEFER. Born at Pittsburg, Penn., December 16, 1855. Farmer, Nokomis, Ill. They were married September 29, 1881. Their children were all born in Christian County, Ill.

1018—J. Will. Born November 4, 1882. Student.

1019—J. Frederick. Born December 22, 1883. Student.

1020—J. Cleveland. Born December 12, 1885. Student.

1021—Jessie M. Born October 6, 1887.

1022—Mary C. Born May 5, 1888.

1023—Lena. Born February 24, 1890.

1024—Birdie R. Born November 30, 1892.

508—WILLIAM F. KINGSTON.

1025—TERRESSA J. WRIGHT. Born at Idaho City, Idaho, March 18, 1864. Milliner. Black Rock, Ark. They were married Junuary 1, 1885. Their children were:

1026—Minnie J. Born at Elk City, Kan., November 3, 1885.

1027—Carrie L. Born at Elk City, Kan., July 23, 1887.

1028—Goldie M. Born at Elk City, Kan., August 6, 1889.

514—LEMEN DOUGHERTY.

1029—CORA A. BAGSLEY. Born near Brooklyn, Iowa., November 11, 1866. They were married November, 1886. Their children were:

1030—Myrtle V. Born in Wichita, Kan., July 12, 1888.

1031—Forest L. Born at Eureka, Kan., August 29, 1890.

1032—Thomas J. Born at Eureka, Kan., February 17, 1894.

NINTH GENERATION.

519—MARY E. COVENTRY.

1033—WM. H. SNIDER. Born May 21, 1848. They were married October 4, 1870. Their children were:

1034—William E. Born Dec. 20, 1871.

1035—Jennie E. Born July 20, 1873.

1036—Charles H. Born December 13, 1875.

1037—Alice M. Born April 4, 1883. Died November 20, 1889.

521—JAMES HENRY COVENTRY.

1038—MARGNORIT B. LeCLAIRE. They were married September 4, 1877. Their children were:

1039—Jennie C. Born October, 1882.

523—SARAH C. EDWARDS.

1040—ALFRED STEVENS. Born in St. Louis, Mo., July 16, 1852. Jeweler, Altamont, Ill. They were married July 29, 1877. Their children were:

1041—Harry E. Born at Collinsville, Ill., June 22, 1878. Died February 2, 1884.

1042—Grace A. Born at Collinsville, Ill., June 13, 1880. Student.

1043—William A. Born at Collinsville, Ill., April 25, 1882. Died March 4, 1884.

1044—Nellie K. Born at Collinsville, Ill, September 15, 1894. Died June 30, 1895.

527—JOSIE C. LEMEN.
1045—DR. JNO. VOISIN. Born in St. Clair County, Ill., February 2, 1853. They were married June 1, 1892. Their children were:
1046—Verna. Born in St. Clair County, Ill., April 21, 1893.
1047—Ada Grace. Born in St. Louis, Mo., April 18, 1895.

536—JESSIE BOSTICK.
1048—DR. CHARLES G. SPRINKLE. Born in Licking County, Ohio, January 14, 1867. Physician in Loveland, Colo. They were married June 12, 1894. They have one child:
1049—Pearl. Born at Millersport, Ohio, March 18, 1895.

538—KATIE B. BOSTICK.
1050—JONATHAN SEAMAN. Born at Lebanon, Ill., August 22, 1867. Merchant, Loveland, Colo. They were married June 19, 1895. They have no children.

544—MARY C. BEEDLE.
1051—(Her Husband.)
        Their children not known.

549—OLIVE OATMAN.

1052—THOMAS R. STOCKETT. Born at Ringgold, Penn., November 6, 1863. Civil and mining engineer, 2602 Locust street, St. Louis, Mo., They were married October 11, 1894. They have one child:

1053—Lewis O. Born in St. Louis, Mo., Nov. 11, 1895.

554—KATIE GARETSON.
1054—JOE WHITE.

Their children were:

1055—(   ).

1056—(   ).

1057—(   ).

555—JOHN W. GARETSON.

1058—ELIZABETH B. DAVIS. Born at Hamilton, Ohio, June 3, 1853. They were married March 13, 1878. Their children were:

1059—James D. Born at Harville, Mo., June 4, 1879. Wentworth, Mo.

1060—Hugh N. Born at Harville, Mo., July 18, 1880. Bill clerk and office boy.

1061—John H. Born at Sorcaxon, Mo., April 18, 1890. Wentworth, Mo.

1062—Worth. Born at Wentworth, Mo., May 18, 1892.

556—JAMES GARETSON.

1063—CAROLINE M. GRIFFITH. Born at Rushville, Ill., January, 1853. Died November, 1890. They were married September 14, 1874. Their children were:

1064—Ella H. Born at Terrehaute, Ind., August 18, 1876.

1065—Katherine G. Born at Terrehaute, Ind., July 1, 1878. Student at Mt. Holyoke College, Mass.

556—JAMES GARETSON.

1066—KATHERINE BOWES. Born at St. Paul, Minn., August, 1862. They were married June 1, 1897.

557—BENJAMIN S. GARETSON.

1067—SALLIE M. COOK. Born at Cape Girardeau, Mo., 1860. School-teacher, Doniphan, Mo. They were married September, 1883. They have one child:

1068—Ben S., Jr. Born at Doniphan, Mo., September, 1884.

558—FRANK A. GARETSON.

1969—JULIA L. METZ. Born at Ullin, Ill., December 5, 1863. They were married September 4, 1884. Their children were:

1070—Sarah E. Born at Harville, Mo., July 18, 1885.

1071—Roy A. Born at Poplar Bluff, Mo., July 10, 1887.

1072—Frank A., Jr. Born at Poplar Bluff, Mo., February 18, 1891.

1073—Julia Louise. Born at Poplar Bluff, Mo., June 26, 1893.

1074—Sylvains H. Born at Poplar Pluff, Mo., November 26, 1895.

559—GEO. EDWARD GARETSON.

1075—IDA ALLIE PURCELL, Born in Johnson County, Kans., March 18, 1864. They were married January 16, 1886. Their children were:

1076—Robert Edward. Born at Vinita, I. Terr., November 14, 1886.

1077—James Lemen. Born at Adair, I. Terr., April 6, 1887.

1078—Lucile. Born at Poplar Bluff, Mo., November 25, 1892.

1079—Benjamin S. Born March 26, 1893. Died June 17, 1895.

560—NELLIE GARETSON.

1080—T. J. KUNEY. Born in Pennsylvania, 1859. Planter, Okolona, Miss. They were married 1885. Their children were:

1081—Buford. Born at Okolona, Miss., 1886. Died November, 1893.

1082—Hester. Born in Okolona, Miss., September, 1888. Poplar Bluff, Mo.

561—ROBT. L. GARETSON.

1082—BIRTHA BALL. Born at Ann Arbor, Mich., 1864. Died 1890. They were married December, 1889. They had one child:

1084—Nellie. Born at Poplar Bluff, Mo., December, 1890.

562—MAGGIE GARETSON.

1085—CHAS. ORCHARD. Born at Piedmont, Mo., 1867. Assistant Agent, I. M. R. R., Poplar Bluff, They were married, January, 1891. Their children were;

1086—Helen. Born at Poplar Bluff, Mo., 1893.

1087—Ruth. Born at Poplar Bluff, Mo., 1897.

597—ADDISON B. McKINLEY.

1088—LAURA AMOS. Born in Iowa, November 7, 1868. Auburn, Cal. They were married June 28, 1888. Their children were:

1089—Robert C. Born in California, March 20, 1889. Auburn.

1090—Addison A. Born in California, April 12, 1893. Auburn

1091—George E. Born in California, May 23, 1895.

575—MATILDA DASHIELL.

1092—G. I. ALISON. Born in Dubuque, Iowa, April 18, 1849. Carpenter, 904 N. Street, Sacramento, Cal. They were married January 31, 1878. Their children were:

1093—George I., Jr. Born in Salem County, Cal., November 14, 1879.

1094—Hester H Born in Dion, Cal., October 19, 1881.

1095—Irma I. Born in Sacramento, Cal., June 24, 1890. Died February 5, 1892.

1096—Clarence. Born in Sacramento, Cal., May 15, 1896.

576—CATHARINE DASHIELL.

1097—CHAS. C. DONOHO. Born in Eldorado County, Cal., June 6, 1856. Salesman, Dixon, Cal. They were married September 20, 1876. Their children were:

1098—Thomas. Born in Dixon, Cal., June 25, 1877. Died June 26, 1877.

1099—William A. Born in Dixon, Cal., October 27, 1878. Berkley, Cal.

1100—James G. Born in Dixon, Cal., November 9, 1881.

1101—Florence R. Born in Dixon, Cal., July 3, 1886.

1102.—John T. Born in Dixon, Cal., May 6, 1890.

1103.—Catharine. Born in Dixon, Cal., December 31, 1891.

1104—Charles. Born in Dixon, Cal., September 14, 1896.

578—AGNES DASHIELL.

1105—HORACE D. OSBORN. Born in Clark County, Ohio, March 23, 1858. Farmer, Courtland, Cal. They were married April 22, 1884. Their children were:

1106—Osborn. Died in infancy.

1107—Myrtle. Born in Sacramento, Cal., October 18, 1885.

1108—Mary H. Born in Sacramento, Cal., April 8, 1887.

1109—Donna A. Born in Sacramento, Cal., April 3, 1889.

1110—Henry R. Born in Sacramento, Cal., July 8, 1890.

1111—Jacob D. Born in Sacramento, Cal., July 15, 1894.

579—GEORGE B. DASHIELL.

1112—MARY E. CROWELL. Born in Dixon, Ill., November 27, 1866. They were married September 1, 1888. Their children were:

1113—Charlotte. Born in Sacramento, Cal., Oct. 6, 1889.

1114—Ray E. Born in Sacramento, Cal., May 13, 1893. Died February 8, 1895.

582—ANNE DASHIELL.

1115—CHAS. F. RICE. Born in Placer County, Cal., June 22, 1868. Telegraph operator, Auburn, Cal. They were married April 29, 1887. They had one child:

1116—Florence A. Born in Sacramento, Cal., January 27, 1888. Died May 22, 1892.

583—BENJAMIN T. DASHIELL.

1117—SADIE CORCORAN. Born in Sunbury, Penn., September 2, 1871. They were married February 2, 1893. Their children were:

1118—Hester. Born in Sacramento, Cal., December 31, 1893.

1119—William A. Born in Sacramento, Cal., November 28, 1895.

584—HESTER DASHIELL.

1120—J. K. BEEDE. Born in Newburgh, N. Y., January 13, 1868. Manager of the Postal Telegraph Cable Co., 121 J Street, Sacramento, Cal. They were married December 10, 1891. They had one child:

1121—Florence A. Born in Sacramento, Cal., June 8, 1893. Died September 10, 1895.

588—GEORGE C. LEMEN.

1122—LAURA AGNEW. They were married August, 1883. Their children were:

1123—Grace I. Born in St. Clair County, Ill., August 25, 1884.

1124—William C. Born in St. Clair County, Ill., August 25, 1888.

590—WALTER W. LEMEN.
1125—**ELIZABETH DARROW.** Born in St. Clair County, Ill., August 26, 1862. They were married January 6, 1881. They have one child:
1126—Robert F. Born in St. Clair County, Ill., June 11, 1882.

592—AKIN PLATT LITTLE.
1127—**MINNIE M. DILL.** Born in East St. Louis, Ill. They were married September 30, 1885. They have one child:
1128—Oral Dill. Born in East St. Louis, Ill., August 15, 1886.

593—SAMUEL H. LITTLE.
1129—**ANNA BOUCHENS.** They were married August 9, 1883. They have one child:
1130—Pearl. Born in St. Clair County, Ill., June 23, 1884.

594—SUSAN C. LITTLE.
1131—**H. R. SCARLETT.** Born in Indiana. They were married in 1881. Their children were:
1132—Maud. Born in St. Clair County, Ill., Dec. 1, 1881.

1133—Harry. Born in St. Clair County, Ill., August 17, 1883.

1134—Ava, Born in St. Clair County, Ill., March 16, 1885. Died October 28, 1894.

1135—Bruce. Born in St. Clair County, Ill., January 2, 1887.

596—WILLIAM L. LITTLE.

1136—MUSIE HALE. Born in East St. Louis, Ill. They were married December 24, 1890. They had one child:

1137—Norman. Born in East St. Louis, Ill., July 11, 1895.

597—EMMA C. LITTLE.

1138—CHAS. T. SMILEY. Born in St. Clair County, Ills. Wiggins Ferry Co., St. Louis, Mo. They were married March 5, 1890. Their children were all born in St. Clair County, Ill., and are:

1139—Gerald S. Born October 5, 1890.

1140—Chas. L. Born July 22, 1892.

1141—Virginia M. Born September 11, 1894.

598—VIRGINIA M. LITTLE.

1142—ANTHONY A. HUNT. Attorney-at-Law, East St. Louis, Ill. They were married April 4, 1895. They have one child:

1143—Dorothy. Born in East St. Louis, Ill., July 18, 1896.

599—IDA MAY LITTLE.

1144—WM. H. HAUSS. Hardware Merchant, East St. Louis, Ills. They were married July 28, 1890. Their children were:

1145—Anna. Died in infancy.

1146—Edward. Born September 5, 1892.

602—HARRY P. ALTMAN.

1147—GRACE SMITH. Born in Champaign, Ill., August 6, 1867. School-teacher. They were married October 7, 1891. Their children were:

1148—Irma. Born in Collinsville, Ill., June 25, 1892.

1149—Stanley P. Born in Collinsville, Ill., December 20, 1894.

1150—Millicent L. Born in Collinsville, Ill., October 5, 1895.

603—PERCY C. ALTMAN.

1151—ANNA RODGERS. Born in Collinsville, Ill., July 15, 1870. They were married 1894. They had one child:

1152—Percell U. Born in Collinsville, Ill., September 17, 1894.

615—CHARLEY MOORE.

1153—(   ) DAVIS.

They have no children.

616—MARIAM MOORE.
1154—(   ) DAVIS.
They have no children.

625—JOE S. HUFFMAN.
1155—MALISSIA LOW. Born January 21, 1856.
Their children were:
1156—Jessie L. Born July 5, 1879.
1157—Charles. Born January 6, 1883.
1158—Louie. Born November 12, 1885.

626—ANGELINE HUFFMAN.
1159—JAMES C. WOODSIDE. Born in Chester Co.,
Pa., October 18, 1842. They were married
December 24, 1890. Their children not
known.

626—ALONZO HUFFMAN.
1160—MARY E. LYONS. They were married April
4, 1885. Their children, as far as known,
were:
1161—Minnie E. Born April 7, 1887.
1162—Pearl. Born February 16, 1891.

654—MARY AGNES PRICE.
1163—JOHN MOYLON. Born in Ireland, March 10,
1858. Stock business, Davenport, Wash.

They were married April 23, 1885. Their children were:

1164—Ellen. Born in Jackson County, Kan., February 7, 1886. Died July 1, 1887.

1165—Katherine. Born in Kansas, February 10, 1887.

1166—Mary Ellen. Born in Lincoln County, Wash., October 18, 1888.

1167—Margaretta. Born in Lincoln County, Wash., September 24, 1890.

1168—Annie G. Born in Lincoln County, Wash., June 7, 1892.

1169—John C. Born in Lincoln County, Wash., March 20, 1894. Died June 27, 1894.

1170—Daniel. Born in Lincoln County, Wash., April 27, 1895.

656- -ANN E. PRICE.
1171—HUGH McFADDEN. Milling business, Halder, Wis.

657—EMMA G. PRICE.
1172—ERNST ALLEN.
Children not known.

663—MARY T. BEGOLE.
1173—CHARLES MILLER. Born in St. Clair County, Ill. They were married December 2, 1885. They have one child:
1174—Floyd.

664—IDA BEGOLE.

1175—ANDY ENTREKIN. They were married April,
1893. They have one child:

1176—Gladys.

670—IDA M. PRICE.

1177—ISAAC W. COOK. Born in Madison Co., Ills.,
Mch. 17, 1845. Farmer. Troy, Ill. They
were married Nov. 26, 1886. Their children
were:

1178—Horrace Blain. Born in Madison Co., Ill.,
January 21, 1888.

1179—Roscoe C. Born in Madison Co., Ill., May
29, 1889.

1180—Maud E. Born in Madison Co., Ill., January
23, 1891.

672—ELLA BOWLER.

1181—JAMES H. KING. Born at Marshall, Clark Co.,
Ill., February 20, 1845. They were married
by Rev. W. S. Post of Chicago, Ill., February 7, 1878. They have no children.

678—NELLIE BEEDLE.

1182—JOSEPH ROCKWELL. They had one child:

1183—Gene Hobart.

981—E. LEE BOWLER.

1184—KATIE PAUSCH. Born in St. Clair County, Ill., April, 1876. They were married September 30, 1897. They have no children.

697—MABEL C. LEMEN.

1185—J. W. WALKER. Born in Union County, Ky. March 5, 1866. Tile Manufacturing. Morganfield, Ky. Their children are:

1186—Ida Madaline. Born at Morganfield, Ky., December 22, 1891.

1187—Wm. Caswell. Born at Morganfield, Ky. September 27, 1896.

708—SARAH V. MURPHY.

1188—JOS. CRAWFORD. They had one child:

1189—William K.

712—ANNA C. HUNTSMAN.

1190—FRANK STANCHFIELD. Their children were:

1191—Ermine.

1192—Ermane.

1193—Erby.

713—SARAH GERTRUDE HUNTSMAN.

1194—WILLIAM FITZER. They had one child.

1195—Harry Huntsman.

716—MARY LOUISE HUNTSMAN.
1196—GEORGE STEWART. Their children were:
1197—Warren H.
1198—Donald.

742—CATHARINE O. DENNY.
1199—PROF. WM. M. VAN ARNAN. They were
married by Rev. J. N. Jessup, January, 1898.

748—HORRACE ROSCOE LEMEN.
1200—IDA AIKINS. Born at Pella, Iowa, February
16, 1873. They were married October 28,
1893. Their children are.
1201—Florence Marie. Born at Pella, Iowa. July
31, 1894.
1202—Ethel M. Born at Pella, Iowa. July 18, 1895.
1203—Helen. Born at Council Bluffs, Iowa, April
14, 1897.

778—FANNIE BOWMAN.
1204—JAMES P. SLADE. Married July 13, 1876.
They have one child:
1205—Leonard Tracy. Born at Belleville, Ill., November 3, 1878. Student at Washington University, St. Louis, Mo.

786—HARRY R. LEMEN.
1206—(His Wife).
They have no children.

807—WILLIAM H. MOWERS.

1207—SALLIE A. McFALL. Born in Mead County, Ky., June 1, 1867. They were married October 4, 1887 They have no children.

845—MARY S. TOLIN.

1208—GEORGE COLE. They were married March 5, 1890.

846—WELTHA P. TOLIN.

1209—CHARLES SHIVERS. They were married January 29, 1896.

857—CLAUDE L. HARRIS.

1210—EMMA RUCHTI. Born in Flora, Ill., January 16, 1870. They were married April 21, 1887. Their children are.

1211—Joseph W. Born in Olney, Ill., January 20, 1889.

1212—Frank J. Born in Flora, Ill., August 17, 1890.

1213—Russell H. Born in Flora, Ill., November, 28, 1892.

859—ETTA B. HARRIS.

1214—GRANT ALCORN. Born July 3, 1869. City officer. They were married May 19. 1892. Their children were:

1215—Eugene G. Born in Olney, Ill. May 28 1893.

1216—Lemen M. Born in Olney, Ill., May 20, 1895.

---

872 — MINNIE B. LEMEN.

1217—JOHN T. COOKSEY. Born November 14, 1871. City officer. Southern Methodist. They were married August 1, 1890. Their children are:

1218—Peck. Born at Canton, Mo., September 2, 1892.

1219—Fannie. Born at Canton, Mo., October 1, 1896.

873—LAURA L. LEMEN.

1220—E. T. EDWARDS. Born November 16, 1863. Book keeper. Cumberland Presbyterian. They were married July 20, 1893. They have one child:

1221—Waldrip. Born July 2, 1894.

932—SELMA HAEBERLE.

1222—THEOPHIL L. MUELLER. Born at Okawville, Ill. March 5, 1863. Minister of the Gospel, 713 Washington St., Jefferson City, Mo. They were married October 12, 1887. Their children were:

1223—Helmut. Born at Millstadt, Ill., January 1, 1890.

1224—Edmund. Born at Jefferson City, Mo., March 4, 1894.

933—HULDA HAEBERLE.

1225—**REV. EDWARD T. BETTEX.** Born in Germany, 1865. They were married 1892. Their children were:

1226—Flora Paula. Born at McCook, Neb. May, 17, 1893.

1227—Harold Frederick. Born at Elyria, Ohio, January 4, 1896.

968—CLEOME I. JOHNSON.

1228—**THOMAS B. COX.** Born in Jackson County, Ill., Nov. 9, 1862. They were married July 12, 1888. Their children were.

1229—Glaydes E. Born in Jackson County, Ill., April 18, 1889. Died September 18, 1889.

1230—Claude. Born in Jackson County, Ill., March 13, 1891.

1231—Sherman. Born in Jackson County, Ill., September 7, 1893. Died July 31, 1894.

1232—Clyde. Born in Jackson County, Ill. September 13, 1895.

969—DUILLA L. JOHNSON.

1233—GEO. HARRIS. Born in Jackson County, Ill., January 18, 1864. They were married September 7, 1890. Their children were:

1234—Kenneth. Born in Jackson County, Ill., August 6, 1892. Died June 16, 1893.

1235—Ardell. Born in Vanderburg County, Ind., March 29, 1894.

992—LUCIAN KING JONES.

1236—NELLIE C. GOUGH. They were married December 24, 1896. They have one child.

1237—Alma Marguerite.

993—EFFIE MAE JONES.

1238—HEBERT G. ELLIS. Teaching school. They were married December 23, 1896.

TENTH GENERATION.

1034—WILLIAM E. SNIDER.

1239—HELEN E. EBI. Born May 9, 1869. They were married Sept. 18, 1894. They have one child.

1240—William H. S., Jr. Born Sept. 19, 1897.

PART II

LEMEN FAMILY HISTORY.

VIRGINIA BRANCH.

Table of Contents of Virginia Branch.

BIOGRAPHIES.

PORTRAITS.

CHAPTER I.

THE EARLY LEMEN FAMILY.

As the early ancestors of the Lemen family in this country, who lived in Scotland formerly and in the North of Ireland later, were only briefly mentioned in a former chapter, and as Virginia was the first home of their descendants who came to America in early times, it is proper, in the Virginia division of this work, to give such details of their lives as are well authenticated in their early family records. Of the three brothers and three sisters who formerly lived in Scotland, Robert and William Lemen, who were soldiers under Cromwell, were married in that country; Robert married Mary Anderson and William married her sister, Elizabeth Anderson. In 1656 Robert and William and wives with their other brother, James, and the three sisters removed from Scotland and settled in the North of Ireland, where the other members of the family were married and where they all reared their families. The three brothers were ship-carpenters.

Among the children of Robert Lemen and wife were two sons, Nicholas and Thomas, the latter their youngest child. Nicholas, who was a navigator and shipbuilder, was married in Scotland to Miss Nancy McKane in 1685, but they settled in the North of Ireland where they reared their family. They were

members of the Church of England and they brought
their family up in that faith. Their family comprised
seven children, four sons and three daughters. Their
first three sons, James, Robert and Nicholas, were on
the sea a great deal, like many of their ancestors,
several of whom were trained navigators. The three
young men, though their permanent home was in
North Ireland, spent much of their time in Scotland,
and when they came to Eastern Virginia, in 1708,
and procured their homes and farms there, they came
directly from that country. After that date they
made several voyages at sea to obtain means to assist
in paying for their homes, and they were eventually
all married in Virginia, where they reared their families. James was married in 1714 to Miss Jane Burns;
in 1715 Robert was married, and in 1714 Nicholas was
married to Miss Ruth Andrews. Nicholas and wife
reared a family of several sons and daughters; Robert and wife had several children but their daughters
only survived, their sons dying in infancy; and James
and wife had eleven children, five of whom died in
infancy and six survived—two daughters and four
sons—the latter were John, Robert, Nicholas and
Thomas. The three brothers, James, Robert and
Nicholas, were members of the Church of England, of
which there was an organization in the community
in which they and their families were members.
Their occupation at times was that of seamen, but
their regular vocation was that of shipbuilders, and
later they became planters.

In 1728 their father, Nicholas Lemen, died at his home in the North of Ireland, and James and Robert with their wives went there to assist in the settlement of his estate and to procure means, and on the return voyage to their homes in Virginia, James and wife had a son, Thomas, born to them on the sea on June 20, 1730. In 1732 James, Robert and Nicholas made their last voyage at sea, visiting both Scotland and Ireland before their return; and it was the dates of these several voyages at sea which have caused some confusion by later writers of their sketches, who have mistaken the dates of their several arrivals here and have confounded the date of their first arrival with those of some of their later ones. But their first arrival in Virginia was in 1708. They and their wives died at their homes in that State before reaching very old age; nor did the four sons of James (John, Robert, Nicholas and Thomas Lemen) live to very old ages, as many of their descendants have done.

Old Robert Lemen and wife, of Scotland formerly and of North Ireland later, had another son besides Nicholas, Thomas Lemen, their youngest child, who was also married in Scotland but settled in North Ireland with his wife, where they reared a family, two members of which, Robert and Thomas Lemen, with a relative, Stephen Lemen, came to America and settled in the South of Virginia in 1733. All were married. Robert in 1719, Thomas in 1720, and Stephen in 1722, and they brought their wives and young families with them; but presently they removed further South. Some writers of the early family sketches confused the dates of the arrivals of the several members of the family here, and their names, which was very natural considering the uniform similarity of them; and in consequence some lines of the later families have confused the names of their ancestors with others. But it is the aim and purpose of this history to correct these errors and to so designate the several branches, that any descendant of James, Robert or Nicholas Lemen in the North, East, West and South, as far as Virginia and Kentucky, may, with the aid of their own family records now in their hands, ascertain their true lines, and thus connect their ancestral lines without break back to Robert Lemen and wife of Scotland formerly, and North Ireland later.

The sources from which this history is derived are entirely trustworthy. A large part of it is based upon facts, notes and records furnished from the official data on record in the archives in Virginia, by Mr. Joseph Baker Kearfott, a member of the family who resides in Martinsburg, W. Va., and who, in addition, has collected and prepared the large, full and accurate genealogical tables of large branches of the Virginia family which will be found elsewhere; and for his arduous and excellent services the thanks of all branches of the family are due and are cheerfully accorded. Much useful information has also been derived from the correspondence of the venera-

ble Robert Lemen, of Williamsport, Md. ; while much
of the earlier information has been derived from facts,
notes, incidents and records copied from the early
dates, sketches and records of the family in Scotland,
Ireland and America, by the aid of which it is hoped
and believed that all our families, whether of both
name and blood, or of blood only, can trace and connect their lines and establish their actual relationship
with each other.

CHAPTER II.

20—NICHOLAS LEMEN.

Nicholas Lemen, the subject of this sketch, was a son of James Lemen and Jane Burns Lemen, his wife, and was born at his parents' home in Eastern Virginia in 1725. The details of his marriage, procuring of his farm and settlement in Frederick County, now Jefferson County, West Virginia, are given in the first chapter of the Illinois Family History of the Lemens, to which the reader is referred. Nicholas came into the years of manhood, with a stature above the medium, with a strong constitution and an active, well-stored mind with the practical affairs of life, but a limited education because of the privations of the early times. His wife was a lady of Pennsylvania, of good culture and some means, but they were married in Virginia in 1747, and settled on their farm in what is now Jefferson County, West Virginia. The farm comprised 570 acres of land, the original title vesting in Nicholas Lemen by a grant or patent from Thomas Lord Fairfax, under the seal of the crown, bearing date September 5, 1756, Nicholas having had it first surveyed. Lord Fairfax was then Lord Proprietor of the Northern part of Virginia, and, under the crown, had the power of the granting and disposition of the lands there.

We have not the original grant, that being now on file among the papers of some members of the family in West Virginia; but through the kindness and researches of Mr. Joseph Baker Kearfott, of Martinsburg, W. Va., we have before us an exact *fac simile*, except as to the name and numbers. The said grant conveys certain lands in Frederick County, Virginia, to Jonathan Edwards, and bears date April 4, 1768,.and is signed by Lord Fairfax. The name is in his own hand, but the instrument itself, which is on parchment (sheep skin), is finely executed in writing type, and for artistic type work it is not excelled to-day by our fine steel engravers.

Nicholas Lemen and Christian Lemen, his wife, in their religious preferences, were members of the Church of England, as there was a church of that faith in their community. Their children, who were all born at their home in Frederick County, were: John, born December 14, 1749; Robert, born November 6, 1750; Nancy, born March 4, 1754, Mary, born January 7, 1756; Thomas, born February 4, 1758; and James, born November 20, 1760. The children were fortunate in having parents who provided bountifully for their wants, and in every respect they, the parents and children were a very happy family. Nicholas Lemen's health began to fail in 1760, and eventually being admonished that his recovery was very uncertain, he made a will bearing date May 8, 1761, making such provisions for his wife and children as he deemed satisfactory. The witnesses were Richard Mercer and Mary Mercer. He died at his home on July 20, 1761, and was buried on his farm where his wife was afterwards buried. The will was duly proven before the proper court in Frederick County on August 4, 1761, and admitted to record. The will appointed his brothers, John and Robert Lemen, to look after the management of the property and the interests of the family, which trusts they faithfully executed. In due time after Nicholas Lemen's death, his widow, Christian Lemen, married Rev. Henry Eaty, a member and minister of the Presbyterian church, and from this union two children were born, namely, Sebastian Eaty and a little daughter who died in infancy.

Nicholas Lemen, realizing that the division of his farm into so many small parts would not be practicable, he provided in his will that the farm should go to John and Robert, his two oldest sons, setting apart one-third of it to his wife during her life, and a monetary consideration to be paid by John and Robert was provided for his two daughters and the younger sons. From John and Robert the farm largely descended by inheritance or by purchase to other members of the family, and at this time 270 acres of the original tract are owned by Mr. John P. Kearfott, a great grandson of Nicholas and a grandson of Robert Lemen. The village of Kearneysville is now situated on part of it, and the Baltimore & Ohio Railroad and a turnpike road cross it.

Nicholas Lemen was a good provider and an excellent planter, and in all matters he was a man of large natural capacities, and for a man not largely educated he had a wonderful insight into public affairs. As a subject of the British king he was not satisfied with some of England's acts toward the colonies at that early day; and in 1758 he declared in the presence of a British officer, "that the colonies would throw off the British yoke inside of twenty years," to which the officer objected in a most furious and threatening manner; but Nicholas Lemen defiantly repeated his prophesy and the Briton had to submit.

Christian Lemen, his wife, also had many noble characteristics. She was a devoted wife and a loving mother, and was highly esteemed by all her neighbors. She survived her first husband many years and died at the old homestead.

Of the children of Nicholas and wife, James and family have been mentioned in former chapters, and Robert and family will be referred to in another place, as will also the others who survived.

The old plantation of Nicholas Lemen was the scene of several skirmishes between the armies during the war for the Union. His house consisted of a heavy log structure one story and a half high, with a porch on the front and shed rooms behind. The land around is gently undulating. There is a never-failing lime-rock-spring near the site of the old house, and the old family cemetery is some 200 yards away where sleeps the dust of many of the pioneers. The old house was removed in 1880 and a large brick structure now occupies the place. The old farm is six miles from the historic Potomac at Shepherdstown, and thirteen miles from Harper's Ferry, made famous by the raid and final execution of John Brown, one of whose jurymen was William Lemen, of Jefferson County, West Virginia, an uncle to Mr. J. Baker Kearfott, and a cousin to the old pioneer Lemens of Illinois.

CHAPTER III.

(21) THOMAS, (18) JOHN AND (19) ROBERT LEMEN.

Thomas Lemen was a son of James Lemen and wife, Jane Lemen, nee Burns, whose home was in Eastern Virginia. In 1730 his parents were on their return from a visit to Ireland, and Thomas was born on board the ship in that year on June 20. He acquired an ordinary education, and in later years was a large reader and became a man of broad general information. He removed from his parents' home when of age and procured a home near Harper's Ferry, now in West Virginia. He was united in marriage with Miss Margaret Slough on January 11, 1757, and they settled at his home in Virginia. Their family comprised five children, namely: William Slough, James, Mathias, Thomas and one daughter. Thomas was reared in the faith of the Church of England. He gave his children good educational and religious training, was a bountiful provider for all their needs, maintained strict family government, but was warmly devoted to his family's best interests, as was also his wife. In 1767, with wife and children, he removed and settled in Pennsylvania, and in 1772 he became a judicial officer under the crown by a commission from George III; the duties of which he faithfully and impartially executed until his death in 1775, which occurred at his home in Pennsylvania.

He was a man deservedly esteemed by all who knew him for his many noble characteristics. He was also a good composer of both prose and verse.

Of the marriages of the children of Thomas Lemen and wife, we have before us a record of the marriage of James, who was born December, 1757. He married Miss Rachel Fleming, of Middletown, Pa., in 1787. Their family comprised nine children, namely: Thomas, Percipher, George, Martha, Margaret, Rachel, Rebecca, James and William. James, the father, died in 1842, and his wife, Rachel, died in 1840.

Rebecca Lemen, their fourth daughter, was born on April 4, 1803, and died June 29, 1893, living some ninety years, which exceeds by a few years the age of any of our family yet mentioned. She was a lady of culture, a devoted wife and an affectionate mother. She married Hugh McWilliams, a grandson of Hugh McWilliams, who was killed by the Indians at the Massacre at Wyoming, Pa. He was also a grandson of Lieutenant Robert Curry, who was also killed by the Indians, and his grandmother, wife of Lieutenant Curry, was taken prisoner by them.

Mr. Hugh McWilliams and wife reared a family of whom three daughters are yet living, namely: Harriet, who married Gilbert Voris, land owner; Regina, who married Dr. Simington; and Annie, who married Frank R. Hain, now deceased, who was Vice-President and General Manager of the Manhattan Elevated Railway. None of the children of the latter are living.   Mrs. Hain resides in New York City, 165 West Fifty-eighth street.

Thomas Lemen, like one or two of his kinsmen among the pioneer Lemens of Illinois, had the gift of poetry so naturally that he could compose very good verse extemporaneously.   He was of a very practical turn of mind, and he regarded the art of making poetry as rather a trivial occupation, but sometimes, for the gratification of his friends, he would extemporize a few verses and let them write them down if they wished; but he would scarcely ever trouble to write it himself.   The following verses, entitled, "Our Three Homes," were composed by Thomas and written and preserved by some of the early Lemens in Virginia, a copy of which was sent to Rev. James Lemen, Jr., of Illinois, in 1840, by a William Lemen from Richmond, Va.   The poem is as follows:

OUR THREE HOMES.

Our fathers bold, the facts agree,
Were quite at home on land and sea;
They lived on Scotland's rugged height,
And fought with Cromwell for the right.

Their second home was Erin's Isle,
Forgetting not their craft the while—
Of making ships with skillful hand,
That sailed to many a distant land.

And then in seventeen and eight,
They sought again a new estate;
And made America their home,
From which their children will not roam.

JOHN LEMEN, a son of James Lemen and Jane Lemen, nee Burns, his wife, was born at the home of his parents in Eastern Virginia, in 1715. In early life his education was limited, but in later years he became a man of large practical information. He was reared in the faith of the Church of England. He was married in Eastern Virginia in 1737, and with his wife settled on his farm there, where their older children were born. Their children were: Alexander, born December 10, 1738; Mary, born in 1740, and John, James, William, and two other daughters in the order named. In 1746 he and wife with their young family removed and settled on a farm near Harper's Ferry, in what is now West Virginia. He was a good planter, and a man much esteemed for his excellent character and other noble qualities. He died at his home on May 10, 1774. The name of his wife is on our old records, but it is faded out and is illegible, though our old family notes mention her as yet living in 1777 with her son William.

John's oldest son, Alexander, married Miss Mary Reynolds on June 8, 1773, and their children were: Elizabeth, Jane, William, Margaret, John, Ann, Alexander and Mary. James, another son, married in 1775, had one child, Ruth; his wife died in 1776, and he died July 10, 1777. John, one of the older sons, was also married and reared a family. William, the other son, married Miss Margaret Martin in 1781. Of the three daughters, Mary married Jacob Morgan, the second daughter married John Barns, and the other daughter married John Taylor, and they all had families.

(33) James, who lived near Harper's Ferry, in West Virginia, and who died in 177·, made testamentary disposition of his property before his death, conveying his land to his wife and daughter (73) Ruth, conditional upon her survival to majority, but if otherwise to go to his brother William, the latter and his mother, meanwhile, to enjoy its benefits. To (56) Elizabeth, a little daughter of his brother Alexander, he gave a legacy, but she died in 1778. To John Barns' son (84) Joseph and daughter (85) Reeca, he gave a colt each, and to John Taylor's son (87) Levi, and his brother John's son (89) Alexander, he gave certain legacies, and a mare to Mary Morgan, one of his sisters.

Of the families or descendants of John Lemen and wife, some members yet live in or near their old community in West Virginia, but chiefly, in early times, they removed into Ohio and thence at a later period many of them removed and settled in Central and Northern Illinois and elsewhere in the West. In Ohio the members of the family were chiefly communicants of the M. E. Church, but they are represented in all the churches, and generally they have been and are an intelligent, useful and influential family.

ROBERT LEMEN, a son of James Lemen and Jane Burns Lemen, his wife, was born at the home of his

parents in Eastern Virginia on August 3, 1716. In
early life his education was meager, but in later years
he became a large reader and a man of liberal information.   He was a member of the Church of England.
In 1737 he married, and with his wife settled on his
farm in Eastern Virginia, where their older children
were born.   In 1746 with his wife and young family
he removed and settled near Harper's Ferry, now in
West Virginia, where he procured a farm.   His vocation was that of a planter.   He was a man of excellent and popular traits of mind and character, and
was warmly esteemed by all of his neighbors.   He
died at his home near Harper's Ferry in 1766.

    Among his older children were Robert, John and
William Lemen, all of whom married in Virginia.
Among his grandchildren, according to our old family
notes, was George Lemen, said to have been a son of
Robert Lemen, who was the oldest son of Robert,
Sr.   George Lemen was married in 1785 and reared
a family, and among his grandsons (according to the
recollections of Robert Lemen, now living in Wil-
liamsport, Md.,) were John, Robert and Ward
Lemen, who were brothers.   They spelled their name
Lemon, and sometimes Ward spelled his name *Leh-
man* or *Lamon*, in order to give it the pronunciation
which the early family name had in Scotland and
Ireland, and during the first generation in Virginia.
Robert Lemen, brother to Ward, was at one time
Sheriff of Berkeley County, West Virginia.   Ward
Lemen or Lamon was Lincoln's law partner in Spring-

field, Ill., and afterward he was Marshal of Washington City, D. C.   He became an eminent attorney, and he wrote Pres. Lincoln's first history.   He died some years since, and was buried in a cemetery near Martinsburg, W. Va.   Some of Robert Lemen's (Sr.) descendants removed to Pennsylvania and New York, and others settled in Ohio and Central and Northern Illinois.   Some of them have filled high positions of trust and honor, and, as a family, they have been excellent citizens and influential members of society.   This sketch of Robert Lemen, Sr., is necessarily meager, as we have lost a part of our old family notes relating to his family; but it is sufficiently comprehensive to enable his descendants, with the aid of their own later family records (probably now in their own hands), to properly connect and trace the several lines of the family.

CHAPTER IV.

(43) ROBERT LEMEN AND (42) JOHN LEMEN.

Robert Lemen, second son and second child of
Nicholas Lemen and Christian Lemen, his wife, was
born at the homestead of his parents in Frederick
County, now Jefferson County, West Virginia, on
November 6, 1750. In early life he enjoyed the
advantages of a good religious training, and acquired
a common school education, and in later years he
became a man of extensive reading and large general
information. He was a member of the Baptist Church
in Virginia, becoming a deacon, in which relation he
faithfully and acceptably served his church for a long
term of years, and his hospitable mansion was ever
open to ministers and other friends. Physically, he
was of large build, well proportioned, of great strength
and endurance; while in the attributes of manhood,
morals and mind, he was brave, generous and intelligent, just and patriotic, and he enjoyed the confidence and esteem of everybody who knew him.

Mr. Lemen was a good manager and a good planter, owning that part of his father's farm in Frederick
County, set apart to him by will, and on which he
and his wife settled when they were married, and
where they reared their family. His wife was Miss
Esther Banes, formerly of Pennsylvania. They were
married in Virginia on May 19, 1779, and their chil-

dren were James, Sarah, Thomas, Elizabeth, Eli,
Christian, Robert, Nicholas, Adrian, John, Mary,
Nancy, Hester and William, born in the order named.
For further records of the children see the family
records elsewhere.   In his rules of family government Robert Lemen, like his father, Nicholas, and
his brother, Rev. James Lemen, Sr., of Illinois, was
very strict; but as his requirements were always
reasonable and just, his children rendered a willing
and cheerful obedience, and altogether they constituted a well regulated, contented and happy family.
He was warmly devoted to his family's interests, providing abundantly for their wants, and giving them a
good religious training and such educational advantages as his means and environments permitted.   He
always kept family worship, and both by precept and
example, instilled into the hearts and minds of his
children true standards and ideas of sound morality
and a profound respect for everything that was
honest, virtuous and upright.

He possessed a remarkably even temper, but when
the right was involved he was resolute and uncom-
promising. He was generous, charitable and patriotic,
and could forgive an injury or an affront under proper
circumstances; but he was a stranger to fear, and
with his large stature and great strength he was well
equipped to defend and maintain his rights.   Upon
occasion, in Eastern Virginia, where he was called on
business in 1775, he was denouncing the King of
England for his heartless oppressions in America,

when a British officer, armed, assaulted him for his
brave words; but with a blow from his right arm
with the force of a sledge hammer he landed on the
officer's mouth, knocking him down, and he instantly
relieved him of his sword, much to the delight and
satisfaction of the crowd, who were largely with
Robert in their feelings. He finally served as a soldier under Washington, and was in the American
army at Yorktown when Lord Cornwallis and his
British army surrendered. He and his brothers were
intimate associates of the Lees in Virginia, and warm
friends and admirers of Thomas Jefferson, who in
later years was often at Robert's house and enjoyed
many a meal at his hospitable table; and the young
men often consulted Jefferson and sought his advice.
Like the Lees and Thomas Jefferson, Robert and
the several branches of the Lemens in Virginia were
intensely loyal to the colonial side of the contention
against George III. and his parliaments several years
before the war began; and their determined opposition and influence against the minions of monarchy
and misrule were important factors which at an early
stage hastened the action of Virginia to unite with
her sister colonies in declaring for independence.

The marked influence of Robert and his wife upon
the religious preferences of their children resulted
generally in their conversion to the Baptist faith.
With but few exceptions they united with the Baptist
Church, one of their daughters, Hester, having her
membership in that church for half a century, one of

their sons, Nicholas, born March 31, 1792, was a
soldier in the war of 1812, where he contracted a
fatal illness which resulted in his death on February
27, 1815. The descendants of Robert and wife now
number many hundreds, with about the usual per
cent living, and they represent every honorable and
upright profession, calling or trade in which people
seek an honest living. Their descendants in part are
now not only living in West Virginia, but also here
and there throughout the Union, and many of them
have occupied important positions of honor and trust
in their several communities and States. After a
well spent, upright and useful life, full of years and
beloved by all his neighbors, Robert Lemen died at
his home in Jefferson County, Virginia, on January
25, 1827. His wife, Esther Banes Lemen, a daughter
of John Banes and Elizabeth Phaxton Banes, his
wife, was born in Virginia on October 20, 1761, and
died at the old home in Jefferson County, Virginia,
on March 2, 1841. She was a devoted wife, an affectionate mother, and an excellent Christian lady, who
was deservedly esteemed by all for her many virtues
and noble endowments. The marriages and family
records of Robert's sisters, Nancy and Mary, will be
found elsewhere.

JOHN LEMEN, first child and son of Nicholas
Lemen and Christian Lemen, his wife, was born at
the home of his parents in what is now Jefferson
County, West Virginia, on December 14, 1749. He

was married in Virginia in early manhood, and he and his wife settled on that part of the original farm of his father, Nicholas Lemen, which was given to him by will, now in Jefferson County, West Virginia, where they had a family of sons and daughters. His wife, Martha Lemen, died at their home in 1786, in which year, on March 12, he sold and conveyed by deed, 110 acres of his farm in Jefferson County, to other parties, and at an early period he and his children moved further West and settled in Ohio. In 1798, one of his sons, Nicholas Lemen and Mary Lemen, his wife, sold to his (Nicholas') uncle, Robert Lemen, a small interest, some five acres of land (being a part of the original 570 acres of his grandfather Nicholas' land), the deed bearing date of June 25, 1798. At a later period some members of the family moved from Ohio and settled in Northern Illinois and elsewhere in the West. A few of John and Martha Lemen's descendants yet live in West Virginia, quite a number in Ohio, some in Chicago, and quite a number in other parts of the country, generally well respected and good members of society. John Lemen was a man of good character, large influence and excellent capabilities, and justly commanded the esteem of all his acquaintances and associates. When and where he died our family notes do not say. His occupation was that of a planter.

CHAPTER V.

NOTES, FACTS AND INCIDENTS.

The following chapter contains quite a number of facts and incidents relating to events and members of the early family in Virginia:

When the Lemen family first located in Frederick County, Virginia, that county included quite a large area, but in 1775, a part of Frederick County, where they lived, was cut off and formed Berkeley County, and in 1800, a part of Berkeley County, where many of them then lived, was cut off and formed Jefferson County; and these facts will explain why it appears in the Lemen History that at times they lived in the several different counties. The reader will bear this in mind.

Robert Lemen (a son of Nicholas and Christian Lemen), who married Miss Esther Banes, left his lands in Jefferson County, West Virginia, to their sons. Their oldest son, James, and youngest son, William, bought out the others' interests and lived on the home place. James never married; was a member of the Baptist Church; was a farmer and lived in the old mansion built by his grandfather, Nicholas Lemen. He died June 14, 1866, aged eighty-six years. Sarah Lemen, second child of Robert and Esther Lemen was a devout member of the Baptist Church. She married John Burns, and

they had four children. Thomas Lemen, the third
son, is mentioned elsewhere. He was a prominent
farmer, an excellent citizen and a man of large
influence, and justly esteemed by all his acquaintances. He married Barbara Amos after his first
wife's death, and they had three children, Sarah E.,
Virginia E. and Samuel R. Lemen. He was enrolled
as a soldier in the war of 1812, but the war ended
shortly afterwards and he was not in any battles.

John Lemen, a son of James Lemen and Jane
Burns Lemen, of East Virginia, made a will on April
2, 1774, giving his youngest three sons, John, James
and William, his farm near Harper's Ferry, Va., in
equal parts, and his wife a third interest for life.
He had previously given his oldest son, Alexander,
his part. His wife and son, Alexander, were execu-
tors.

On March 3, 1773, John Lemen and Martha, his
wife, with his brother Robert and their mother,
Christian Eaty (who after the death of her first husband, Nicholas Lemen, had married Rev. Henry
Eaty), made a deed conveying a part of the original
570 acre tract of land of their father to Andrew
Fouts, their brother-in-law.

At the request of the compiler and publisher of
our Family History, Mr. Frank B. Lemen, and other
members of the family, the writer, Joseph B. Lemen,
of Collinsville, Ill., has written and prepared this and
the preceding chapters in this, the Virginia Division
of our Family History; and he desires to express his

sincere thanks to prominent members of the family in West Virginia, Maryland and elsewhere, for the intelligent and excellent services which they have rendered in compiling many of the facts for this work. In executing the family request, the writer has necessarily had large correspondence with many parties in the interest of our Family History, and often writing to them from mere memory respecting many names, dates and incidents in our large collection of old family notes, it is very likely that he has committed some errors in dates or names; but in the final preparation of that part of our Family History committed to his care and preparation, he has compared every statement, date and name with the old records, notes and names, or with accurate copies of them in his possession, and thus avoided, as far as constant care might do, all inaccuracies or errors.

In the great labor and care expended by the compiler and publisher of this work, Mr. Frank B. Lemen, of Collinsville, Ill., he has brought to the task a degree of untiring patience, a persistent perseverance and a consummate skill, at a large expenditure of means, time and labor, which have made our Family History a success. Not, however, as a monetary venture, because he will be exceedingly fortunate if he ever recovers the actual funds expended; but rather in that higher sense in which success means merit. For the labor, time and skill expended, worth in themselves several hundred dollars, Mr. Lemen will receive nothing except the satisfaction of having rendered his large and widely extended family a noble service, which, but for him, would not have been rendered during the lifetime of our present generation, and probably never.

In this connection we are not only justified but fully authorized on behalf of our large family in West Virginia, Maryland, Pennsylvania, New York and elsewhere, to extend to Mr. Lemen their grateful remembrance and sincere gratitude for the great labor of love he has performed for the family in making our History a success.

In concluding this chapter it is proper to say, that our Family History contains in its different parts, every name, fact, date, record and incident mentioned in our large collections of old family notes, records, etc., so far as prolonged and diligent researches can discover; and the many members of the family and other readers who would familiarize themselves with their contents can only do so by securing a copy of this History.

CHAPTER VI.

THE WILLIAMSPORT FERRY.

BY S. D. CALDWELL.

This is perhaps the oldest ferry on the Potomac. In looking up its history the writer finds that the first grant of lands adjacent to this ferry was made by Charles II. of England to Ralph Lord Hopton and others (1 Car. II.), the tract being known as "The Northern Neck of Virginia," which is described in the second grant of this tract by Charles II. (2 Car. II.), to Earl St. Albans and others, as all that tract bounded by and lying within the heads of the rivers Rappahannock, etc., together with the rivers themselves, etc., and that the third and last grant was by James II. to Thomas Lord Culpepper, in 1736. By Act of Assembly (Rev. Code, vol. 1, ch. 3, p. 5) the title was confirmed to Rt. Hon. Thomas Lord Fairfax, the heir-at-law of Lord Culpepper. In 1748, Lord Fairfax, at his own expense, opened a land office and disposed of large tracts of waste and ungranted lands, in fee, to various persons, among whom was one Watkins, a son-in-law of Lord Fairfax, who became the owner of a large section of land in the vicinity of the above mentioned ferry, of which Watkins was undoubtedly the first owner and operator. This ferry is referred to in (vol. 2, p. 43) of Penn's Archives for the years 1748–1756, wherein Thomas Cookson, of Lancaster, reporting under date of March 1, 1749, to Governor Hamilton, as to the proper situation for the county town of Cumberland County, Pennsylvania, mentions the fact that "Lord Fairfax was laying out a town at *Watkins' Ferry* on the Potomac." Watkins sold a large tract of his land, containing several thousand acres, laying in the vicinity of this ferry, to one Rolly Colston, who in turn disposed of a part of his holdings, including the Virginia terminus of the ferry, to Peter Light, by whose name the ferry afterwards went. These lands descended to his son Peter, and in 1854 a part of them were purchased, including the ferry, by Robert Lemen, whose wife was a niece of Peter Light, Jr. Mr. Lemen lived most of his life on his property, and managed the ferry until recent years, when his children being all grown up and married, he rented his farm and went to live with his son-in-law, Charles A. Ardinger, who had built a house near the ferry landing, and has been in charge of the ferry ever since.

Mr. Lemen informed the writer in a conversation recently, that no wire was used on the ferry until he placed one there; that shortly after he purchased the property he began to experiment to devise some means of crossing the river in a direct line in spite of the current, the old way being to start the boat at some point on the one shore considerably above where it might be expected the current would land it on the opposite side, and on return it was necessary to tow the boat up the river a corresponding distance so

that it would land about the same place from where
it started. He first took a bed cord and fastening it
to the shore carried it out into the stream some distance, making it fast to the bottom of the river. He
then put a ring on the cord which ring was connected
with the boat, and by inclining the boat to the rope
at an angle he found that the current would force the
boat along the rope, that end nearest the rope moving
forward, and to return all he had to do was to reverse
the program, bringing the other end of the boat
nearest the rope. Having demonstrated the principle, he went to Trenton, N. J., in 1857, and bought
the identical wire now used, and stretched it across
the river. This wire cost about $260.00, or 13 cents
a pound, it weighed about a ton. The same kind of
wire can now be bought for 3 cents a pound. This
wire was cut on the Virginia side in the spring of 1861,
by his own nephew (Billmyer) who was in the Confederate service at the time. Mr. Lemen had three
sons in the Union army and five nephews in the Confederate army, the latter living in Jefferson County.
They all came out of the war without hurt except
Robert Billmyer, who was slightly wounded. Mr.
Lemen's situation on the west bank of the Potomac
was a very dangerous one, as both armies crossed
and recrossed at his ferry and passed his house, and
the two armies had gun practice across the river at
whatever object came in sight, which made it extremely dangerous for him and his family to show
themselves. The members of his family had many

narrow escapes during the war from this rifle and gun practice.

Upon inquiry of Mr. Lemen as to whether he was the first to use the wire on a ferry, and whether he had ever applied for a patent, he said he was not certain, but thought his arrangement was at least an improvement upon anything that had been used before, and could not remember whether he had ever seen anything like it before he constructed his, and that he never applied for a patent. He also stated that when he went to New Jersey to buy the wire, he was referred to a place somewhere on the Delaware River, where, he was told, some such arrangement was used, though he never saw it.

As to the amount of business the ferry did, Mr. Lemen stated that during the four years of the Rebellion, the average number of trips per day was about twenty, though as high as a hundred had been made. Since that period the average was perhaps ten.

Quite a fine stick of timber is required to make the planks forming the sides of the boat which is fifty feet long, as they must be six inches thick, and the small end of such a stick must measure from twenty-four to twenty-six inches in diameter. The planks in the old boat which has just been laid aside for a new one after twelve years' service, cost $65.00 in Cumberland, Md. The boat will carry a loaded wagon with six horses attached, the charge for the transportation of which is $1.00.

Mr. Lemen is a Republican, and believes the cause of the present depression in all kinds of business is to be attributed to over-production, both in products of the farm and workshops and in the family. Mr. Lemen has thirty-five grandchildren, thirty-one of whom are living.

Mr. Lemen spoke of the time Washington visited Williamsport, on the search for a location for the Nation's Capital, and said Washington had made his headquarters in the old building now owned and occupied by his son Thomas Lemen; that Washington had presented an old colored woman named Kitty Warren, with a silver dollar which she used to show with much pride; that Kitty had only been dead about twelve years—perhaps fifteen—and that she and her son were owned by Mr. Syester who sold her son to a slave dealer, or "soul driver," as he said they were then called, and when the purchaser came to Kitty's house, which was in an obscure alley, to get his man, she, butcher knife in hand, chased the fellow out of her place, though he returned and got her son. In connection with the slave business, Mr. Lemen related, that when Fred Douglas was being led through the streets of Baltimore, shackled and fastened to other slaves, on the way to the slave market, Fred raised his voice and sang, "Hail Columbia Happy Land," and that a bystander was so affected by the sight and sentiment that he sought out the owner of Fred, bought him and set him free.

CHAPTER VII.

103—MRS. HESTER LEMEN KEARFOTT.

Mrs. Hester Lemen Kearfott, youngest daughter of Robert Lemen, and Esther Lemen, his wife, was born November 2, 1801, in the farm house built by her grandfather, Nicholas Lemen, in what is now Jefferson County, West Virginia; and in August, 1827, she was united in the bonds of matrimony with John Pierceall Kearfott. Soon after they were married they assisted in organizing and united with the Baptist Church at Mt. Zion; and during all their lives they were earnest and devoted Christians. To their union were born eight children, two of whom died in infancy. She died January 6, 1862, aged 81 years, 3 months and 4 days.

John P. Kearfott, her husband, was a school teacher for more than twenty years in connection with being a County Surveyor of Berkeley County, West Virginia, for about forty years. Was in early life elected deacon and clerk of the Mt. Zion Baptist Church, which position he held until death, and being a man of deep piety, exemplary character and kindly disposition, he was deservedly esteemed by all his acquaintances, and commanded a large and helpful influence in his community; and by reason of his liberal acquirements and thorough mathematical training, he was often called to give much time and

235—JOSEPH BAKER KEARFOTT.

attention in the arbitration and settlement of estates, either as executor or administrator. His death, which occurred very suddenly, was in June, 1881, aged 76 years.

235—JOSEPH BAKER KEARFOTT.

Joseph Baker Kearfott, second son of John P. and Hester Lemen Kearfott, was born November 2, 1830, in Berkeley County, Virginia (now West Virginia). In early life he received a common school education and engaged in teaching school and surveying. At the age of seventeen years he united with the Mt. Zion Baptist Church, and in 1869, assisted in organizing the First Baptist Church in Martinsburgh, W. Va.. at which time he was chosen one of the deacons.

In 1855 he was united in marriage with Mary Ruth Gorrell, and from this union were born seven children, two of whom died in infancy. Those living are Clarence P., a druggist in Martinsville, Va.; Joseph Gorrell, a druggist in Amhurst, Va.; Hettie Bell, who married Milton S. Miller, a farmer; Mary Baker, who married Henry Bogert, of Martinsburg, W. Va.; and Fannie Quick, unmarried.

Mr. Kearfott, from his large experience, ready perception, thorough acquaintance with the intricacies of titles and records and liberal knowledge of the higher mathematics, is well equipped as a successful antiquarian and investigator, and his labors in that

field have been large and creditable; and in addition
to his life pursuits he has made and published a map
of Berkeley County, West Virginia.   He is also a
very careful, accurate and ready surveyor.   In 1875
his second marriage occurred, which was with Miss
Rachel A. Brotherton, of Jefferson County, West
Virginia.

181—ROBERT LEMEN, JR.

Robert Lemen, Jr., was a son of Thomas Lemen,
who was a son of Robert Lemen, one of the brothers
of Rev. James Lemen, Sr., who settled in Illinois in
1786.   Thomas Lemen married Mary O. Williamson.
His home was in Berkeley County, West Virginia.
They had nine children, namely: Eliza, Jane, Mary,
Robert, Nicholas, Christopher, Joseph, William and
Hester.   Nicholas was a minister of the gospel, and
his son, Miner, is now a minister in the M. P. Church.
Robert Lemen, Jr., who bought the farm owned by
his father, Thomas Lemen, married Sallie E. Light,
of Berkeley County.   They had nine children, which
are Peter Light Lemen, Jacob F., Thomas J., Nicholas
S., Mary A. L., William and Virginia, living, and
Sallie and Robert, dead.

Robert Lemen, Jr., bought the Peter Light farm
and ferry near Williamsport, Md.   During the war
Gen. Robert E. Lee crossed the ferry here to and
from Gettysburg with his army.   Robert Lemen's
oldest son, Peter, was in the Union army, in the

First Maryland Cavalry, and part of his time during the war was in the Provost office. After the war he was deputy clerk in the Berkeley County Court. In 1801 he was elected Judge of the Orphan's Court in Maryland; he is now a merchant in Williamsport. He was born December 14, 1840. Married Miss Helen Stake, and three children were born to them, Bessie, Nellie and Robert. After his first wife's death he married Nannie Hatler, and they have three children, Mary, Louis and Herman.

Jacob F. Lemen was born July 24, 1842. He lives in Washington County, Maryland. Married Miss Sallie Hyser, of Hagerstown, Md., and one child was born to them, George. After her death, he married a widow lady, Mrs. Nancie Wilson, and from this union there were six children, John, Jacob, Mary, Sallie, Robert and Newton. Jacob Lemen was in the Union army.

Thomas J. Lemen was born August 31, 1843. He married Miss Anna Ensminger. They have three children, John, Thomas and Bessie. He served in the Union army; is now a merchant in Williamsport, Md.

Nicholas Lemen was born April 14, 1845. He married Miss Virginia Shoop. They had eight children, five of whom are living, Samuel, John, Mary, Ross and Sallie. John is a postal clerk.

Mary Lemen was born April 27, 1847. Married W. B. Price, of Illinois, now of Louisville, and owns three well-improved farms. They had three children, Walter and Sallie, living, and Daisy, dead.

William E. Lemen was born April 2, 1851.
Bought a fine farm in Kansas, then went to California,
and after having been away seventeen years, returned
home.

Virginia Lemen was born January 3, 1852.   Mar-
ried Charles Ardinger.   They have nine children,
Robert, John, Thomas, Lena, Dixie, George, Hollie,
Sallie and Kearfott.

A branch of the Lemen family has not been men-
tioned as yet.   Robert Lemen, Jr., says he can go
back to George Lemen, who was a second cousin to
Thomas Lemen, his father.   He says among George
Lemen's grandsons were John, Robert and Ward
Lemen, brothers.   Robert Lemen was sheriff of
Berkeley County, West Virginia.   They spell their
name L-e-m·o-n; Ward Lemen spelled his name
Lehman, though they are brothers, according to
Robert Lemen's statement—grandsons of George
Lemen.   Ward Lehman was law partner of Abraham
Lincoln, and when Lincoln became president he made
him Chief Marshal of Washington, D. C.   He was
attorney for a tribe of Indians in Kansas; he gained
the suit and they paid him $250,000 for his services.
He also did valuable service for Robert Lemen, Jr.
When his horses were taken by the army he went
after them himself and returned with them.   He
also did all of Robert's business in Washington in
collecting his war claims, and did not charge for his
services.   Ward wrote the first history of Lincoln's
life.

Robert Lemen, Jr., had three sons in the Union
army, Peter, Jacob and Thomas. Had one brother,
Jacob D. Lemen, in the Confederate army, also one
brother-in-law, Henry Hagen, who married Hester
Lemen. He also had six nephews in the Southern
army, Thomas Jones, James Jones, Capt. Milton
Billmyer, Lieut. John Billmyer, Robert Billmyer and
White Williamson; they all came out safe and sound.
Robert Lemen, Jr., has thirty-one grandchildren,
and two great grandchildren.

(177) MRS MARY WILLIAMSON LEMEN AND (458) MRS. SALLIE LIGHT LEMEN.

Robert Lemen, Jr., of Williamsport, Md., has
written the following sketches of his mother and
his wife, with mention of some members of their
families. He says: My mother, Mary Williamson Lemen, was a Baptist. She was baptized in the
Potomac River near where I now live, and was a
member of the Mt. Zion Baptist Church, of Berkeley
County. She had four brothers: namely, Jacob,
Dorris, John and William. Dr. Jacob Williamson,
who was an eminent physician, adopted my brother,
Jacob Lemen, and at his death left him a large
estate in lands and negroes, the latter were all
emancipated after the war. Dorris Williamson emigrated to Ohio in 1800, and there raised a large
family, and all settled in sight of his home, except

one, who removed to Michigan. The old gentleman, Dorris Williamson, received a very fine carriage from his sons, and as it was too fine for him, he cut the top off; and for the same reason, he also cut the posts off of a very fine bedstead which they sent him, preferring to sleep in the old continental bedstead. John Williamson was a man of considerable wealth. Had a very large family. William Williamson was never married.

My aunt, Ollie Williamson, married a Mr. Thornburg and reared a large family. All were Presbyterians.

Joseph Lemen, one of my brothers, now lives in Champaign, Ill. My youngest sister lived in Springfield, Ill., went to the Illinois College, and while there became acquainted with Prof. Strong's son and they were married. She died some years ago and left a family of four children; they are living in Decatur, Ill.

We have made it a rule to hold an annual Lemen Reunion which has been kept up for the last thirty years. It is always held at the Sulphur Springs, at Bedington, W. Va., at the place where my father-in-law lived, about seven miles from the Lemen Ferry. The picnic is largely attended every year.

I married Miss Sallie E. Light in 18?8. Her father was Jacob F. Light, of Bedington. Her uncle, John Light, was a very distinguished minister in the Methodist Protestant Church. Her uncle, Robert

185—JOSEPH R. LEMEN.

Wilson, was a traveling minister for many years. Her brother-in-law, Thomas Ward, was the founder of the Western Maryland College, one of the most prominent institutions of learning in the State. He used a great deal of his own funds for the school. Was also President of that college. Peter Wilson, her cousin, was a minister in the Methodist Protestant Church. All of her family were Methodist Protestants. We are a branch of the Episcopal Church, and withdrew from that church on account of church government, which we considered as a one-man power. The Methodist Protestant is a representative church with a republican form of government. At the meeting of our conference we send a lay delegate with every minister, and in the trying of members for violations of rules of the church, they are tried by a committee, and the member accused can challenge any one of the committee, and if they are not satisfied with their trial they can then appeal to the quarterly conference, and from the quarterly to the annual conference, and from the annual to the general conference, which is final.

Jacob F. Lemen, my son, is the patentee of the great perforated strap fence. I am the inventor of the machine to punch that strap—will punch a hundred weight of strap in thirty minutes. The end of the strap is put into the machine, it feeds itself and punches a hole every two inches, with only the labor of a young boy; it was a great success for the strap fence.

185—JOSEPH R. LEMEN.

Joseph Roberts Lemen, son of Thomas and Mary
O. Lemen, born January 13, 1823, in Berkeley
County, Virginia. His mother's maiden name was
Williamson. She was a descendant of an old French
family, De Grot, driven out of France during the
Hugenot trouble. He served in the army during the
Mexican war, and was honorably discharged. He
was married January 29, 1852, to Mary Catharine
Price, at Harper's Ferry, W. Va., and resided there
until 1858, was in the employ of the United States
Government. From there he went to Pittsburg, Pa.,
and was there four or five years, still in the employ
of the government. He then went to Baltimore
County, Maryland, and opened a blacksmith shop,
and continued that business until 1868, when he
came to Champaign, Ill. He has lived there ever
since, and has been continuously in the employ of the
Illinois Central Railroad. He has no children. He
receives a Mexican war pension.

161—DR. MILTON LEMEN.

Dr. Milton Lemen, was born March 1, 1819, in
Clark County, Ohio. He was a son of Judge John
and Rebecca (Donelson) Lemen. Judge Lemen's
wife was an aunt to Gen. Andrew Jackson's wife.
The Lemens were natives of Virginia, and emigrated
to Ohio. He studied medicine with Dr. Robert

Houston, of South Charleston, O., and located at
Midway, in 1843, and had an immense practice. He
was a man of great energy, tall, wiry, restive and
impetuous. He was a skilled and popular physician. In the fall of 1860, he was elected to the Ohio
Legislature. He removed to London, in 1862, and
was appointed by President Lincoln an examining
surgeon for the counties of Madison, Clark, Green
and Franklin. He was attacked with paralysis in
1865, before his discharge from the service. He died
at his home in London, O., April 24, 1878. He led
a very inactive life for fourteen years preceding his
death, owing to his paralytic condition. He married
Sarah, daughter of Samuel and Elizabeth Smith, of
Clark County, Ohio, May 5, 1840. His wife died
June 27, 1890, of heart trouble. Her last and fatal
illness was at her daughter's, Mrs. Y. B. Woosley,
of London, O. Of their eight children, three are
living, Mrs. Elizabeth Woosley, Mrs. Alice Curtain,
of Los Angeles, Cal., and Mrs. Ida Stroup, of South
Charleston, O.

164—WILLIAM FISHER LEMEN.

William Fisher Lemen, son of Judge John R.
Lemen, was born and reared on a farm east of Springfield, Clark County, Ohio. In 1848 he was married
to Susanna E. Bishop and lived on the farm till 1859,
when he sold his farm and moved north to Round-
head, Hardin County, Ohio, where he engaged in the

grocery business, and from 1862 was postmaster several years. He enlisted as a Union soldier in 1864 for one year, but was finally rejected owing to ill health. In 1868 he with his wife and family moved to a farm in Dewitt County, Illinois, thence to Bloomington, McLean County, Illinois, in 1872, where he engaged again in the grocery business and remained until his death. He was of the Methodist faith, and his family are devout members of the M. E. Church.

425—MAUD-EOLINE LEMEN.

Maud-Eoline Lemen was born in Dewitt County, Illinois, and at the age of two years with her parents came to Bloomington, Ill., where she now resides. She received her education in the Bloomington public and high schools, also State Normal University, at Normal, Ill., during that time a musical course was pursued. At the age of eighteen she began her career as teacher in the public schools at Maroa, Ill., two years in public school at Hudson, Ill., thence in city schools at Bloomington. During the past three years of teaching she completed a three years' course in oratory. As a reader, and having given many recitals, she exhibits gifted elocutionary talent and is an adept in the art of "pantomime." She is a member of the M. E. Church, having united with that church in early life.

425—MAUD-EOLINE LEMEN.

331—PROF. WILLIAM S. LEMEN.

Prof. Wm. S. Lemen was a young man of marked ability and of high social standing. At the time of his death, June 21, 1892, he had charge of the biological department in the high school, which position he had successfully filled for three years. His death resulted from an introversion of the intestines, a trouble similar to that which caused the death of Emmons Blaine and Judge Howland. His uncle, Dr. Samuel G. Dorr, of Buffalo, N. Y., attended him during the last week of illness, and his sister, of Danville, N. Y., was also at his bedside.

Prof. Lemen was born August 22, 1858, at Danville, N. Y. He graduated from Rochester University in 1883. He spent four years in teaching at Tonawanda and Kingston, N. Y. For two years he made special studies in biology at Johns Hopkins University. In the high school he taught zoology, botany and geology, and under his direction, Principal W. W. Grant says, these branches reached a high standard in the school.

Prof. Lemen was also active in church work. He was a deacon of the First Presbyterian Church and a leader in the Christian Endeavor Society.

130—JAMES B. LEMEN.

Mr. James B. Lemen, of South Danville, N. Y., was born on the first day of October, 1816. He died

at his residence, on Sandy Hill, November 12, 1894.
Mr. Lemen lived his long life on his parental farm.
He was the eighth child of Major William S. Lemen,
a Revolutionary patriot, and Agnes Ewart Lemen.
He was the first white child born in that part of the
township known as Sandy Hill.   One sister only survives him at the age of eighty years.   His father
came to this State from Pennsylvania.   His brother,
Samuel Lemen, deceased, was twenty years his senior.
This brother and his father cut their way through
the forest from Ossian to the present farm sometime
previous to 1815.   They built a log house in the
woods very near where the present residence now
stands.   Here James B. was born, his childhood being
spent, like most children of those early pioneers, with
limited school facilities and assisting in work of clear-
ing forests, and surrounding himself with those comforts which made his declining years so pleasant.
Seven years prior to his death Mr. Lemen had a stroke
of paralysis, from which he never recovered.   While
in feeble health so many years, with his naturally
cheerful and social disposition, he retained his interest in home and friends by whom he will be greatly
missed and mourned.

May 1, 1845, he married Dina M. Dorr, the eldest
daughter of Samuel G. and Selina Phelps Dorr, of
Danville, who survives him.   Seven children were
born of this union, four of whom are living: Mrs.
Emma J. Campbell, of Danville; R. Dorr Lemen, of
Alma, Mich.; Orlo H. Lemen and Miss Martha E.,

328—ROBERT D. LEMEN.

of Danville. Mr. Lemen's life was the highest type of the true farmer—honest, industrious, neighborly, a friend to all that was good and right. In these days of rapid changes in families it is remarkable that four generations have in continuous succession occupied the old home.

50—MAJ. WILLIAM SLOUGH LEMEN.

Major William S. Lemen, was a son of Thomas Lemen and Margaret Lemen, nee Slough. He was born in Lancaster, Pa., in 1760. About 1815, he with his son Samuel cut their way through the forest from Ossian to near Danville, N. Y., where he located on Sandy Hill; here they cut logs and built a house near where the present Lemen residence now stands. Major Lemen was a soldier in the Revolutionary war, where his bravery and intense devotion to the cause won for him the rank to which he attained, that of Major. He, by indomitable push and enterprise, gathered around him that competence that has been a recompense not only to him but also to three generations who have had a birthplace at the parental homestead. From this home of intelligence and virtue have gone out on the four wings of the wind, as it were, to various parts of the United States, the descendants of this noble patriot, to disseminate the virtues, the patriotism and the intelligence that have brought the nation from the wilds of nature to the enlightened and elevated plane of civilization it now occupies. The influence of a worthy life cannot be lost, but will be felt not only through the representatives of that life, but through all with whom it comes in contact.

Major Lemen was thrice married. First at Williamsburg, Pa., to a lady whose name has been lost; the result of this union was two sons. Second marriage was to Lydia Dunwoddy; the result of this union was four children. Third marriage was to Agnes Evart, of Genesee, N. Y.; the result of the last was nine children.

328—ROBERT D. LEMEN.

Robert D. Lemen, the leading insurance agent in Alma, Mich., was born on a farm in Steuben County, New York, in 1850. He attended the district school until fifteen years of age, when he was sent to the seminary at Danville, N. Y., until his 18th year. At this time he taught his first term of school for four months, then worked on the farm for one year, when he took a commercial course at the L. L. Williams Business College in Rochester, N. Y. After this time he taught school for fourteen terms. Coming to Michigan in 1876, he settled on a farm near Fenton. He came to Alma in the fall of 1889 and settled, buying out the insurance business of A. Yerington. Mr. Lemen does a general insurance business, representing some of the oldest and best-known fire com-

397—ELIZA ANN FISHER.

panies in the United States, among which are the Hartford of Connecticut, Home of New York, Fire Association of Philadelphia, New York Underwriters', Germania, New York; Liverpool, London and Globe; Niagara, New York; Continental, New York; N. B. Mercantile and other reliable companies.

He was married in 1873 to Estella, second daughter of Judge Dunham. They have one son, Major, who is at present attending the Ohio University, at Ada, O.

669—J. MAJOR LEMEN.

J. Major Lemen, only son of Robert D. and Estelle Lemen, was born on a farm in the Township of Tyrone, Livingston County, Michigan, July 22, 1877. He entered the Union School at Fenton, Mich., in 1888. In the fall of 1889, he came with his parents to Alma, Gratiot County, Michigan. Entering the Union School at this place he graduated in a class of six in June, 1896. Entering the Business Department of Alma College, he completed the two years' course in one year, graduating at the head of the class in June, 1897. Having worked in a drugstore all his spare time for nearly three years while pursuing his school work, he decided on the profession of a pharmacist, and in the fall of 1897 entered the Ohio University at Ada, O., where he intends to complete a two years' course in pharmacy.

Major Lemen is a member of the Presbyterian Church at Alma, Mich., and an active member of the Young Men's Christian Association.

CHAPTER VIII.

GENEALOGICAL.

FIRST GENERATION.

1—**ROBERT LEMEN.** Born in Scotland. Ship carpenter.

2—William Lemen. Born in Scotland.

3—James. Born in Scotland.

6—Three sisters. Born in Scotland.

SECOND GENERATION.

1—**ROBERT LEMEN.**

7—**MARY ANDERSON.** Born in Scotland. After marriage they moved from Scotland to North Ireland, 1656. They had children, two of whom were:

8—Nicholas. Born in Ireland. Ship builder and navigator. Died 1728.

9—Thomas. Born in Ireland.

THIRD GENERATION.

8—NICHOLAS LEMEN.

10—NANCY McKANE. Born in Scotland. They were married 1685. They had four sons and three daughters. Three of the sons came to America in 1708. They were all three mariners and ship builders :

11—James. Born in North Ireland.

12—Robert.

13—Nicholas.

16—Three daughters.

FOURTH GENERATION.

11—JAMES LEMEN.

17—JANE BURNS. Born in Virginia. They were married in 1714. Their children were

18—John. Born in Virginia, June 4, 1715. Died May 10, 1774.

19—Robert. Born in Virginia, August 3, 1716, Died 1766.

20—Nicholas. Born in Virginia, 1725.

21—Thomas. Born on the sea, June 20, 1730.

23—Two daughters.

28—Five children. All died in early life.

FIFTH GENERATION.

18—JOHN LEMEN.

29—(His Wife.)

They were married in East Virginia, 1737. Their children were:

30—Alexander. Born December 10, 1738.

31—Mary. Born in 1740.

32—John.

33—James. Died 1777.

34—William.

35—Daughter.

36—Daughter.

19—ROBERT LEMEN.

37—(His Wife.)

They were married 1737. Their children were:

38—Robert.

39—John.

40—William.

20—NICHOLAS LEMEN.

41—CHRISTIAN (   ) They were married in Virginia, 1747. Their children were:

42—John. Born December 14, 1749.

43—Robert. Born November 6, 1750.

44—Nancy. Born March 4, 1754.

45—Mary. Born January 7, 1756.

46—Thomas. Born February 4, 1758.

47—James. Born November 20, 1760. Died January 8, 1823.

21—**THOMAS LEMEN.**

48—**MARGARET SLOUGH.** Born in Virginia, 1735. Died 1822. She was the daughter of Judge Slough, and sister of Col. Mathias Slough. They were married January 11, 1757. Their children were:

49—James. Born in Lancaster, Pa., near the close of 1757.

50—William Slough. Born in Lancaster, Pa., 1760. Died 1845, at Danville, N. Y. He was Major in the Revolutionary War.

51—Thomas.

52—Elizabeth.

SIXTH GENERATION.

30—ALEXANDER LEMEN.

55—MARY REYNOLDS. They were married June 8,|1773. Their children were born in Berkeley County, West Virginia, and were:

56—Elizabeth. Born January 22, 1775. Died September 4, 1778.

57—Jane. Born July 11, 1777. Died 1858 or 1859.

58—William. Born January 12, 1779. Died September 20, 1849.

59—Margaret. Born July 7, 1781. Died 1840.

60—John Reynolds. Born December 7, 1783. Died July 21, 1854.

61—Ann. Born May 3, 1786. Died May 5, 1792.

62—Alexander. Born April 6, 1788. Died May 12, 1792.

63—Mary. Born December 13, 1790. Died 1859.

31—POLLY LEMEN.
64—JACOB MORGAN.
65—Names of children not known.

32—JOHN LEMEN.
66—(His Wife.) They had a son and perhaps other children.

67—Alexander.

71—Names not known.

33—JAMES LEMEN.

72—(His Wife.) They were married 1775, and his wife died 1776. They had one child:

73—Ruth.

34—WILLIAM LEMEN.

74—MARGARET MARTIN. They were married in 1781. The names of their children are not known.

35—(Name not known.)

83—JOHN BARRIS. They had two children:

84—Joseph.

85—Reeca.

36—(Name not known.)

86—JOHN TAYLOR. They had a son:

87—Levi.

38—JOHN LEMEN.

88—MARTHA (   ) They had one son:

89—Alexander.

43—ROBERT LEMEN.

90—ESTHER BANES. They were married May 19, 1779. Their children were:

91—James. Born March 5, 1780. Died June 14, 1866.

92—Sarah. Born April 20, 1781. Died November 26, 1839. Baptist.

93—Thomas. Born March 16, 1783. Died January 23, 1838. Baptist. Farmer.

94—Elizabeth. Born August 31, 1784. Died July 9, 1855. Baptist.

95—Eli, Born June 15, 1786. Died October 25, 1786.

96—Christian. Born January 11, 1788. Died February 18, 1875.

97—Robert. Born May 23, 1790. Died November 13, 1870. Farmer.

98—Nicholas. Born March 31, 1792. Died February 27, 1815.

99—Adrian. Born February 8, 1794. Died July 6, 1794.

100—John. Born June 10, 1795. Died June 1, 1875.

101—Mary. Born June 18, 1797. Died December 25, 1840.

102—Nancy. Born September 11, 1799. Died May 24, 1865. Baptist.

103—Hester. Born November 2, 1801. Died January 6, 1882.

104—William. Born March 2, 1806. Died August 27, 1877. Lived on and owned the old Lemen homestead.

49—JAMES LEMEN.

105—RACHEL FLEMING. Born near Northumberland, Pa. She died in 1840. They were married 1787. Their children were:

106—Thomas. Born 1789. Died June 13, 1849. Judge.

107—Percipher. Born 1791. Died 1864.

108—George. Born 1796. Died 1882.

109—Margaret. Born 1798. Died 1857.

110—Rachel. Born 1801. Died 1872.

111—Rebecca. Born in Pennsylvania, April 4, 1803. Died May 29, 1893.

112—James. Born 1805. Died 1844.

113—William. Born 1808. Died 1846.

50—WILLIAM S. LEMEN.

114—MARGARET FLEMING. They were married at Williamsburg, Pa. They had two sons:

115—William. Born October 19, 1785. Died, 1881. He was married. Children all dead.

116—George. Born October 6, 1787.

These children went to Michigan at an early day where their descendants still reside.

50—WILLIAM S. LEMEN.

117—LYDIA DUNWODDY Their children were:

118—Thomas. Born October 29, 1790. Died 1863.

119—Lydia. Born January 14, 1793. Died October 1793.

120—Margaret. Born December 18, 1794. Died April 1, 1864.

121—Lydia. Married but left no descendants.

— — — — — —

50—WM. S. LEMEN.

122—AGNES EWART. Born at Geneseo, N. Y. October, 1776. Died December, 1851.

They were married in 1797. Their children were:

123—Samuel. Born December 1798. Died June 1870.

124—Rachel. Born 1800. Died March, 1886.

125—Mary. Born 1802. Died 1873.

126—Susan. Born 1805. Died April, 1874.

127—Hannah. Born 1808. Died 1875.

128—Lucinda. Born 1812. Died 1876.

129—Jane. Born October 4, 1814. Died June 1897.

130—James B. Born October 1, 1816. Died November 12, 1894.

131—Helen. Born April, 1819. Died October, 1890.

— — — — —

51—THOMAS LEMEN.

132—(His Wife). Their children were.

133—Sarah.

134—William. Born January 22, 1794.

135—Rachel.

52—ELIZABETH LEMEN.

136—MR. ENGLE.   Their children were:

137—Siles.

138—Susan.

139—Mathias.

140—George B.

141—Mary Eliza.

SEVENTH GENERATION.

57—JANE LEMEN.

142—JOHN REYNOLDS. He was a judge for several years at Urbana, Ohio. Their children were:

143—Sarah. Deceased.

144—Mary Jane. Deceased.

145—Daughter. Deceased.

58—WILLIAM LEMEN.

146—MARY DONALDSON. She died in 1854. They were married 1804. Their children were:

147—Thornton. Deceased.

148—John. Deceased.

149—Mary Jane. Deceased.

150—Rebecca. Deceased.

151—James Wesley. Deceased.

152—William.

153—Newton. Physician, Catawba, O.

154—Eliza.

60—JOHN REYNOLDS LEMEN.

155—REBEKAH DONALDSON was the daughter of John and Rachel Donaldson, was born March 7, 1789, died March 17, 1854. They lived in Clark county, Ohio, after 1804. He was judge at Springfield, O. for 15 years. He also was justice of the peace and a deacon in the M. E. church. Their children were:

156—James Alexander. Born October 23, 1806. Physician, Clinton, Ill.

157—George Bruce. Born October 1, 1809. Died January 27, 1886.

158—Eliza Ann. Born November 10, 1811. Died August 30, 1840

159—Mary Vance. Born February 18, 1814. Died May 24, 1874.

160—John Reynolds. Born August 31, 1816. Died February 6, 1892.

161—Milton. Born March 1, 1819. Died April 24, 1878. Physician, London, Ohio. Served two terms in the House of Representatives, and was Examining Surgeon during the late war.

162—Lemuel Newton. Born June 24, 1821. Died September 25, 1824.

163—Rebekah Donaldson. Born March 15, 1823. Died February 5, 1833.

164—William Fisher. Born July 9, 1825. Died February 27, 1882.

165—Joseph Vance. Born September 6, 1827. Died February 7, 1833.

166—Leander. Born July 31, 1830. Died September 19, 1831.

63—MARY LEMEN.

167—JOSEPH VANCE—He was Governor of Ohio in 1840. Their children were:

168—Frank.

169—Duncan. Physician.

170—Mary. Deceased.

67—ALEXANDER LEMEN.

171—MARY MORGAN. They were married 1793.

92—SARAH LEMEN.

172—JOHN BURNS—Their children were:

173—Mary. Baptist.

174—Hester.

175—Robert.

176—Magdelane.

93—THOMAS LEMEN.

177—MARY WILLIAMSON. Baptist. Their children were:

178—Eliza M.

179—James M. Farmer. Prot. Methodist.

180—Mary O. Shepherdstown, W. Va.

181—Robert. Williamsport, Md. Prot. Methodist.

182—Nicholas. Prot. Methodist Minister.

183—Jacob W. Farmer.

184—Christopher.

185—Joseph R.

186—William W. Martinsburg, W. Va.

187—Hester A. Shepherdstown, W. Va. Episcopal.

93—THOMAS LEMEN.
188—BARBARY AMOS. Their children were:
189—Sarah E.
190—Virginia E.
191—Samuel K.

— — —

94—ELIZABETH LEMEN.
192—WILLIAM ROBERTS. Their children were:
193—Rebecca. Baptist.
194—Agnes C. Baptist.
195—Lemen.
196—William H. Farmer.
197—Hester L. Vanclevesville, W. Va.
198—Samuel.
199—Mary.
200—Edmond H.
201—Elizabeth. Baptist.
202—Sarah B.
203—James L. Miller, Leetown, W. Va.
204—Joseph L. Leetown, W. Va.

— — —

96—CHRISTIAN LEMEN.
205—SAMUEL ROBERTS. Baptist. Their children were:
206—Rebecca.
207—James L. Large miller.
208—Nancy L.

97—ROBERT LEMEN.
209—WINIFRED BOLEY.
They had no children.

97—ROBERT LEMEN.
210—MARGARET ORSBORNE. Their children were:
211—David P.
212—William.
213—Hester.
214—Thomas L.

101—MARY LEMEN.
215—JOSEPH ROBERTS. Their children were:
216—George W.
217—James.
218—Thomas.
219—Hetty A.
220—Mary E.
221—Alfred H.
222—Frances C.
223—John William, Summit Point, W. Va.
224—Joseph.
225—Robert L. St. Joseph, Mo.

102—NANCY LEMEN. Baptist.
226—ALFRED HOWARD. Their children were:
227—Thomas.

228—James W.
229—Mary C.
230—Robert L.
231—George W.
232—Virginia.

103—HESTER LEMEN.
233—JOHN P. KEARFOTT. Their children were:
234—Robert W.
235—Joseph Baker.
236—Levi H.
237—Cynthia A.
238—Hester L.
239—James L.
240—John P.

104—WILLIAM LEMEN.
241—CATHERINE GRIGGS.
They had no children.

107—PERCIPHER LEMEN.
242—MARY BEACH. Their children were.
243—Susan A.
244—Rachel M. Born in Northumberland, Pa.,
May 13, 1824.

109—MARGARET LEMEN.

245—THOMAS BEACH, of Beach Haven, Pa., son of Judge Beach. Their children were:

246—Susan.

247—George. Deceased.

248—Martha. Deceased.

249—Emily, Deceased.

250—James Lemen.

111—REBECCA LEMEN.

251—HUGH McWILLIAMS. Died 1877. They were married 1830. Their children were:

252—Harriet. Born at Mooresburg, Pa.

253—Regina. Born at Mooresburg, Pa., July 3, 1833.

254--Annie—Born at Mooresburg, Pa.

116—GEORGE LEMEN.

255—(His Wife). Their children were:

256—William.

257—George.

258—Samuel.

259—Katherine. Married a Mercer.

118—THOMAS LEMEN.

260—(His Wife). Their children were:

261—James.

262—William.

263—Lydia.
264—Ann.
265—Thomas.
266—John.
267—Mariette.
268—Margaret.
269—Lewis.
270—Archibald.
271—Manervia.

123—SAMUEL LEMEN.
272—HANNAH PERINE.
280—They had eight children, all deceased.

124—RACHEL LEMEN.
281—PHINEAS ALVORD, of Mt. Morris, N. Y. They had ten children.
291—Three sons and three daughters still survive.

125—MARY LEMEN.
292—ELISHA BROCKWAY, of Whitmore Lake, Mich.
298—They had six children. All deceased.

126—SUSAN LEMEN.
299—EDEN BOOTHE, of Danville, N. Y. To them were born five children.
304—A son and daughter still survive.

127—HANNAH LEMEN.

305—LEWIS CARROLL. They had seven children.

312—Four daughters and two sons still survive.

128—LUCINDA LEMEN.

313—JOHN P. FAULKNER, of South Dansville, N. Y. To them were born six children.

319—Two sons and two daughters still survive.

129—JANE LEMEN.

320—ORLO HOPKINS of Scottsburg, N. Y. Died 1854. Their children were:

321—Helen.

322—Juliette.

323—Lemon O.

324—Agnes.

325—Florence.

325½—Phoebe.

130—JAMES B. LEMEN.

326—DINA M. DORR. Born in Dansville, N. Y., January 22, 1824. They were married May 1, 1845. Their children were:

327—Emma J. Born November 9, 1847.

328—Robert Dorr. Born May 18, 1850.

329—Orlo H. Born March 25, 1853.

330—James A. Born February 17, 1856. Died November 28, 1877.

331—William S. Born August 22, 1858. Died June 21, 1892.

332—Mary S. Born December 15, 1862. Died November 9, 1879.

333—Martha E. Born June 1, 1866.

334—Emma J.

131—**HELEN LEMEN.**

335—**JOHN SMIITH** of Salamanca, N. Y. To them were born six children.

341—Three sons and three daughters survive.

133—**SARAH LEMEN.**

342—**JACOB SHOLL.** Died 1826. They had two children:

343—Wm. H. Born 1821.

344—Catharine Lemen. Born June 21, 1824.

133—**SARAH LEMEN.**

345—**GEORGE HYLAND.** Dansville, New York, married in 1833. Their children were:

346—George. Born December 27, 1834. Died June, 1896.

347—John. Born January 27, 1837.

348—Rachael. Born September 3, 1838. Died May, 1842.

134—WILLIAM LEMEN.

349—CATHARINE SPANGLER. Married December 30, 1828. Their children were:

350—Anna. Born October 27, 1829. Died March 8, 1892.

351—William. Born October 11, 1831. Died January 6, 1833.

352—Catharine. Born July 25, 1832.

353—Mary. Born May 28, 1837. Died August 5, 1892.

135—RACHAEL LEMEN.

354—CHAS. PATRICK. They had six children.

360—Five sons and one daughter.

EIGHTH GENERATION.

143—SARAH REYNOLDS.
361—WILLIAM FISHER.
They had no children.

144—MARY JANE REYNOLDS.
362—PHILANDER ROSS.
They had no children.

151—JAMES WESLEY LEMEN.
333—MARY (   ) She lives at 34 West North
Street, Indianapolis, Ind. Their children were:
364—Laura. Bloomington, Ill.
365—Three daughters.
366—Son.

156—JAMES A. LEMEN.
367—ALMIRA GARFIELD. They were married
1831. Their children were:
368—Mary. She and her father went to California
and did not return.
369—Reynolds. He and his father went to California in '49. He returned in 1851. His
father returned in 1853.
370—Calvin. Has a sheep ranch in Texas.
371—Frank V.
372—Frost. With Frank V. own a large show.

157—GEORGE B. LEMEN.
373—CHARITY SWISHER. Their children were:
374—Rachael.
375—Mary Jane.
376—James.
377—John.
378—Newton.

157—GEORGE B. LEMEN.
379—MARY JANE WOOD. Their children were:
380—Martha.
381—George.
382—Joseph.
383—Scott.
384—Orilla.
385—A. Lincoln.

158—ELIZA A. LEMEN.
386—WILLIAM LAFFERTY. Their children were:
387—James. Deceased.
388—Mary.

159—MARY V. LEMEN.
389—JOSEPH WOLFE. Born June 10, 1811. Died
April 1, 1888. They were married November
22, 1832. Their children were:
390—George B.
391—Rebecca D. Born January 4, 1836.

392—John H.   Born November 2, 1844.   Died
    January 21, 1849.

160—**JOHN R. LEMEN.**

393—**LUCINDA FLUMMER.** Their children were:

394—John. Died in childhood.

395—Mary. Died April, 1858.

396—Milton.

397—Eliza A. Born January 25, 1849.

398—Calvin. Deceased.

399—Franklin. Deceased.

400—John R.

401—James.

402—Orange. Died in infancy.

403—Edward.

404—Lucind.

161—**MILTON LEMEN.**

405—**SARAH SMITH.** Born in Clark County, Ohio,
    May 5, 1840. Died June 27, 1890. Their
    children were:

406—Elizabeth. Born at Midway, O., November
    30, 1844.

407—Alice. Los Angeles, Cal.

408—Eva.

409—Milton.

410—Louise.

411—Rebecca.

412—Johny.

413—Ida. Born November 2, 1851.

164—WILLIAM FISHER LEMEN.

414—SUSANNA E. BISHOP. Daughter of Aquilla and Isabella Ann Bishop. Born July 15, 1833. They were married May 11, 1848. Their children were:

415—Arabella Jane. Born September 22, 1849.

416—Anna Josephine. Born September 15, 1852, in Ohio.

417—Mary Rebekah. Born June 23, 1854. Died March 9, 1887.

418—Willhelmina Alice. Born June 22, 1856.

419—Ada Myrtilla. Born April 14, 1858. Died April 5, 1868.

420—Lizzie Dingess. Born August 18, 1860. Died February 7, 1891.

421—Louie Della. Born December 10, 1862.

422—James Alban. Born January 7, 1865. Electrician. Chicago, Ill.

424—Milton O. Born March 9, 1867.

425—Maud-Eoline. Born February 24, 1870. She took high school and normal courses, then a three-years' course in oratory. Teaching at Bloomington, Ill.

173—MARY BURNS.

436—JOSIAH ROBERTS. Farmer. Baptist. They had no children.

174—HESTER BURNS.

427—THOMAS G. FLAGG. They had no children.

175—ROBERT BURNS.

428—RAITH DOWNCY. Their children were:

429—John D.

430—Samuel D.

431—Ruhama.

432—Hester.

433—Josiah.

178—ELIZA LEMEN.

434—JOHN BILLMYER. Farmer. Their children were:

435—Martin T.

436—David Frank. Shepherdstown, W. Va.

437—John T.

438—Milton J.

439—Susan M.

440—Elizabeth A.

441—Jacob.

442—Robert.

179—JAMES M. LEMEN.

443—SARAH E. LEMEN. Their children were:

444—William Manning. Born May 25, 1834. Jefferson County, W. Virginia.

445—Josephine. Monmouth, Ill.

446—Nicholas.

447—Adrian W. Martinsburg, W. Va.

458—Willoughby M.

449—Jas. Thomas.

450—Henry Hagen.

180—MARY O. LEMEN.

451—ADRIAN JONES. Their children were:

452—Thos. F.

453—James F.

454—John R.

455—Emma S. Shepherdstown, W. Va.

456—William F.

457—Sarah E.

181—ROBERT LEMEN.

458—SARAH F. LIGHT. Their children were:

459—Peter L. Born December 14, 1840.

460—Jacob F. Born July 24, 1842.

461—Thomas J. Born August 31, 1843. Williamsport, Md.

462—Nicholas S. Born April 14, 1845. Williamsport, Md.

463—Mary A. Born April 27, 1847.

464—Sarah E.

465—William E. Born April 12, 1851.

466—Eliza V.

467—Robert.

182—NICHOLAS LEMEN.

468—CATHARINE MINOR. Their children were:

469—Catharine.

470—Willie.

471—Minor. Minister M. P. Church.

472—John.

473—Willoughby.

183—*JACOB W. LEMEN-WILLIAMSON.
474—MARTHA E. WHITE. Their children were:
475—K. New Market, Va.
476—M. White. New Market, Va.
477—T. L. New Market, Va.
478—Gilbert M. New Market, Va.
479—D. J. G.

185—JOSEPH R. LEMEN.
480—CATHARINE PRICE. Married January 29, 1852. They had no children.

186—WILLIAM W. LEMEN.
481—MARGARET RUTHERFORD. Their children were:
482—Geo. T.
483—Hester A.
484—Virginia E.
485—Eliza W.
486—Sally B.
487—James W.

187—HESTER A. LEMEN.
488—HENRY HAGAN.
They had no children.

---

*Jacob W. Lemen when a young man visited an uncle, Jacob Williamson, who had no children. Williamson was very wealthy, and having no living children he had him change his sirname, i. e., drop the Lemen and assume the Williamson. Then he made him his sole heir.

190—VIRGINIA E. LEMEN.
489—J. STRONG.
Their children not known.

193—REBECCA ROBERTS.
490—HENRY FURRY. Their children were:
491—Ruth B.
492—Elizabeth A.
493—Lucy.
494—Martin L.

195—LEMEN ROBERTS.
495—ELIZABETH SIMMONS. Their children were:
496—William H.
497—Samuel.
498—Agnes C.
499—Rebecca.
500—Ruhama.
501—Lucy.
502—Amelia.
503—Sallie.
504—Ruth.

166—WILLIAM H. ROBERTS.
505—NANCY SCHOPPERT. Their children were:
506—Mary E.
507—J. W.
508—Chas. B.
509—Laura V.

510—Virginia.
511—Georgiana.
512—Cordelia.
513—Ashby.

197—HESTER L. ROBERTS.
514—JOHN SUTTON.
They had no children.

199—MARY ROBERTS.
515—JAMES YOUNG.   Their children were:
516—Maggie.
517—Fannie.
518—John.
519—Annie.

200—EDMOND H. ROBERTS.
520—AMELIA SEIBERT.   Their children were:
521—George D.
522—E. Seibert.
523—Emma S.
524—Charles J.
525—Alice M.
526—Rosa L.

201—ELIZABETH ROBERTS.
527—HARRISON SEIBERT.   Their children were:
528—Eliza V.
529—Mary A.   Martinsburg, W. Va.
530—John E.   Farmer.   Presbyterian.

202—SARAH B. ROBERTS.
531—JOHN SUTTON. Their children were:
532—Mary E. Vanclevesville, W. Va.
533—Hester L.
534—Charles M. Vanclevesville, W. Va.

203—JAMES L. ROBERTS.
535—SALLIE KRANTY. Their children were:
536—Campbell.
537—Lillie.
538—Willie.
539—Nora.

207—JAMES L. ROBERTS.
540—ELIZA RIDGEWAY. Their children were:
541—Charles M.
542—Sarah C.
543—James C.
544—Richard S.
545—Robt. M.
546—Birdie V.

208—NANCY L. ROBERTS.
547—JAMES H. ROBERTS.
They had no children.

211—DAVID P. LEMEN.
548—MARY E. ROBERTS. Their children were.
549—Robert.
550—Maggie.

551—William.
552—Laura.
553—Samuel.
554—Mamie.
555—David.

213—HESTER LEMEN.
556—MICHAEL NICKOLS.   Their children were:
557--Robert.
558—Hester.

216—GEORGE W. ROBERTS.
559—MARGARET SNOWDEAL.   Their children were:
560—Elizabeth.
561—Mary E.
562—Alice.   Parkersburg, W. Va.
563—Fanny.
564—Hester.
565—Robert A.
566—Willie.
567—Martha L.

219—HETTY A. ROBERTS.
568—WILLIAM MYERS.   Their children were:
569—Rosalie.
570—Mary E.   Charleston, W. Va.
571—Frances R.
572—Jessie S.   St. Louis, Mo.
573—Rose A.   Charleston, W. Va.
574—Willie R.

220—MARY E. ROBERTS.
575—JAMES WAGELY. Their children were:
576—Chas. W. St. Louis, Mo.
577—Mary E.
578—James W.
579—Martha.

225—ALFRED H. ROBERTS.
580—CATHINNE BURNS. Their children were:
581—Minnie.
582—Nettie. Charleston, W. Va.
583—Willie.

222—FRANCES C. ROBERTS.
584—JOSEPH SIEBERT. Their children were:
585—Annie. Gerrardstown, W. Va.
586—Robert K. Martinsburg, W. Va. Baptist.
587—Charles M.
588—Joseph L. Martinsburg, W. Va. Baptist.
589—Berkely.
590—D. Clinton. Parksburg, W. Va.
591—Lillie L. Pine Bluff, Ark.

222—FRANCES C. ROBERTS.
592—DAVID M. DECK.
They had no children.

223—JNO. WM. ROBERTS.
593—JULIA A. BOGGISS. Their children were:
594—Thomas.
595—Nettie.

596—Emma.
597—Alice.
598—Laura.
599—Clinton.
600—Bertie.
601—Fanny.

225—ROBT. L. ROBERTS.
602—M. E. SHRECKHISE.
　　They had no children.

228—JAMES W. HOWARD.
603—MARY JENNINGS.　Their children were
604—Sadie.
605—Ida.
606—Eva.
607—Virginia.

234—ROBERT W. KEARFOTT.
608—ANNA DUNHAM.　Their children were:
609—Corrinne.
610—Thornton.
611—William D.

235—JOSEPH BAKER KEARFOTT.
612—MARY RUTH GARRELL.　Their children were:
613—Clarence P.
614—Hetty Bell.
615—Mary Baker.

616—Joseph Garrell.

617—Fannie Quick.

618—Ella Rose.

619—James Lemen.

235—JOSEPH BAKER KEARFOTT.
620—RACHEL A. BROTHERTON.
They had no children.

236—LEVI H. KEARFOTT.
621—ELIZABETH DAILEY. Their children were:
622—Sally S.
623—Elizabeth.
624—William P.
625—Charles C.
626—Hester L.

236—LEVI H. KEARFOTT.
627—RUTH DECK. Their children were:
628—David D.
629—James.
630—Amelia.
631—John P.

237—CYNTHIA A. KEARFOTT.
632—JONATHAN MILLER. Their children were:
633—John P. K.
634—Robert B.
635—Hetty A.

636—James W. S.
637—Amelia R.
638—Arthur R.

239—JAMES L. KEARFOTT.
639—AMELIA BOLEY.
They had no children.

240—JOHN P. KEARFOTT.
640—MARY SIDNEY DECK. They had one child:
641—William H.

243—SUSAN LEMEN.
642—EZRA CONLEY VINCENT.   Their children
were:
643—Mrs. J. Sharon McNair.   Hazleton, Pa.
645—Two daughters.

244—RACHEL M. LEMEN.
646—JOHN PFONTS. They were married May 27,
1843.   Their children were:
647—Helen M.
648—Nancy J.
649—Pierce Lemen.
650—J. Leonard.
651—Frances S.

250—JAMES L. BEACH.
652—SARAH GUEIST. Their children were:
653—Edward Lemen.

654—Margaret.

655—James D. Physician.

252—HARRIET McWILLIAMS.

656—GILBERT VORIS. They were married 1854.
Their children were:

657—Annie McWilliams. Born 1856. Died 1897.

658—John Lemen. Born 1858.

658½—Hugh. Born 1864. Now deceased.

659—Harriet Evelin. Born 1873.

253—REGINA McWILLIAMS.

660—DR. R. S. SIMINGTON. Born in White Deer
Valley, Pennsylvania. Died 1889. He was
Surgeon of the Ninety-third Pennsylvania Vol-
untcer Infantry in the late war. They were
married December 28, 1854. Their children
were:

661—Rebecca Gertrude. Born at Danville, Pa.

662—Harriet E. Born at Danville, Pa.

663—Anna J. Born at Danville, Pa.

254—ANNIE McWILLIAMS.

664—FRANK K. HAIN. Born near Reading, Pa.
Died May 9, 1896. He was Vice-president
and General Manager of the Manhattan Elevated Railway of New York City. They were
married 1861. They had one child:

665—Rebecca McWilliams. Born 1862. Died 1866.

327—EMMA J. LEMEN.
666—DUNCAN CAMPBELL, of Dansville, N. Y.
  They were married July 15, 1886.   They have
  one son:
667—Robert D.   Born August 14, 1889.

328—ROBERT D. LEMEN.
668—ESTELLA DUNHAM.   They were married
  1873.   They have one son:
669—Major.   Student at the Ohio University,
  Ada, O.

329—ORLO H. LEMEN.
670—MARY SHEELEY.   Married March, 1878.
  Their children are:
671—Frederick M.
672—Frank J.
673—Floyd A.
674—Dorr S.
675—Hortense.
676—William S.

343—WILLIAM H. SHOLL.
350—ANNIE LEMEN.

344—CATHARINE LEMEN SHOLL.
677—ED. A. SCOVILL, of Cleveland, O.   They had
  two children:
678—Wm. Sholl.
679—E. T.

352—CATHARINE LEMEN.

680—GEO. W. HOWE. They were married November 16, 1854. Their children not known.

———————

353—MARY LEMEN.

681—WALTER MORRISON. They were married November 16, 1854.

NINTH GENERATION.

368—MARY LEMEN.
682—MORTON PIATTE. Their children were
683—Ida U. Died December 10, 1883.
684—Almira.

374—RACHAEL LEMEN.
685—(   ) CHAPIN.
    Their children not known.

375—MARY JANE LEMEN.
686—CAPT. JOSEPH DENISON. They have one
    daughter:
687—Hulda.

376—JAMES LEMEN.
688—SIDNEY FOLEY.
    Their children not known.

377—JOHN LEMEN.
689—ETTIE WOOD.
    They have no children.

380—MARTHA LEMEN.
690—MR. HALL. They had one child:
691—Maud.

384—ORILLA LEMEN.

692—I. N. BAILOR. Born in Lancaster, O., April 26, 1850. They were married October 24, 1877. They had one child:

693—Lena E. Born June 23, 1880, in De Witt County, Illinois.

391—REBECCA D. WOLFE.

694—G. C. WEEDMAN. He was born July 9, 1836. Died December 11, 1887. He was Captain of Company G, 107th Regiment Illinois Volunteer Infantry. They were married February 25, 1864. They had one child:

695—Lawrence W. Born July 14, 1876.

397—ELIZA ANN LEMEN.

696—(   ) FISHER.
Children not known.

406—ELIZABETH LEMEN.

697—THOS. B. WOOSLEY. London, O. Married November 19, 1879. Their children were:

698—Bertha Alice. Born December 19, 1880.

699—Percy M. Born May 4, 1887. Died September 12, 1888.

407—ALICE LEMEN.

700—JEROME CURTAIN. London, O., February 9, 1870. Their children were:

701—Napoleon. Born September 27, 1874.

702—Milton F.   Born August 26, 1876.

703—Forrest.   Born August 20, 1877.   Died September 20, 1877.

413—IDA LEMEN.

704—**WILLIAM L. STROUP,** Born September 14, 1841.   Died October 4, 1884.   They were married May 27, 1880.   Their children were:

705—Alfred.   Born Elk Falls, Kans., June 30, 1882.

706—William M.   Born at Elk Falls, Kans., July 7, 1884.

415—ARABELLE J. LEMEN.

707—**LAWSON D. WELCH.**   Real Estate and Loans, Bloomington, Ill.   They were married September 22, 1869.   Their children were:

708—Annie L.   Graduate of Wesleyan College of Music.   Teaching music, Bloomington, Ill.

709—Boydton.   Deceased.

710—John Edgar.   Graduate of Wesleyan College, and now at Columbian Medical College, N. Y.

711—Gertrude.   Born March 17, 1879.

416—ANNA J. LEMEN.

712—**JOHN M. MIKLE.**   Farmer, Webster City, Ia.   They were married September 17, 1871.   Their children were:

713—Claude.   Born November 16, 1872.

714—Rosalia.   Born October 1, 1874.

715—Louisa Belle. Born June 28, 1877.

716—James Arthur. Born December 6, 1881.

717—Ray. Born August 28, 1884.

718--Carrie. Born May 2, 1886.

719—Iris. Born August 16, 1889.

720—Lorene. Born in Iowa, January 10, 1892.

417—MARY R. LEMEN.

721—ALBERT P. DOWNS. Farmer, Downs, Ill. They were married November 12, 1874. They had three children:

722—Josephine May. Born August 19, 1875.

723—Robert. Born February 15, 1877.

724—Edna. Born February 20, 1887. Died October 2, 1889.

420—ELIZABETH D. LEMEN.

725—CHARLES TETER. Farmer. They were married April 12, 1882. Their children were:

726—Ormand. Born March 13, 1883. Died September 8, 1884.

727—Gertie Belle. Born April 22, 1885.

728—Roscoe C. Born September 21, 1886.

729—Maude Grace. Born September 8, 1888.

730—Howard. Born October 8, 1890.

429—JOHN D. BURNS.

731—BARAH JOHNSON. Their children were:

732—Sarah E.

733—Marah E.

429—JOHN D. BURNS.
734—ELMIRA RITTER. Their children were:
735—Samuel C.
736—Winifred V.
737—Henry C.
738—Jonathan L.

431—RUHAMA BURNS.
739—GEORGE NAVE. Their children were:
740—Sarah.
741—Dorah.
742—Samuel.
743—Florence.

432—HESTER BURNS.
744—CYRUS JOHNSON.
  They had no children.

432—HESTER BURNS.
745—LEVI ROBINS. Their children were:
746—Robert.
747—Alice.

436—DAVID F. BILLMYRE.
748—SALLIE RANDLE. Their children were:
749—Ida.
750—Sidney.
751—Eliza.

437—JOHN T. BILLMYRE.
752—SUSAN RANDLE. Their children were:
753—Bettie.
754—Charles.
755—Adrian.
756—Eliza.

438—MILTON J. BILLMYRE.
757—ELIZABETH VANMETRE. Their children were:
758—Anna.
759—Robert.
760—Rose.
761—Herman.

439—SUSAN M. BILLMYRE.
762—WILLIAM T. LEMEN. Their children were:
763—Elizabeth Ann.
764—Hester H.
765—Robert N.
766—Susan M.

442—ROBERT BILLMYRE.
767—EMMA HUYATT. Their children were:
768—Charles.
769—Mazie.
770—Archie.
771—John.
772—Earnest.

444—WM. MANNING LEMEN.

773—ELIZABETH TRUMPHOWE. Born at Washington, Md., July 5, 1835. Died November 25, 1874. Their children were:

774—Sarah Ellen. Born in Knox County, Illinois, March 15, 1858.

775—Susie D. Born in Knox County, Illinois, January 23, 1860.

776—Mary Elizabeth. Born in Knox County, Illinois, May 16, 1862. Died March 22, 1876.

777—Phoebe V. Born in Knox County, Illinois, May 4, 1864. Died February 17, 1883.

778—Hattie A. Born at Monmouth, Ill., December 9, 1866.

779—William M. Jr. Born at Monmouth, Ill., January 6, 1869. Railroad man, Beardstown, Ill.

780—James E. Born at Monmouth, Ill., August 10, 1871. Farmer. Red Oak, Ia.

781—Matty M. Born at Monmouth, Ill. January 5, 1874. School-teacher.

445—JOSEPHINE LEMEN.
782—JONATHAN MACKEY.
Children not known.

447—ADRIAN W. LEMEN.
783—ELIZABETH WALKER. Their children were·
784—James.

785—Willoughby.
786—Adrian.
787—Robert W.
788—Mary J.

448—WILLOUGHBY M. LEMEN.
789—SALLIE KERNEY. Their child was:
790—Mary F.

449—JAMES T. LEMEN.
791—ANNA BUSSEY. Their children were:
792—Alma.
793—Elsie
794—Benjamin.

450—HENRY HAGEN LEMEN.
795—MARGARET RANDLE. Their children were:
796—Alice.
797—Harvy.
798—Joseph.

452—THOMAS F. JONES.
799—ANNIE REYNOLDS. Their children were:
800—Estell Hagan.
801—Mary L.
802—Agile.
803—Armstrong.
804—Thomas B.
805—Sallie F.

453—JAMES F. JONES.
806—ROSE H. ROBINSON. Their children were:
807—Charles R.
808—Sidney N.
809—Adrian W.
810—William F.
811—Mary L.
812—Martha.

454—JOHN R. JONES.
813—ELIZA V. SEIBERT. They had one child:
814—Mary.

455—EMMA S. JONES.
815—MILES W. STARR. Their children were:
816—Bessie May.
817—Ruth.

457—SARAH E. JONES.
818—CHARLES M. FALK. They had one child:
819—Agga Eliza.

459—PETER L. LEMEN.
820—HELLEN STAKE. Their children were:
821—Robt. E.
822—Sally L.
823—Eliza M.
824—Mary E.

459—PETER L. LEMEN.

825—NANCY A. MOTTER. Their children were:

826—Mary M.

827—Joseph L.

828—Herman L.

460—JACOB F. LEMEN.

829—SALLY HYSER, of Hagerstown, Md. Their children were:

830—George F.

831—Thomas.

460—JACOB F. LEMEN.

832—MARY WILSON, nee LIGHT. Their children were:

833—John L.

834—Jacob H.

835—Mary A.

836—Robt. L.

837—Sally E.

838—Newton W.

461—THOMAS J. LEMEN.

839—ANNIE ENSMINGER. Their children were:

840—John E.

841—Bessie F.

842—Thos. W.

462—NICHOLAS S. LEMEN.

843—JANE L. SHOOP. Their children were:

844—Samuel C.

845—Daisey.
846—John L.
847—Annie M.
848—Edgar.
849—William.
850—Sallie C.
851—Jennie S.

463—**MARY A. LEMEN.**
852—**W. BAKER PRICE.** Their children were:
853—Daisey.
854—Sally L.
855—Walter.

466—**ELIZA V. LEMEN.**
856—**CHAS. ARDINGER.** Their children were:
857—Charles R.
858—John W.
859—Thomas J.
860—Lena L.
861—Albert Z.
862—Geo. L.
863—Hollingsworth.
864—Sally L.
865—Kearfott.

469—**CATHARINE LEMEN.**
866—**P. C. ARCHIBALD.**
They had no children.

470—WILLIE LEMEN.
867—EDWARD NELLOR.
They had no children.

475—K. WILLIAMSON.
868—A. T. WALDEN. Their children were:
869—William E.
870—J. W.
871—A. A.
872—G. L.

476—M. WHITE WILLIAMSON.
873—M. L. HARRISON. Their children were:
874—Morgan.
875—Rush II.
876—Martha.
878—Isabella.

477—T. L. WILLIAMSON.
879—B. K. B———. Their children were:
880—J. W.
881—C. B.
882—K. L.

478—GILBERT M. WILLIAMSON.
883—LUCY RUTTER. Their children were:
884—W. W.
885—Elizabeth.
886—Linn.
887—Mathew.

479—J. G. WILLIAMSON.
888—F. A. RIPLEY. Their children were:
889—Mary.
890—Thomas.
891—Virginia.
892—Paxton.
893—John P.

482—GEO. T. LEMEN.
894—EMMA HYATT. Their children were:
895—Ward.
896—Arthor.

483—HESTER A. LEMEN.
897—JOHN YOUNG. Their children were:
898—Ella May.
899—Willie M.
900—Robert L.
901—Rena Bell.
902—Raymond B.

484—VIRGINIA E. LEMEN.
903—JOHN F. MADDOX. Their children were:
904—Edith.
905—James H.
906—Bessie O.
907—Julia.

486—SALLY B. LEMEN.
908—REV. HENRY L. HOUT. Their children were:
909—Della.
910—Bessie.

_____ _____

494—MARTIN L. FURRY.
911—MARY C. HENRY. Their children were:
912—Florence B.
913—Blanch L.
914—William H.
915—Mary R.
916—Philip C.

506—MARY E. ROBERTS.
917—BAILEY S. HEDGES. Their children were:
918—Nannie L.
919—Maud.
920—Minnie.
921—Pearl.
922—Bessie.
923—Leaton.
924—Robert.

_____ _____

507—J. W. ROBERTS.
925—ELIZA C. CUSHWA. Their children were:
926—John W.
927—Lena.
928—Bessie.
929—Cora.

508—CHAS. B. ROBERTS.
930—SALLY ROBINSON.
931—They had one child.

509—LAURA V. ROBERTS.
932—GEO. RIDINGS. Their children were:
933—Bell.
934—Charles.
935—Daisey.
936—Clarence.
937—Nellie.
938—Claude.

511—GEORGIANNA ROBERTS.
939—HENRY HAVEY.
They had no children.

512—CORDELIA ROBERTS.
940—NICHOLAS THUANY.
Their children not known.

516—MAGGIE YOUNG.
941—JOHN SIGLER. Their children were:
942—William.
943—Nettie.

517—FANNIE YOUNG.
944—JOHN HOLLIS. Their children were:
945—James.
946—George.

947—William L.
948—John E.
949—Fred B.
950—Chas.
951—Walter.

519—ANNIE YOUNG.
952—WM. WOLFENSBURGER. Their children were:
953—Silas.
954—Albert.
955—Dora.

521—GEO. D. ROBERTS.
956—ELIZABETH REUCH. Their children were:
957—Florence W.
958—Clara E.

522- -ELI SEIBERT ROBERTS.
959—FANNIE KRAUTZ. Their children were:
960—Charles.
961—Clarence.

523—EMMA S. ROBERTS.
962—ALEX. C. DRAWBAUGH. They had one child:
963—Edward.

525—ALICE M. ROBERTS.
964—JAMES W. BURR. Their children were:
965—Mary.
966—Charles.

529—MARY A. SEIBERT.
967—DAVID. L. EUBANK. Their children were:
968—Emma V.
969—Carrie R.
970—George H.
971—Charles.
972—Harlan.
973—Raymond.
974—Alice.

530—JOHN E. SEIBERT.
975—EMILY C. OTTO. Their children were:
976—Elizabeth.
977—John F.
978—Elmer.
979—Lucy G.

532—MARY E. SUTTON.
980—FRANCIS MILLER. Their children were:
981—Cora.
982—Clinton.
983—Savilla.
984—John.
985—Hettie.
986—Ruth.

987—Grant.
988—Lucy.

534—CHAS. M. SUTTON.
989—DOLLY HAZLEWOOD. Their children were:
990—Maggie.
991—Leonard

534—CHAS. M. SUTTON.
992—LAURA WINEBRENNER. Their children were:
993—John.
994—Elma.
995—Virginia.
996—Ira.
997—Gay.
998—Bettie.

537—SALLIE ROBERTS.
999—CHAS. CHAPMAN.
They had no children.

541—CHAS. M. ROBERTS.
1000—FANNY A. SWAN. Their children were:
1001—Edward S.
1001 —Chas. S.

542—SARAH C. ROBERTS.
1002—EDWARD YINGLING. Their children were:
1003—Laura B.
1004—Ida M.
1005—Manzella.

543—JAS. C. ROBERTS.
1006—MARY THOMAS. Their children were:
1007—Ira T. N.
1008—Lena M.

546—BIRDIE V. ROBERTS.
1009—JAMES H. CARTMELL. Their children were:
1010—Nannie.
1011—Mary E.

549—ROBT. LEMEN.
1012—MARGARET E. McKITTRICK.
Their children not known.

550—MAGGIE LEMEN.
1013—ROBERT NICHOLS.
1014—They had one child.

557—ROBT. NICHOLS.
1015—MAGGIE LEMMEN.
Their children not known.

560—ELIZABETH ROBERTS.
1016—ROBERT McKITTRICK. Their children were:
1017—Margaret E.
1018—Mary.
1019—Nancy.

562—ALICE ROBERTS.
1020—DANIEL SAMUELS. Their children were:
1021—Marie.
1022—Lola.
1023—Gail.

563—FANNIE ROBERTS.
1024—JOHN BLAKELY. Their children were:
1025—George.
1026—Franklin.
1027—Francis A.

564—HESTER ROBERTS.
1028—DANIEL W. ROBERTS. Their children were:
1029—Edward.
1030—Thomas.
1031—Leonard.
1032—Alice.

565—ROBT. A. ROBERTS.
1033—MOLLIE ANDERSON. Their children were:
1034—John.
1035—Florence.

566—WILLIE ROBERTS.
1036—MINNIE PEACOCK.
Their children not known.

567—MARTHA L. ROBERTS.
1037—MATTHEW WARD.
   They had two children.

570—MARY E. MYERS.
1038—MAYBERRY SMALL.   Their children were:
1039—Mary E.
1040—Hester.
1041—Beuba.
1042—Rose.
1043—Fannie.
1044—Frank.

571—FRANCIS R. MYERS.
1045—HOWARD ANDERSON.
   They had four children.

572—JESSIE S. MYERS.
1046—MILDRED WAGELY.   They had one child:
1047—Mabel.

576 —CHARLES W. WAGELY.
1048—MAGGIE SNYDER.   They had one child:
1049—Archie.

577—MARY E. WAGELY.
1050—CONRAD JOHNSON.
   Their children not known.

578—JAMES W. WAGELY.
1051—ANNA GRANTHAM.
Their children not known.

581—MINNIE ROBERTS.
1052—W. EASTERDAY. Their children were:
1053—Cora Bell.
1055—(Two not known).

582—NETTIE ROBERTS.
1056—ROBERT ROLAND.
Their children not known.

585—ANNIE SEIBERT.
1057—WALTER BUSEY. Their children were:
1058—Minnie.
1059—Ernest.
1060—Florence.
1061—Gertrude.
1062—Edgar.
1063—Eva L.
1064—Geo. M.

586—ROBT. K. SEIBERT.
1065—MOLLIE THOMBURG. Their children were:
1066—Lena.
1067—Nannie.

588—JOSEPH L. SEIBERT.
1068—SARAH E. REILLY.
    Their children not known.

591—LILLIE L. SEIBERT.
1069—REV. F. SAPP.
    Their children not known.

596—EMMA ROBERTS.
1070—(   ) SHEWBRIDGE.
    Their children not known.

604—SADIE HOWARD.
1071—ROBT. WILSON.
    Their children not known.

606—EVA HOWARD.
1072—GEO. JEWELL.   Their children were:
1073—Daisy.
1074—Ruby.
1075—George.

607—VIRGINIA HOWARD.
1076—GEO. HEIRBIG.   They had one child:
1077—Howard.

609—CORRINNE KEARFOTT.
1078—REV. FRED B. DE VAL.   Their children were:
1079—Genivive.
1080—Lina.

1081—Lorram.
1082—Fred.
1083—Ed. William.
1084—Robert K.
1085—Anna C.
1086—Paul
1087—(.   )

611—WILLIAM D. KEARFOTT.
1088—MARY R. JACKSON. They had one child:
1089—Thornton.

613—CLARENCE P. KEARFOTT.
1090—REBECCA KRATZ. Their children were:
1091—Clarence B.
1092—Joseph Conrad.
1093—Mary Low. ·
1094—Ruth.
1095—Robert R.
1096—Rebecca.
1097—Hellen V.
1098—Hugh S.

614—HETTY BELL KEARFOTT.
1099—MILTON S. MILLER. Their children were:
1111—Mabel L.
1112—Florence S.
1113—Mary B.
1114—Chas. J.

1115—Anna R.
1116—Frederick M.
1117—Joseph.

615—MARY B. KEARFOTT.
1118—HENRY BOGERT. Their children were:
1119—Henry K.
1120—Elma B.

624—WILLIAM P. KEARFOTT.
1121—SARAH A. TOWN. Their children were:
1122—Emma M.
1123—Wm. David.

628—DAVID D. KEARFOTT.
1124—NANCY DECK. They had one child:
1125—Bessie.

633—JOHN P. K. MILLER.
1126—SADIE PEGG. Their children were:
1127—Carrie M.
1128—Eugene K.
1129—Frank.
1130—Charles.

634—ROBERT B. MILLER.
1131—MATTIE DUNCAN. They had one child:
1132—Jessie K.

635—HETTIE A. MILLER.
1133—WALTER BOGERT. Their children were:
1134—Walter.
1135—Raymond.
1136—Roland.
1137—Corinne.

637—AMELIA R. MILLER.
1138—LAWRENCE BYERS. They were married March 11, 1895. They have one child:
1139—Sarah M.

641—WILLIAM H. KEARFOTT.
1140—NANNIE B. HERR. Their children were:
1141—Mary G.
1142—John P.
1143—William.
1144—Sidney W.

647—HELEN M. PFONTS.
1145—H. E. BROWN.

648—NANCY J. PFONTS.
1146—EDWARD GORMAN.

649—PIERCE L. PFONTS.
1147—HELEN CAMPBELL.

651—FRANCES S. PFONTS.
1148—W. MURRAY ALEXANDER. They were married August 14, 1889.

655—JAMES D. BEACH.
1149—JENNIE BOUERS.
They have no children.

657—ANNIE McWILLIAMS VORIS.
1150—DR. H. M. EMORICK. They were married 1882. Their children were:
1151—Harriet Anna. Born 1884.
1152—Rebecca Lemen. Born 1890. Deceased.

658—JOHN L. McWILLIAMS.
1153—MARY HAMOR. They were married 1883. Their children were:
1154—Gilbert. Born 1884.
1155—Emily H. Born 1886.
1156—Frank H. Born 1888. Deceased.
1157—John H. Born 1889.

659—HARRIET E. McWILLIAMS.
1158—LUTHER M. MALL. They were married 1896.
1159—They have an infant son.

661—REBECCA G. SIMINGTON.
1160—CALVIN LEINBACK. They were married January 15, 1885. He died December 24, 1886. They had no children.

663—ANNA J. SIMINGTON.

1161—CHARLES A. SIDLER, of Sunbury, Pa. Attorney at Law. They were married November 11, 1896. They had no children.

683—IDA U. PIATTE.

1162—WALTER NICKELS, of Bellefontain, O. They were married November 23, 1881. They had no children.

684—ALMIRA PIATTE.

1163—CHARLES McKEE, of Bellefontain, O. They were married November 15, 1882. She lives at 99 South Victoria street, St. Paul, Minn. Their children were:

1164—Marie V.

1165—Myle.

1166—Donald F.

TENTH GENERATION.

749—IDA BILLMYRE.
1167—FRANK HILL.
Their children are not known.

753—BETTIE BILLMYRE.
1168—GEO. FOLK.
Their children not known.

756—ELIZA BILLMYRE.
1169—OSCAR SPERON.
Their children not known.

758—ANNA BILLMYRE.
1170—SEATON MILLER.
Their children not known.

759—ROBERT BILLMYRE.
1171—ELLA CAMERON.
They had two children.

760—ROSE BILLMYRE.
1172—EDWARD DROWBAUGH.
Their children not known.

763—ELIZABETH A. LEMEN.
1173—ROL. C. CRISWELL. They have one child:
1174—Stewart H.

764—HESTER H. LEMEN.
1175—DAVID FOLK. Their children were:
1176—William.
1177—Sarah.
1178—Daniel H.

765—ROBT. A. LEMON.
1179—MAUD HEDGES.
Their children not known.

766—SUSIE LEMEN.
1180—(   ) JOHNSON. Their children were:
1181—Foletta M. Born May 14, 1889.
1182—Chas. E. Born May, 1890.
1183—Horrace I. Born December 4, 1891.
1184—Iva M. Born November 8, 1895.

778—HATTIE LEMEN.
1185—(   ) COLLINS. Their children were:
1186—Gertrude.
1187—Mildred.
1188—Foster.
1189—Fanny.

778—HATTIE COLLINS, nee LEMEN.
1190—**WM. M. TUNIG.**   They had one child:
1191—Mabel.

1001—**EDWARD S. ROBERTS.**
1192—(   ) **HALL.**
    Their children not known.

1003—**LAURA B. YINGLING.**
1193—**CHAS. CRAWFORD.**
    Their children not known.

THE END